AMERICA'S THIRD REVOLUTION

AMERICA'S
THIRD
REVOLUTION

PUBLIC INTEREST AND THE PRIVATE ROLE

IRVING S. SHAPIRO
with Carl B. Kaufmann

A Cornelia & Michael Bessie Book

HARPER & ROW, PUBLISHERS, New York
Cambridge, Philadelphia, San Francisco, London
Mexico City, São Paulo, Sydney

FIRST EDITION

Designer: Sidney Feinberg

Library of Congress Cataloging in Publication Data

Shapiro, Irving S.
  America's third revolution.
  "A Cornelia & Michael Bessie book."
  Includes index.
  1. Business and politics—United States.
2. Industry—Social aspects—United States.
I. Kaufmann, Carl B. II. Title.
JK467.S52   1984   322'.3'0973   83-49059
ISBN 0-06-039034-4

84 85 86 87 88 10 9 8 7 6 5 4 3 2 1

For
Charles Brelsford McCoy
A man who personifies the best
in thoughtful business leadership

Contents

Introduction

Organizations, like explorers, find themselves crossing watersheds. America's political and economic institutions have traveled across such a ridgeline in recent years and now operate in an environment different from the one they left behind. It is so different that it has forced substantial changes in both the public and the private sectors, and demands a new working relationship between them. That is what this book is about.

Behind us is a world in which government largely left the private sector alone and in which many leaders of private organizations, those in business being prime examples, were isolated from societal problems. We have moved to a world in which the affairs of private and public organizations are interrelated, interdependent, and nearly impossible to untangle.

What informs this book are three ideas, scattered through its pages: that institutions are means and not ends, and therefore are subject to change; that the private sector can and should contribute more than it has to the public-policy process, and that if it does so properly, the community as a whole will be the net gainer; and that leaders in the private sector have quasi-public status and must accept the public responsibilities that go with this. Private gain remains a necessary condition of commerce, but it is no longer a sufficient one. The objective now should be not just to make individual companies perform better but also to make the whole system work better.

There is a distressing amount to be done. National governance today is characterized by a politics in disarray; by legislation and regulation that try to do too many of the wrong things; and by a judiciary almost tied in knots. One reason we have come to this pass is because the nation has for years failed to acknowledge that some sort of parity must exist between social goals and economic resources. All sorts of institutions in society have been unwilling, for one reason or another, to restrain immediate wants in favor of longer-term benefits, their own included. Leaders in government, labor, and business have worn blinders, and seen issues too narrowly. Each group has maneuvered for its own gains without asking where such a chain of events would probably, even inevitably, lead.

The question of means and ends is not by itself a real issue. Society decided long ago that secular institutions do not exist by holy writ but are merely instruments for reaching certain human ends. There is, though, a compact, a social contract for the private sector, and it has been substantially rewritten in the past generation. According to our political philosophy, whether a private-sector organization be a university, manufacturing corporation, or community organization staffed largely by volunteers, it ought to be left as free as possible, short of denying equal freedom to others. Practical experience says that is the way most organizations can best be encouraged to do their jobs well; but there is a *quid pro quo:* Private organizations are obliged to operate within the ground rules, and society writes those. For business, there must be a correspondence between capitalism and decency.

The precepts change. For commercial organizations, which provide my focal point, there have been dramatic shifts over the years in what is expected in the way of performance and what is acceptable in the way of conduct. Partly because of economic necessity, partly of political choice, the nation has converted from a relatively freewheeling version of capitalism to one that is more circumscribed. Private businesses have become more ruled than ruling. One reason for writing this book is to explore that shift, accepting as a premise that the changes are mostly irreversible, but also with the conviction that the private sector in this country remains more free than its counterparts in other countries, and ought to be at least as vigorous as any of them.

Another reason is to explore the relationship that has developed between private and public sectors. To a degree that is unique among democratic nations, government and business in this country have approached one another with suspicion and ill-will. It is my conviction that the adversarial climate has served both sides badly and the country still worse. What is needed is not just a cease-fire but a new economic and social attitude, one that recognizes the imperatives for successful enterprise in world competition, and one that also realizes that economic units must accept some responsibilities in the realm of social change.

I see the present as a time comparable in some ways to the 1930s. At that point in history, there was a breakdown of the economic system, and the public sought new political leadership to restore the nation. Now we are looking at change brought about by two factors: some public questioning of the performance of the private sector over a period of decades, and governmental mismanagement of economic resources over the same period. The changes that come out of this may be no less wrenching than those that came out of the Depression of the Thirties. The times call for a political leadership capable of delivering consistent and coherent policies, at arm's length, with the nation's well-being standing above the interests of particular groups. The policies we have are too fragmented and too factional in their origins or their impact. They come from governmental units so consumed with immediacies that their people cannot think through the implications of their own actions. We need a new style of governance.

We need as well a new breed of managers in the private sector, one that respects the ability to operate in the public-policy arena equally as much as it lauds the ability to manage the internal affairs of a business. It must be a group that is sensitive to public needs and that knows how to communicate effectively through the public media, for it can succeed only if it has public understanding and support.

I believe that practically all the leaders in the private sector understand (could any not know this, today?) that their own success or failure hinges to a considerable degree on decisions reached in government through the political process. What is being sorted out now is how the private and public sectors can fit together in this process, without either trying to do the other's job. The private sector cannot expect to dominate—the contract gives business a voice, but denies it control—but neither can it afford to be a bystander. Nor is there reason for it to be silent, for it has a stake in the public-policy process so large that it is measured in terms of the livelihood of tens of millions of people. It is also a part of my argument that the private sector has skills and perspectives that ought to be melded into governmental decisions. It has ideas that deserve to be heard on their merits. It has talents that cannot be duplicated elsewhere. Thus, to my way of thinking, the private sector does not merely have a right to participate in the public sector's work; it has that duty.

One reason that fortune might smile on such a notion as it applies to business is that the rationale is not so much altruism, a quality for which businessmen are not famous, as it is simple practicality, for which they are noted. No one stands to gain more from peace and harmony in the town than the folks running the shops on Main Street. Putting that more broadly, the better the Federal executive and regulatory offices function, the more efficient the operations of the judicial system, the more responsive and efficient the state and local governments, the better the climate for profit-seeking enterprises. Any business executive who believes that—and it is not a hard idea to sell—should have no trouble squaring his obligations to private masters with a sensitivity to community needs and a sense of duty to contribute to good governance when he can. Those things go with the territory.

There is more to this than pragmatism, though. I argue a principle behind the practicality. Like millions of people of my generation, I came from a family that had no distinguished background and no great means. The American Dream was not an abstraction to people like me. It was our only hope. We had to believe in that, or nothing; and the nation delivered on the dream. In the 1930s it was government, more often than the private sector, that offered opportunity to many able young people. In the 1940s and afterward, the open doors were more frequently found in the private sector, and notably in business. Among the men and women with whom I have worked in business are many who built their careers out of those opportunities and their own energy. They have recognized the changes of which this book speaks, and have come to represent the first generation of the new breed of leadership that is needed.

It is not an accident that they think and behave as they do, and that I write as I do. We are products of what can fairly be labeled America's third revolution. We recognize that the American system, for all its faults and foolishness, has treated most of its people very well, and us most generously. Working in enterprise is an exciting way to make a living, but we have also found it is a way one can pay his dues. The effort to make the business contribution fit better against society's needs is a step in that direction.

This set of essays begins with an explanation of what I mean by "the third revolution" and "the new breed." What follows are some thoughts on the problems of government today, the effect these have on organizations and people in the private sector, and the steps that are being or might be taken to bring improvement in the executive, legislative, and judicial branches. After that, the relationship of business and the public media is explored at some length. The book concludes with a chapter on corporate governance and the climate inside big businesses, a chapter built on the discovery—which surely is not new with me—that the skills needed to manage the internal affairs of a corporation today are much the same as the skills required to run its external affairs, and that a management team seriously deficient in one of those areas is not likely to excel in the other.

The closing thought of this introduction is not repeated elsewhere in this book in so many words, but it is a short explanation for the ideas that follow, and for my attempting the book. With many of my colleagues in the private sector, I work from a belief that we ought not take more out of the system than we try to put back. The private sector needs to expand its sense of public commitment.

AMERICA'S THIRD REVOLUTION

1

America's Third Revolution

AMERICA has launched three revolutions. The first was for political freedom. The second, the Industrial Revolution, was technological and material in focus. It took a nation rich in potential and made it rich in fact. Though we think of that revolution as history, it is still going on. The third revolution, unnamed, lies even more in the column of unfinished business. It is a revolution to make real the notions of social justice and equality, a revolution driven by a vision of a nation as rich in quality as in quantity. It is an economic as well as a social revolution, and one of its premises is that a wealthy society has few if any excuses for not being just and humane. It is built on the principle that a society may fairly be judged on the way it cares for its weakest members, and the opportunities it offers the individual. On that logic, the third revolution could have been expected as an outgrowth of the second, as well as an overdue attempt to live up to the promises of the first.

This third revolution began about a half-century ago and has since become the central fact of domestic life in the United States. It has changed the fabric of society and all manner of relationships among individuals, mostly for the better. It has brought voting rights to blacks; put millions of students through college who never would have attended before; given the poor and elderly higher baseline living standards; and launched national programs of improvement in areas where there were none before, such as pollution abatement.

There have been companion events, both causes and effects: more government (the U.S. holds no record here, but the 37 percent of the Gross National Product that goes to government at the federal, state

1

and local levels is a far larger fraction than it was fifty years ago); a greater centralization of power; a growth in big organizations in both the private and the public sectors; a surfeit of regulations, some of which have been necessary or at any rate productive, others of which have been merely expensive without being effective; and a redistribution of national income, marked by a steady rise in the share of the nation's economic output going to people in the form of wages and salaries, with a proportionately smaller share going to property-owners in the form of returns on their invested dollars.

Not incidentally, this third revolution also has had more than a little to do with one of the nation's recurring problems: inflation. This is important to this book because inflation comes out of the clash between social wants and economic means. As social ambitions have grown, we have let the nation's accounts get badly out of balance. Not wanting to make guns-or-butter choices, lacking easy political mechanisms for removing from the wish-list anything the least bit popular with large numbers of voters, we have simply ordered up large amounts of everything on the menu. That would be all right were it not for the fact that expenditures were not matched by tax revenues. Government printed the money to cover the deficits, and we call the result inflation.

It is easy to point the finger at an irresponsible Congress for this, but, as is true a surprising fraction of the time, the nation's elected officials were doing what most voters thought at the time they ought to do. The large middle-income group, which is where most of the votes are in this country, is the principal long-range victim of inflation, but it also is the short-term beneficiary of the programs that emerge from an inflationary strategy, and it provided the political support for these. Inflation is just a shorthand label for our national unwillingness to pay bills as they fall due and to go easy on the expansion of credit. Following Mr. Micawber's simple arithmetic in *David Copperfield,* "Annual income twenty pounds; annual expenditure nineteen, nineteen, six—result happiness. Annual income twenty pounds; annual expenditure twenty pounds nought six, result misery."

All that is familiar, and it is not my purpose here to preach social economics or to rerun history except as it is useful as stage setting. My main concern is with the present and future relationships between the private and public sectors, and with the question of what it will take for the two of them to deliver on the promises of the nation's revolutions. One of the more obvious facts of our times is that the units of society on each side of that border do not get along particularly well with each other. This is especially true of big government and big business, which have for years been open adversaries. If the two kinds of organizations have nonetheless survived, it is largely in spite of each other's efforts, or because there was no alternative. As John Maynard Keynes said of an earlier era, "Those governments which attack business are fast rendering impossible a continuance of the social and economic order. But they have no plan for replacing it." Just so in the modern setting; government has made life increasingly difficult for countless private organizations, many of them have returned fire with fire, and neither side has demonstrated that it can do the other's work satisfactorily, though at times both have tried.

My argument, simply put, is that this hostile relationship is not necessary or useful, nor is it innocent. It is not just fun and games among the gladiators. Setting aside the rhetoric about small being beautiful, and agreeing that it sometimes is, the fact remains that big business and big government both are here to stay. Our social as much as economic progress requires that those two kinds of institutions understand one another and develop a more productive relationship. The constant bickering only hurts the country. One of the important tasks of our times is to replace the ingrained hostility with attitudes that are more constructive. This is not easy, but it can be done, as some evidence reported here should make clear.

If any point is certain, it is that the world we live in is not the world we came from. It is not business alone but all sorts of organizations that today find the rules of conduct redefined and more confining. A medical school can no longer admit whomever it pleases, using whatever screening standards it elects. A university buildings superintendent may not decide on his own what fuel will be burned to heat the dormitories, there being restrictions on the sulfur content of the oil or coal going to the boilers. A police department may not promote anyone it wants, or skim the top-scoring candidates on its entrance examination, but must achieve a balance that meets a minority-hiring goal, often under the gaze of a Federal judge. A philanthropic foundation may no longer deploy its assets, or hoard them, as its board members may wish, without risking a court challenge and Internal Revenue action. A labor union may not run its elections of officers any way it wants, but must instead submit to overseers and conform to a large body of rules.

As the list of options has been narrowed, the list of expectations has been expanded. Some goals that were sought in past generations—minimum health care without reference to ability to pay, decent living standards for the aged, a safety net for employees put out of work—are now seen as entitlements, "rights." The first principle of "do no harm," as with the doctors, has been extended to include a "do some good" demand placed on people in all walks of life. Employers are expected to treat their people as individuals, not "hands," and to accommodate organizations to human needs. Vendors of products and services are expected to think about potential hazards as well as benefits of what they offer, and not let their customers be taken by surprise. When there is an accident that imperils health or safety—when a tank car is derailed, when hazards are recognized in an abandoned toxic dumpsite—it is expected that organizations that know how to deal with such problems will clean up the mess promptly and sort out the responsibilities and costs later. No one is much impressed by the excuse that "It's not my tank car," or even "You told me I could put it there."

While all types of organizations live under new ground rules, none has felt greater pressures for change than has private business. The modern commercial organization, and especially the large, stockholder-owned corporation, operates today under markedly different conditions from those that prevailed for earlier generations of owners and managers. The profit motive is still endorsed—survey after survey has shown that the public has no objection to business making money—but the allowable limits of behavior have changed. The community has drawn a line in the dirt, and when business steps over it, the message is quickly heard: "It's okay to make money, but not that way." There is no point in the leaders of organizations waiting for times to "get back to normal." These times are as normal as any. We will not be turning back. Oliver Wendell Holmes once said that ". . . a mind once stretched never returns to its former dimensions." That applies to a society as to an individual, and the third revolution has stretched our community mind. That is what dictates the need for a new kind of management for business firms.

Just as the third revolution has given business a new stake in politics, it has created the need for a new politics of business on the part of society. America could not have won its political independence without powder and shot, food and transport, and lines of credit. By the same token, a social revolution as sweeping as this one cannot succeed without a strong economic underpinning, the chief component of which is the production of goods and services by private-sector commerce and industry in a manner efficient enough to meet world competitive conditions. Economics is rarely irrelevant, though social decisions often pretend it is, and the U.S. has finally learned to its sorrow what many other nations have long known: that prosperity and a vigorous economy cannot be taken for granted.

The recession of 1979–82 and the declining position of the United States in world trade over a much longer time span ought by now to have convinced everyone that America's celebrated economic machine is not invulnerable. It makes mistakes on its own, it responds as readily to external disincentives as to incentives, and increasingly its fates have been manipulated by government. Today, to a far greater extent than in the early days of industrial capitalism, whatever government does about business or to it, by action or neglect, makes a difference in the strength of the support base for the whole of society, and influences such mundane matters as the rise and fall of particular companies, the growth or decline of different industries and geographic areas, and the creation of new jobs or the loss of old ones. The downstream effects of economic performance on social objectives, as much as on material living standards, can neither be ignored nor wished away by good intentions. The unanswered question is whether this is now understood within government, and whether the public-sector apparatus can adapt itself to this reality.

Within the private sector, there has been a visible shift toward public concerns. It can be seen, for example, in the composition of boards of directors. The boards are becoming more diverse in membership and more open in disclosure of facts about the businesses. It can be seen in the changing relationships between employers and employees. It is evident in a slow but sure opening up of relationships with the press, television, and radio. It can be seen in the participation of business representatives in community programs of all kinds—not just in safe, noncontroversial charities which have always enjoyed support from the well-heeled, but also in organizations trying to cope with such touchy problems as urban race relations. Finally, it is made visible by the presence of corporate leaders in Washington and the state capitals, doing in person the sort of work previously done only by paid lobbyists and trade associations, if done at all.

The most important change, though, is one that began to appear many years ago but crystallized only in the 1970s, and that is the change in the way that business people see themselves and their organizations. Increasing numbers of businessmen are seeking a new fit for themselves in society. They speak now of their organizations not merely as machines cranking out profits but as organizations useful for other reasons, enjoying public sufferance because they help society meet society's objectives. The way people in the private sector think of their work says something worth knowing about their sense of accountability. Profit alone may be all that many stockholders want or expect from their corporations, but other signs of utility and performance are necessary to legitimize business in the public eye: useful products and services (the old standbys), plus (in this competitive world) contributions that strengthen the nation's technology, add to its security, and improve its international economic position. Some will claim that many people outside corporate life have always looked upon these as being part of the social charter for the private corporation, and maybe that is so. What is noteworthy now is how many business people are saying the same.

Is all this defensive, nothing more than a tactic to put business on the side of the angels? I do not think so. I read it as a fundamental change in thinking. There is in it something of the antique notion of service which at one time was held up as the model for American citizenship and which businessmen, among others, were not ashamed to endorse. It is not an exaggeration to say that we have seen a return at least in part of the private sector to an idea that fell from fashion during the Depression of the 1930s: namely, that skills honed in business may be of some use to the solution of public problems, and that where those skills apply, the private citizen or organization is duty-bound to apply them.

Quaint words—"duty," "service"—and what interests me is how many business leaders dusted them off in the 1970s and began to use them without embarrassment. The trend hardly fits the stereotype of the modern executive as a portfolio manager who is all numbers and no heart, a person who either uses other people or steps on them as he sees fit, and whose sole tests of worth are the last quarter's earnings and the next quarter's expected increase. Such "macho managers" have always been with us, but one has to wonder whether they were ever as prevalent as was supposed. They have surely been more noticed than admired, and, whatever the limited successes of their organizations in the past, they have a dismal future. In the social climate of today, the "damn the torpedoes" style of management is obsolete. I think there is good evidence that it always was.

Perhaps this is too much to hope for in the short range, but it is not beyond belief that the third revolution could restore throughout the private sector a historic sense of place and community. It could bring back the once widespread notion of public duty first, private interests later. That eighteenth-century point of view had much to do with the creation of these United States. Many of the leaders of the period when the Constitution was being written were businessmen, farm-owners, or self-employed professionals (Washington, Hamilton, Jefferson, the Adamses, Madison). As the founders and early builders of the republic, they regarded public service as having the first call on their time and energy, before family, before private gain. The parallel today is admittedly a loose one. Those early leaders expected to set aside their farm ledgers and lawbooks to make time for the public's work, while my reference is to contributions to the public welfare that for the most part will be made by people in the private sector as part of their work. It is nonetheless a trend worth remarking, for it reflects a mind-set that is in keeping with one of the nation's finer traditions.

(The reason I am not willing to press the parallel very far is that the nation has fallen into a habit of treating its private-sector "volunteers" shabbily. Calls to duty do go forth and are answered by some, but ill-will and suspicion have distorted the conflict-of-interest rules to a point where neither George Washington nor Caesar's wife could pass through the screen. Many a would-be public servant today finds he is expected to sacrifice much of any personal fortune he is assembling, as a penalty price for being allowed to help his country. Such is the fear that the foxes will take over the chickenhouse that even the most knowledgeable of counselors, and sometimes especially those, are turned away from public service. Years of experience in an area of importance—energy supply is a good example—stand for naught if the individual in question suffers from guilt by association with commerce. It is a giant leap to suppose that an ex-executive will dishonor the public trust by favoring his former employer, while other kinds of people taken into government service—say, college professors—are presumed to be made of better stuff, but that is a leap made all the time. This says much about our society's low opinion of chickens as well as foxes, a point on which I will say more later.)

When the United States was founded, most people were self-employed. Now the ratio is nine-to-one the other way. Working in organizations, frequently large ones, is the fact of life not just in business and government but even in occupations that traditionally we think of as independent. Most lawyers no longer work in little offices and see private clients. Most doctors, as television shows correctly inform us, bear no resemblance to the folksy general practitioner of a Norman Rockwell picture on the cover of the *Saturday Evening Post*. The cottage industry of medicine has given way to General Hospital, and the largest single organization in that field today, apart from government-run facilities, is a private corporation which runs a chain of hospitals for profit. Schools have become systems, some with thousands of employees. Small colleges have been joined by big universities, some of which have a score of satellite campuses. There were no large corporations in the nation's early days, and not many organizations of any kind that would qualify today as even middle-sized. Now that there are large numbers of private-sector organizations of every size, and in view of the influence these have on economic and social affairs, questions about the public responsibility of private organizations are on the agenda.

A bit of perspective is in order regarding these questions: Should privately owned enterprises drive for profit alone, or should they be encouraged (compelled?) to consider other needs? Must they answer to constituents other than stockholders, beginning with employees? Should they be required to go still further and accept accountability to the community in a general sense, or even "deprivatized"? Proposals rising out of the "social responsibility" questions filled the pages of the business and popular press in the 1960s and early 1970s and continue to be debated now, but *déjà vu:* It was all said long ago, in the first stirrings of the third revolution. The questions really have not changed much since then, and neither have the answers. What has changed is the support level for ideas once considered radical. The views of the practical visionaries of an earlier generation have become society's majority opinion.

At least a generation ago, it seemed that the debate about duties of private organizations had been satisfactorily resolved. It was evident that the "social responsibility" debate was tripping over false dichotomies. It was departing on tangential arguments: "either-or," profit or public service. It soon dawned on people that this is a phony issue. An organization can admit to being accountable to its first constituency without turning its back on all other claims on its resources or its concern. Leaders at all in touch with the world around them could see that it is not possible for them to wear one hat only. As the late Abe Fortas once put it, in occupying an office of responsibility one does not forfeit membership in the human race. In the early years of this century, as now, leaders with wisdom realized that running any complex organization calls for a balancing of various competing and sometimes conflicting interests, and they have known that a democracy will not long tolerate organizations that pursue policies blind to their public consequences.

Then as now, the argument reduced not so much to beliefs about institutional duties as to a question of the time frame. It is not easy to find successful corporations today that care for nothing but the next quarter's earnings, or to find leaders who echo Commodore Vanderbilt's nineteenth-century expletive: "The public be damned." With twentieth-century realities in sight, it does not take genius to see that society is no longer willing to let people like that run loose. It will put them out of business if not into jail. Neither outcome is profitable, and therefore any corporation whose goals stretch across years or generations can be expected to take a different approach. That would be true even if one were willing to assume that private-sector leaders are driven by no goal more noble than profit.

The conventional wisdom in the private sector today is that organizations can best win needed friends and avoid crippling sanctions if they pay due respect to the needs (and political clout) of all groups significantly affected by their activities. The only thing remarkable about that modern view is how old it is. It was advanced in the early years of the century, and among its champions were some well-known business leaders including Gerard Swope and Owen Young of General Electric; Theodore Vail, Walter Gifford, and Arthur Page of AT&T; and members of the du Pont family running the company they owned. All of them worked from the premise that a business was something that should be around for their children and grandchildren, and that time horizon was translated into policies and actions reflecting responsibility toward employees, customers, and the public.

These are a few of those voices from the past:

"The larger the corporation becomes, the greater become its responsibilities to the entire community" (George Perkins, a director of

U.S. Steel and International Harvester, 1908).

"We feel our obligation to the general public as strongly as to our investing public, or to our own personal interests" (the Bell System's annual report for 1913).

"Today a much higher proportion of corporate leaders realize . . . their obligation of service to the public, and their duty to their employees" (Swope, 1927).

"We know that real success in business is not attained at the expense of others. Business can succeed only in the long run by acquiring and holding the good will of the people. . . . [Most of] the best upper class men in business would not consider a policy which enriched them or their company and was at the same time against the public interest" (Charles Cason, Chemical National Bank of New York, 1927).

There were precedents much earlier. A British court in 1883 handed down the famous "cakes and ale" decision, in which Lord Justice Bowen said that a company might provide free cakes and ale to its workers because that "sort of liberal dealing with servants eases the friction between masters and servants, and is, in the end, a benefit to the company."

The most eloquent advocate of the businessman-as-citizen was not one from the ranks of businessmen or from the judiciary, though, but was instead the philosopher Alfred North Whitehead. In lectures at Harvard University, Whitehead examined public and private interests against one another, and pressed the conclusion that the first condition for steady prosperity in an economy is the general greatness of the community. He added, in lines that have been quoted countless times, that in a great society businessmen would think greatly of their function.

Whitehead said that in 1931. Two years earlier, the stock market had crashed. One year later, the national election brought the New Deal administration into power. The United States economy was in the worst depression in history.

The years on each side—the mid-1920s through the mid-1930s— are particularly important to the theme developed here. In that ten-to-twelve-year period, sweeping changes were made in the management of the economic system by government, and private business went from the top of the heap to the bottom in terms of reputation and government relations. At the beginning of this period, the status of business was reflected in words that President Warren Harding had used: "This is essentially a business country [and] we need business sense in charge of American administration." By the late 1930s, as the Chamber of Commerce accurately reported, business had become "the country's Number One whipping boy."

I leave to historians the question of what might have been, had the leaders of business and politics found a way to work together on the problems that wracked society. What is a matter of record is that the needle swung the other way, toward antagonism and away from any serious effort toward collaboration. Business and government could not agree on the causes of the nation's agony, and even less on the correctives. What business leaders had read in the 1920s as a sense of public support and harmony became, in fact, a legacy of bitterness and distrust that still pervades the business-government relationship.

Trouble signs were there for all to see. The New Deal was preceded by (maybe produced by) a churning of ideas in universities and colleges, in the political system, and in the press, ever more critical of real and presumed failings on the part of businessmen. Investigations run in 1932 by the Senate Banking and Currency Committee made it clear that the house of commerce was in far from good order; gross, widespread misconduct was brought to public view. As the Depression tightened its hold, there was a growing political conviction that the economic system as it had run in the past simply could not survive unchanged. The public had lost confidence in it.

By the time Franklin Roosevelt took office in March 1933, the pressures for action were irresistible. What followed were social-welfare and insurance programs, launched to provide people with economic help and security in greater measure than the private sector had delivered: veterans' pensions (1933), the Social Security system and Aid to Families with Dependent Children (1935), the railroad retirement system and housing assistance (1937), and wage-and-hour laws (1938).

On the same timetable, new laws drew power into Federal hands and created a string of new agencies regulating the private sector: the Securities and Exchange Commission (1934); the National Industrial Recovery Act (creating the NRA), and the Federal Communications Commission (1935); the Robinson-Patman Act (an effort to load the antitrust laws in favor of small business) and the Commodity Exchange Commission (1936); and the Civil Aeronautics Authority

(1938). With the exception of the NRA, declared unconstitutional by the Supreme Court, and parts of an agricultural assistance program which met a similar fate, all of the New Deal laws and agencies remained in existence (some in amended form) for decades thereafter.

The style was control and command: many sticks, few carrots. The result is today's bulging library of regulations setting forth in detail the approved relationships between businesses and employees, customers, competitors, suppliers, neighbors, and the public at large.

In 1935, simply to keep track of the new rules laid down each year, government set up the annual Federal Registry. Two years later, it contained 3,400 pages. In the next forty years, it climbed to 65,000 pages.

Through the 1930s, business stood firm, heels dug in against the New Deal "reforms," Social Security and wage-and-hour laws included. The more conservative element reacted in horror to what it regarded as the invasion of business' turf. Some leaders feared a deliberate "sell-out" of free enterprise, into socialism or worse. Closer to the political center, the view of business leaders was that the New Deal's policies, if well-intentioned, were so wrongheaded economically that they could not restore prosperity, and would produce only a vast centralization of power in a Federal bureaucracy endangering personal freedom. Some believers in that view are still alive, and argue that history has proven them right. At the time, however, business' reasons for opposition carried little weight. The leaders presenting them were elbowed aside.

It must be conceded that many of the people who spoke for business did more to hurt their cause than help it. Through the 1920s, along with some visionaries, business produced leaders who were proud of themselves and not afraid to say so. Humility was not in fashion for captains of industry. Some saw themselves as especially wise, farsighted, and ordained, and deserving of privileges not to be offered to the great unwashed.

"Without these great minds," one spokesman claimed of business leaders, "the multitude would eat their heads off and, as history proves, would lapse into barbarism...."

"The manufacturer is the great constructor," said A. B. Farquhar of the National Association of Manufacturers. "[His] is by far the most important of all classes.... We would be living in caves, dressed in skins, except for him...."

Invidious comparisons seemed entirely in order to some enthusiasts. In *Nation's Business,* the Chamber of Commerce magazine, E. W. Howe said that "businessmen have better ability and philosophy, and are more useful, than writers, soap box orators, politicians and statesmen. . . ."

The all-time record for unfortunate expression with bad timing probably goes to James Edgerton, who, as president of the National Association of Manufacturers, contended that business leaders are "the relatively few who can see far into the distance. . . . Of such is the kingdom of leadership, and upon them the mass advancements of civilization itself depend." He said that in the fall of 1929, just before Black Friday took the stock market apart.

Hubris was not universal. Just as some critics of business were temperate and sympathetic, some business leaders saw the need for changes and recognized that business, in seeming to oppose everything, was shooting itself in the foot. As was said in 1934 by Milo Perkins, a manufacturer from Houston, "The capitalist system can be destroyed more effectively by having men of means defend it than by importing a million Reds from Moscow to attack it. Unless we work out a program [to solve the nation's economic problems] so simple that children can grasp it and then carry the fight for its adoption to the front-line trenches, we'll be museum pieces in fifty years."

Donaldson Brown, a General Motors executive, worked within the NAM, trying to restrain its public statements. AT&T, having seen in the 1920s that antibusiness sentiment was building, took itself out of a NAM publicity campaign which was meant to polish business' image and silence its critics, but which failed to deal with the real issues. Those calmer voices failed to prevail, though. They were overwhelmed by the strident noises coming from the Chamber of Commerce and the NAM, and unresponsive arguments from such organizations as the American Liberty League.

The League existed for only a few years, but its story is particularly instructive. Its rise and fall show how people dedicated to principle but out of touch with their times can make judgment calls that cancel out their own influence and provide ammunition to their opponents.

The League was founded as a result of an exchange of letters in 1934 between two executives, R. R. M. Carpenter of Du Pont, and John J. Raskob, an official at different times in Du Pont and General Motors. It was financed by wealthy individuals led by members of the du Pont family.

The Liberty League's announced purpose sounded reasonable

enough. It was to teach "the necessity for respect for the rights of persons and property." It declared it to be "the duty of government to encourage and protect individual and group initiative and enterprise, to foster the right to work, earn, save, and acquire property, and to preserve the ownership and lawful use of property when acquired." Good old American virtues, those.

Yet others did not react that way. Looking at the list of League sponsors, opponents decided that what the League sought to protect was the privileged position of the owners of large amounts of property, at others' expense. Retention of power was taken to be the true goal. The League's boosters did little to counter that impression. Carpenter complained privately about the problems President Roosevelt's policies were creating, and gave as examples the fact that the five blacks at his place in South Carolina "refused to work this spring . . . stating they had easy jobs with the government," and "a cook on my houseboat at Fort Myers quit because the government was paying him a dollar an hour."

Raskob, writing to Carpenter to encourage support for the League within industry, said that big companies ought to organize "to protect society from the suffering which it is bound to endure if we allow communistic elements to lead the people to believe that all businessmen are crooks, not to be trusted, and that no one should be allowed to get rich."

(Raskob's presence in the cast is worth special note, for he was a Democrat. In addition to being an executive and investor—he helped finance the Empire State Building—he was chairman of the Democratic Party, 1928–32, between the campaigns of Al Smith and Franklin Roosevelt. While the League's backers were strongly conservative, it was ideology rather than partisanship that bound them together.)

By the League's philosophy, "small is beautiful" pertains, but only for government: Larger slices of power ought to be reserved to private-sector leaders. Demarest Lloyd, one of the League's major supporters, held that Congress "should delegate its powers and functions to a small group, not over a hundred of the most well-informed, intelligent and patriotic men in the country." William Perkins, a member of a lawyers' committee of the League, claimed that the public owed business leaders its support. "Who but they developed and established this great country of ours commercially?" he asked, echoing the faith of the 1920s.

The Liberty League was too much even for probusiness *Fortune* magazine, which labeled the organization's backers "self-righteous" and "self-satisfied." For a less friendly group, the New Deal strategists, the Liberty League was a target as big as a barn. They could not have fabricated an enemy as easy to attack as the one given to them. The leaders of the League could be held up to the public as people who looked upon privilege and authority as "givens," but who themselves had proven they did not have the capacity to lead; people who lived in the past, resisted change, and would not even admit complicity in the policies that had brought the nation to its knees economically. Whether any of that is a fair description of the real qualities of the people in the League is quite beside the point.

The fatal flaws of the American Liberty League were its insensitivity to everyday problems and a paucity of ideas for overcoming them. What the public wanted—from business, from government, from anybody—was not a lecture on property rights or sermons on self-reliance, but action. The League was against much, but stood for little that had practical application for ordinary citizens. Milo Perkins put his finger on it. As a class, he said, "We businessmen are offering no program of action to the American people which would make tomorrow seem more attractive than today. We who have done such an amazing job of selling the public everything from soap to radios are failing miserably in selling ourselves."

As L. L. Golden wrote in the book *Only by Public Consent: American Corporations Search for Favorable Opinion,* "[The League] failed because it had to fail, not because the virtues [it] supported ... were untenable but because the kinds of freedom and liberty stressed and campaigned for by the League had no relevance to the man who needed a job badly, could not get one, and was bitter with frustration."

The pertinence of jobs is emphasized by the fact that in the year the Liberty League was founded, the unemployment rate in the United States was close to 20 percent. It had been even higher the previous two years; and, as labor economist Arnold Weber has more recently pointed out, one of the truths of American politics is that the nation will not tolerate prolonged high unemployment rates. We are not willing to run a social system with a discard pile. That is as much worth remembering in the 1980s as in the 1930s.

The League was an enthusiastic backer of Alf Landon in his campaign against Roosevelt in 1936. Landon's lopsided defeat set a record for voter nonsupport (he carried only Maine and Vermont) that stood until George McGovern ran in 1972 and carried one state less. Following the 1936 election, the League declined and disappeared.

The Liberty League is forgotten. The old NAM and Chamber of Commerce are gone: Organizations bearing the same names thrive today but are entirely different in focus, purpose, and operating style. The U.S. has since been through several wars, through the longest and most vigorous period of economic growth in the nation's history, and through several recessions. During World War II, the public focus was on business' constructive talents: It excelled in forced-draft production skills and technological prowess. In the years that followed, the emphasis was on restoring and expanding the civilian economy. Doing its basic jobs well, business drew away from much of the criticism that had overwhelmed it during the Thirties.

For American enterprise, the late 1940s and the 1950s were days of wine and roses. Markets existed for almost any product or service one could offer. The U.S. dollar was strong and the foreign competition, weak. Other industrialized nations were behind the U.S. on the technology and productivity curves, and were preoccupied with their own problems of rebuilding war-torn economies: Germany, the United Kingdom, Japan. The U.S. accounted for more than one-half of all of the world's industrial production. The American workman was the best-educated in the world, had the highest output per man-hour, and earned the highest real wages.

Business developed a false sense of security. It paid too much attention to the favorable comments in public-opinion polls, and not enough to the fact that there had been no shift in people's basic views about business' responsibilities and the public welfare. The mood of New Deal reform was still there, with its central assumption that the Federal government should be the moderator between citizens and commerce. Pressures for societal improvement did not decline with prosperity, but increased, strengthened by the notion that economic wealth was now assured. No more depressions: The U.S economy would grow indefinitely except for shallow, short corrections. It was time to attend to unfinished business: civil rights, equality of opportunity, better housing, better medical care, improvements in job safety and working conditions, the correction of abuses and reduction of hazards in the marketplace.

I believe it was an ecologist at Yale, Paul Sears, who created the most memorable phrase of this era. He suggested that the time had come for the nation to stop paying so much attention to the quantity of its goods and begin paying more to the quality of its life. At the time, the mid-1950s, not many people knew what an ecologist was, but the professor proved to be the man on the front edge of the wave. Within a few years, all of America was talking about "quality of life." The environmental movement was under way.

In response to public pressure for social change, government launched new rounds of regulation. The peak years were 1964 through 1972, when the Equal Employment Opportunity Commission, Council on Environmental Quality, Environmental Protection Agency, Occupational Safety and Health Administration, and Consumer Product Safety Commission came into being. Business found itself on the outside, looking in. Its leaders were regarded not as positive contributors but as impediments to social and political change.

As in the past, cases of wrongdoing chipped at business' reputation. Leading firms in the electrical industry were convicted of price-fixing, a *per se* violation of the antitrust law. Officials of prominent companies in numerous industries were found to have made political contributions in Federal elections with corporate funds. Various other kinds of questionable payments were turned up, not here and there but by the handful. The Securities and Exchange Commission ended up with more than 400 companies on its confessors' list. Some infractions were nothing worse than bad judgment calls on the part of managers, but many cases were clear-cut violations of clear-cut laws. Shades of the Senate investigations of 1932. Where government officials were the principal malefactors, as in Watergate and lesser White House scandals before and since, it often developed that there had been business accomplices in the wings. Shades of Teapot Dome.

Whether there was more or less nonfeasance and malfeasance during this period than in earlier times is impossible to know, but beside the point. Failings did exist and there were enough of them to fan embers back into flames. ("I told you so." "Business ethics is a contradiction in terms." Etc.) It would be a mistake, though, to conclude that it was *per se* offenses that most corroded the public's confidence in business. Crimes were compounded by more general concerns about corporate performance: consumer dissatisfaction with products and services, business' overemphasis on profits, and a perceived disregard for the social impact of corporate actions. There were sins of omission, as for example with company pension funds that evaporated, leaving long-service employees with no retirement benefits when businesses closed shop. Those pension funds had never been protected by vesting.

By an objective measure, it could probably be demonstrated that criticism of business increased in spite of substantially improved performance, and not because of corporate backsliding. In most companies, the quality of products and services, working conditions, and employee- and community-relations programs were better in the 1960s than in any earlier decade; but that, too, turned out to be beside the point. While standards had improved, expectations had ratcheted upward even more. As new goals were agreed upon—clean air, fishable and swimmable rivers, equal pay for equal work, safer autos—the acceptable minimums moved up, and the public became impatient with those who failed to measure up.

Businessmen felt particularly put upon, but they were not alone. This was the winter of our national discontent, the Vietnam War period, when "the system" as a whole was on public trial as a class-action case. Hospital administrators were besieged by angry claimants. University presidents found their offices taken over by students with "nonnegotiable demands." Political rallies disintegrated into mob scenes. Bearers of bad tidings were shouted off lecture platforms. Demands for the reform if not the complete overhaul of society faced public and private sectors alike.

Government as much as business was seen as failing the public. There was a growing gap between what government did and what it had promised people it could do. There seemed to be more truth than ever in the First Law of Bureaucracies: that they take on lives of their own, irrespective of results or the people they are supposed to serve. Urban budgets increased, but cities continued to decay. Urban crime became worse. Progress came slowly in such areas as employment opportunities for blacks and women. After decades of public support for Federal housing projects, a room-count showed that there were fewer rather than more low-cost housing units in the nation.

If you cannot solve a problem, move it. As the public sector gained a reputation for being unable to cope with national problems, many people concluded that the thing to do was to shift a large part of the burden to the private sector and hold its feet to the fire: Tell business it has to move in; establish quotas and timetables; accept no excuses.

Damn the expense. That was the rest of the message. If the U.S. could send a man to the moon, it surely ought to be able to clean up the cities down below and the air above them. Never mind the fact that the cost of earthbound programs was dozens of times higher than the price of a moon walk. It was wrong to speak of dollars when the human condition was at stake. Hubert Humphrey said late in his life that at the time the Occupational Safety and Health Administration (OSHA) was in the planning stages and on its way to the floor of Congress, nobody even raised the question of how much it was going to cost. Senator Humphrey was one of a large number of legislators who later acknowledged that such a view could only leave the nation short in its other accounts, but at the time Congress was in no mood for lectures on the finiteness of economic resources. "Trade-offs" and "cost-benefit analyses" were not yet acceptable in the political vocabulary.

It is beyond dispute that the 1960s and 1970s brought gains that were and are strongly endorsed by the public. What is worth considering is how much of the real progress was of government's doing and, where it was, how much the political and economic systems were warped in the process. What other important work was deferred? Perhaps the point can be made for any period in history, but it seems in retrospect that equal or better results could have been achieved if the government had pursued a different tack.

EPA and OSHA, for example, could have helped produce environmental-improvement and better employee-protection programs at less expense by using more carrots and fewer sticks. In 1980, after OSHA had been in business for ten years, the list of industries and companies with the poorest safety records still looked much the same as the list of 1970. The industries and firms with the best records were the ones that had excelled before. Worse for the government's case, the companies that had maintained good records had done so mostly by following practices they had developed on their own and installed before OSHA was created.

There were suggestions in advance, from people with firsthand experience in such matters, that such might be the results, but the command-and-control voice prevailed. Volunteerism was nowhere in favor. Business was back in the woodshed, being instructed on proper behavior and being told, "You had your chance and you blew it."

Government further extended its reach into the private sector. It had long been a corporate partner in the sense that it took about one-half of the profits in the form of taxes. Now it became a partner in a new sense, as an overseer of operations. The government helped General Motors design the bumpers on its cars, and passed judgment on the webbing width of seat belts. Government helped Sears, Roebuck select the right words for warning labels and warranties on merchandise, and monitored product-performance claims for truthfulness, deciding on its own how to draw the line between commercial poetry and dishonesty. Du Pont and Dow had government help in engineering the tank cars that carry hazardous materials on the railroads, down to the specifications for the brackets that join the tanks and frames. Employers of every description, beyond being given encouragement in bringing minorities into the work force, were given detailed instructions on how to report the number of people hired and promoted, so that government could decide whether affirmative action was affirmative enough.

The costs of all this were cumulative and large. There is no way to compute the size of the bill with precision. It is like trying to count the trees in Canada—the best you can do is fly over it and make estimates. Some costs would have been incurred anyway, for other reasons. A plant's pollution-control program may pay for itself in part by retrieving valuable materials that can be recycled. Other costs were more clearly red-ink. Everybody chipped in, that much is certain. Some quality-of-life costs were reflected in higher selling prices for products and services. The stockholders paid: Higher operating costs mean lower profits, with less to be passed along in dividends. Not to be overlooked are the tax dollars required to staff the government agencies managing social and regulatory programs. Such programs represent by far the largest portion of Federal and state budgets, where most of their costs are "people costs": wages, salaries, and related expenses.

On the other side, there were direct and indirect gains and savings to business and society alike. A safer workplace equates with higher productivity and lower medical bills. Appropriate high standards for the testing of pharmaceuticals and agricultural chemicals protect manufacturers as well as users. Bringing blacks and women into the economic mainstream and giving them a chance to develop full potential provides society with contributions it would otherwise be denied. As with education, the justification for equal opportunity does not lie exclusively or mainly in an economic calculus, but that surely strengthens its defense.

How does the calculation balance out? That is a judgment call, and it is probably too early to make it. Both the bills and the benefits are still coming in. This much can be said in summary: The postwar expansion of government involvement in the economy has required the spending of hundreds of billions of dollars (environmental programs alone put the numbers in that range). While goals and standards have gone up linearly, costs have gone up geometrically (it costs more to get the last percent of a pollutant out of a river than to remove the first 50 percent). Finally, whether the dollars were spent well or otherwise, they were unavailable for other purposes.

Obvious as that last point is, it bears mentioning for an unhappy reason: As the race toward social goals reached full velocity, the economic means to support those goals began to weaken. The assumption that the American economy could run on autopilot, producing permanent prosperity and sustaining any number of social programs, was plainly and simply wrong. Living with that dream cost this nation dearly.

If the 1960s and 1970s can be read as decades of an activated social consciousness, they should also be remembered as the time when the U.S. lost its economic virginity. Economic differences among major nations became progressively smaller and international economic competition increased. Between 1960 and 1980, leading nations steadily converged in productivity, in their rates of growth in real output, and in their technological capability. Output on a per-capita basis was higher in the U.S. in 1960 than in Germany, France, the United Kingdom, Japan, and a number of other countries, by a large margin. It was also higher in 1980, but by a much smaller margin.

The everyday results of this closure became plain to see. Imported cars filled American streets. Japanese producers effectively took over the U.S. market for television sets and radios. Textile-makers, steel-producers, and chemical-manufacturers based in the U.S. confronted a steadily rising number of able competitors from other nations, selling in both domestic and foreign markets. America's market share, its percentage of the world's total production, declined. Some U.S. jobs went down with it. So did some U.S. companies and a lot of illusions.

U.S. business firms found themselves boxed in. As their competitors became more efficient and aggressive, frequently with help from their national governments, American companies were hit with double-barreled cost increases, once courtesy of government requirements as noted above, and once more by rising wages, pension payments, and other outlays for employee benefits. (Corporate managements have since been criticized for "giving away the store" through rounds of collective-bargaining agreements in which pay was divorced from productivity. These contracts, mostly drawn in the days when American industry was king of the hill, set patterns for unionized and non-unionized companies alike, and made high-cost producers of them all. The criticism is deserved.)

The next most important resource for progress, after people, is capital investment. At a time when industries needed large infusions of dollars to modernize plants and install new technologies, domestic economic conditions and tax policies took away the funds for such reinvestment. With inflation, anything new costs more than what it replaces. The money that companies were allowed to set aside for depreciation was not adequate to cover even one-for-one replacements, let alone machines of newer, more efficient design. After corporate annual reports were adjusted for inflation, and interest was paid on the money that companies were borrowing, it turned out that many of the best-known and presumably best-run companies in the nation were nonprofit enterprises. In real terms, they were making no money at all. With the Red Queen in *Through the Looking Glass,* they were running faster and faster just to stay in the same place.

The souring relationship of business and government made this a no-win period. In some other nations, government and business were combining resources to finance a strong industrial base, to build the unit size of enterprises to gain efficiency, and to establish toeholds in new markets. In the U.S., the comparable private organizations found they had more critics than defenders in the public sector. In many agencies of the Federal government, officials simply did not care whether the companies and industries that came before them survived or not. ("That's not my department." In truth, it was not anybody's department.) There was more political mileage in calling for a break-up of big businesses than in doing anything that appeared to favor them. As for businesses getting together privately with one another, American antitrust law specifically proscribed most such coalitions. Meanwhile, foreign governments arranged them for their companies.

On public issues, American business faced Hobson's choice: It could not decline involvement, and it seemed singularly unsuccessful in affecting the outcome. Many issues fell in its lap, of necessity. No one could argue, for example, that pollution control or occupational safety should not be business' concerns. Moreover, the larger private firms were too much a part of the economy to exempt themselves on any account. For them to try to stay out of sight—"show a low profile," in the jargon of the day—was like trying to hide the elephant in the strawberry patch.

Yet when business stepped forward or was pushed into the limelight, it was put on the defensive. It was supposed to do the government's bidding, do penance for past misdeeds, pay the bills, and wait for further instructions. The private sector not only was expected to have little influence on "the big questions" ("Where is the nation going?"); it was even losing its grip on the tiniest details of running its own shops. The diameter of the pipe used for hand railings on staircases, OSHA proclaimed, should be OSHA's business, not the private sector's.

It understates the case to say that people at or near the top in the private sector felt stymied and irritated. Beyond the sense of personal insult—nobody likes to be treated like an errant schoolboy tugged by the ear to a caning—they decried what they saw as the illogic of many of the rules being imposed and the lack of coherent, workable Federal policies that recognized competitive realities. The after-dinner speeches and Congressional testimony of executives through the 1960s and 1970s were filled with complaints about "excessive regulations" and with pleas for more of a balance between social ends and economic means. They also abounded with warnings that sooner or later the economy would come unstuck.

How much difference the speeches made is questionable—mostly business people were talking to business people, preaching sermons to the choir. What did make a difference, however, were the gathering economic storm plus a conscious decision by a relative handful of business executives to take a new approach to the public-policy process.

Only a little needs to be added to what has already been said about that storm. Soon after the American public began to feel the impact of international competition, the energy crunch of the mid-1970s hit. It was triggered in 1973 by OPEC, the Organization of Petroleum Exporting Countries, through an embargo on shipments to oil-dependent nations, and a rapid run-up in crude-oil prices. OPEC's move was the most massive wealth-reallocating scheme of all time, enriching OPEC nations by taking from everyone else, and penalizing the less-rich, developing nations even more than the wealthier, industrialized countries.

OPEC alone cannot be blamed for America's eroding competitive position, for its persistent Federal-government deficits and their consequences, or for more than a fraction of the inflation of the 1970s. The energy crisis touched off by OPEC did have powerful effects, though. It was at least partly responsible for making economics front-page news, as economics had not been since the days when people were selling apples on the streets and singing, "Brother, can you spare a dime?" As had no event since the Depression, it brought home the lesson that even the strongest economy in the world can be crippled. It also did a lot to convince the public of the lack of foresight in Federal programs steering the economy: People learned, for example, that the net effect of past energy policies was to encourage high consumption and discourage exploration, production, and conservation—the exact reverse of the outcomes the public would want from governmental policies.

Several years before OPEC's major move, some American business leaders decided to try a new approach to government, in the hope that this would produce better policies on issues of economic concern. The individuals in question had come to the conclusion that the nation could no longer afford the adversarial climate, not merely because it was painful to them but because it was producing wrong decisions for wrong reasons. Moreover, this group of businessmen concluded that the private sector might not survive much longer if they themselves remained defensive versus the public and ineffectual in the political arena. As was said in 1978 by Thomas Murphy, head of General Motors, "We have been clobbered in the marketplace of ideas and public issues."

The new approach was for business executives personally to commit time to governmental and public-policy affairs, to do their homework on issues, to learn how the political process works and how to survive in it, to develop the skills needed to accomplish something constructive, to learn how to sell ideas out in the open, in view of the press, radio, and television, and, above all, to earn the credibility and trust that were needed if they were to have any enduring effect on the public-policy process.

It is a different approach in many ways, but, as I have suggested, it was telegraphed long in advance. What it represents is an acceptance by business leaders that they as much as anyone are part of the third revolution, and that they can help move it forward if they are willing to come into the public forum with the desire to contribute without a demand that they be given control. It is a recognition, too, that businessmen have to earn their place at the table, and that if changes are to be made in relationships with government, these have to begin with business.

In an economics classic that few read but many talk about, *The General Theory of Employment, Interest and Money,* John Maynard Keynes made the point that ideas exert a more powerful influence on everyday affairs than most people recognize. He said, "Practical men, who believe themselves to be quite exempt from any intellectual influences, are usually the slaves of some defunct economist." In this instance, businessmen are responding to an idea not from an economist but from the philosopher Whitehead, with his line about businessmen thinking greatly of their function. It is too much to say that business people are now doing that, but it is evident that a new breed of leaders has emerged in the private sector, and at least they seem to understand what Whitehead meant. How much and how fast the ranks of this new breed will grow, and how much of a positive contribution will result in the efforts to build a better society, are the open questions.

2

The New Breed

Bᴜꜱɪɴᴇꜱꜱᴍᴇɴ are supposed to be pragmatists, good at getting results, realistic about the factors that affect their profits. Given the goal of building better relationships between the private and public sectors, business in the 1960s and early 1970s was by its own standards a miserable failure. Business was at an impasse. Companies in the United States faced rising international competition and domestic problems. They were increasingly burdened by the consequences of governmental policies but they were unable to have much effect even on the decisions most important to their operations.

It was at this point that a relative handful of business leaders, responding to the guidance of Arthur F. Burns and others, decided that the future would be bleak unless business started doing things differently. That was a turning point—not the recognition that the climate was extremely bad (anyone in the country who was marginally literate knew that) but the realization that the ball was in business' court. Out of this came a new breed of private-sector leaders.

A way to tell this story is through an organization named The Business Roundtable, and of the relationships some of its members built up with government during the Ford and Carter administrations. At the time Richard Nixon left office and Gerald Ford succeeded him, the private and public sectors were circling each other like sumo wrestlers. Seven years later, when Jimmy Carter left office and Ronald Reagan's administration began, there was a climate that permitted an open, candid exchange between the Oval Office and many corporate executive suites. Pin-striped chief executive officers, Republicans almost to a man, were welcome in the chambers of the most powerful

26

member of the majority party in Congress, Thomas P. "Tip" O'Neill, Speaker of the House, liberal Democrat. Many businessmen had learned how to present their views in a political setting, fulfilling one of the main objectives of the Roundtable's founders. Events had progressed to a point where a businessman with my background, from a company with only a small percentage of employees in national unions, could sort through economic problems with George Meany, longtime head of the AFL/CIO, or with his successor, Lane Kirkland, and find common ground for recommendations to Congress. I vividly remember a day when George Meany and I trooped up Capitol Hill together to present a joint position on what ought to be done about Far Eastern textile imports that were affecting U.S. jobs and the economy, thinking to myself that this was not a companion most executives in my kind of organization would have dreamed of choosing a decade earlier. For all I know, Meany was thinking the same thing.

What had happened was that many leaders of private corporations had learned what political leaders already knew: that the public-policy process hinges mostly on dealings among individuals, and that there is no substitute for personal contact and trust. People from the private and public sectors had built up personal credibility. They had established a basis for discussing issues frankly, without bombast, even with governmental leaders whose philosophy they did not share. They had learned that, because the cast of characters in government and the private sector is always changing, a constant testing process is going on to determine whose judgment is worthwhile and who can be counted on to present straight facts. People in business also discovered that they have to go through that screening process in person, like everyone else.

A number of organizations other than the Roundtable could be used to describe the changes that took place during the Seventies. One was something called the Labor-Management Group, an organization of national union and corporate leaders who met from time to time to discuss national policy questions. It was this group that brought George Meany and me together. An education in the workings of the public-policy process also was gained by some leaders of smaller companies, as represented by the American Business Conference and by a number of trade and industry associations. Good examples also could be drawn from organizations apart from business. Colleges and universities can claim presidents of the new breed, and some of these leaders rose to view before their counterparts appeared in commerce. Foundations, voluntary associations, and leading policy-study centers could yield cases, too. Examples include the Brookings Institution and the American Enterprise Institute, influential Washington-based organizations that are regarded generally (if not quite accurately) as encampments, respectively, of liberal and conservative thought, with each institution serving as safe harbor for political "outs" while the other's team is "in."

The reason to call forth the Roundtable in particular is that it is unique. Only corporate chief executives can be members, and then only by invitation. In temperament, the Roundtable is poles apart from most of the organizations that spoke for business in previous generations. Its goal is constructive action, not opposition. It is unafraid of controversy, and its activities on varied issues have brought the Roundtable considerable press attention, along with a reputation for having that rarely defined (and probably overrated) quality known as political clout. It is doubtful that the Roundtable deserves as much praise or blame as has been heaped on it—it has lost as many as it has won—but it is beyond argument that the organization did gain prominence in the Seventies, and its failures as well as successes serve as evidence of how fast attitudes could be changed once business "started doing things differently."

The Business Roundtable was created by executives who had shared ideas and frustrations with one another at meetings of the Business Council. Founded in 1933, the Business Council has about 200 members. It meets quarterly for social activity and to review economic trends and public-policy developments. Senior government officials up to and including the President speak at meetings. The Business Council is not an action group, however. It mounts no campaigns and dispenses no political funds. It is useful, but only as a forum, and that self-imposed limitation led some of its members to set up separate, action-oriented alliances.

One was a labor-law study group, dedicated to the proposition that the legislative pendulum had swung too far in favor of national labor unions, and that it was time to build political support for what business regarded as needed reforms. Another group was the Construction-Users Anti-Inflation Roundtable, whose title tells all. Year after year, the costs of construction had been rising at 15 to 25 percent annually, which is to say that any given project could be expected to double in price every four to five years. Most of the cost increases could be traced to rising pay scales and benefits in the unionized construction trades. The Anti-Inflation Roundtable brought contractors together with the buyers of construction with the objective of capping costs, revising work rules, and relating workers' pay and fringe benefits to workers' output; that is to say, bringing the notion of productivity back to the bargaining table.

Predictably, both the labor-law and construction-users groups were taken by opponents to be billies for union-busting by big business. However construed, though, the missions of the groups were what the leaders claimed them to be: efforts to constrain runaway inflationary trends which businessmen were convinced were having disastrous economic consequences. That point of view later gained wider respectability when the public recognized inflation as a serious national (and personal) problem. Eventually, even union leaders began to identify themselves as inflation-fighters. At the beginning of the 1970s, however, admitting publicly that those "right-wingers" in business had a point was not a way to rally rank-and-file support in the guild hall.

A third such alliance was the March Group, named for the month of the year in which it met. Its organizers hoped that if business leaders could be persuaded to stop talking to themselves and listen to others, they might come up with workable ideas for reversing some of the negative trends. To that end, three executives, John Harper of Alcoa, Henry Ford II of Ford Motor Company, and Fred Borch of General Electric, met with a group of corporate Washington representatives, arranged through them for interviews with Congressmen and others in public life, and began to pull together the strands that in 1972 were braided into The Business Roundtable. John Harper was the first Roundtable chairman, and half of his executive committee were people from the labor-law or construction-users groups. Over time, those two groups melded into the Roundtable and became part of its committee structure.

The interviews with government officials brought forth a bill of particulars: When business leaders did call on government, which was rare, they were negative, inflexible, and inclined to stonewall problems. They were regarded as long on rhetoric but short on practical suggestions to help a politician handle the issues on his doorstep in ways that could be sold to the voters back home. Trade and industry associations were seen as groups trying to peddle positions reflecting the lowest common denominator, defending the most selfish of interests. When a labor union had something to sell to Congress, its top leaders personally made the contracts, but, with a few exceptions, business' spokesmen were seen as "messengers", i.e., as people lacking the authority to make the compromises that are the bread and butter of politics. One Congressman, complaining to the interviewers about the parade of "corporate reps" programmed to their masters' voices, told them to send "somebody who can commit his company."

My first reaction to the Roundtable was negative. After attending one of its meetings, I told my predecessor at Du Pont, Charles B. McCoy, that all I had heard was industry people talking about their problems without any reference to the larger public-policy issues involved. McCoy's advice to me was to be patient. He said the Roundtable leaders were well aware of this problem and were trying to point the members in a new direction. Like turning an aircraft carrier 180 degrees, this takes time. McCoy was right. John Harper proved to have an excellent understanding of the workings of the political process. He and a core group of others (including John deButts of AT&T, Reginald Jones of General Electric, and, a little later, Thomas Murphy of General Motors and Walter Wriston of Citicorp) set about the task of leading by example, and building an effective liaison with the Federal government.

The first generation of leadership gave the Roundtable its distinctive cast. The central ideas, which survive to this day, are that the Roundtable members should carry the mail in person, dealing with issues on which they had solid background, and offering positive proposals wherever possible. Operating through task forces assigned to specific issues, these executives would be responsible for research, analysis, and the preparation of position papers. When they were ready to "go public" on public-policy issues, they would provide the lead by speaking out at press conferences, and ask for meetings with Congressmen and executive-branch officials.

That is the way it has worked out. The Roundtable has never built a bureaucracy. It has small offices in New York and Washington. Though the membership has grown from a few dozen CEOs to about 200, the paid staff has been kept in the range of a dozen people. The thinking all along has been to avoid building a staff to churn out policy papers to which CEOs sign their names. Rather, the expectation

has been that executives will do their own homework, drawing on
assistance as needed from their own companies or outside consultants.

The value of solid research and of knowing the territory can hardly
be overstated. As one Washington veteran has said, "You better do it
right the first time because in this town you don't get many shots."
His point was reinforced by a government official who said that many
businessmen came to his office "very poorly prepared, with only a
bitch and a groan and without real substance to back up their points
or practical suggestions for dealing with them. Diplomatic and polite
though I am by nature, many of these petitioners went away feeling
that I was unresponsive and unsympathetic."

If the man who said that sounds unsympathetic, others in government could hardly be expected to be more forgiving. The quote comes
from George Shultz, a man who at the time was wearing a government
hat but who knows business' problems at first hand. In addition to
serving as Secretary of Labor, of Treasury, and of State under different
Presidents, he has been president of the Bechtel Group, a multibillion-
dollar construction and engineering organization which has built industrial plants, refineries, and transit systems in different parts of the
world.

"Don't bite off more than you can chew" has been the motto of the
Roundtable's Policy Committee, the group that monitors the task
forces. The Roundtable has tried to deal only with issues with broad
connotations for the economic and social well-being of the nation, and
only with those where the perspective of business can provide significant contributions. There has been no shortage of candidate issues for
the Roundtable. Over the years, its list has grown from the point-of-
entry issues of inflation and labor-management relations, to include
taxation, capital formation and creation of jobs, environment, wage
and price controls, Federal chartering of corporations, antitrust,
criminal-code reform, international trade and investment, energy supply, consumer-protection legislation, product liability law, health-care
systems and cost containment, welfare, Social Security and private
pension systems, the costs of regulation, and the improvement of government staff.

The Roundtable has sought diversity of membership in both geography and types of businesses. The cross-section is shown by a look at
some of the members who chaired task forces or served on the Policy

Committee in the 1970s. Along with the names already mentioned, the list includes Robert Anderson of Atlantic Richfield, J. Paul Austin of Coca-Cola, Charles Brown of AT&T (he succeeded deButts), Frank Cary of IBM, A. W. Clausen of BankAmerica (later named to head the World Bank), Clifton Garvin of Exxon, W. H. Krome George of Alcoa (Harper's successor), John Hanley of Monsanto, Robert Hatfield of the Continental Group, Ralph Lazarus of Federated Department Stores, Ruben Mettler of TRW Inc., Howard Morgens of Procter & Gamble, and Donald MacNaughton of Prudential (later CEO of Hospital Corporation of America). Donald Regan of Merrill Lynch was a Policy Committee member until he became Secretary of the Treasury under President Ronald Reagan, as was George Shultz when he was with Bechtel.

It would be wrong to imply that many Roundtable members came on the scene with personal exposure to Federal government operations. There are not many George Shultzes. Very few Roundtable members had held senior posts at the state or national level, and only a few more, myself included, had served time in subordinate posts in government before switching to corporate careers. In my case, it was as a lawyer in the Department of Justice, a job I left to go to the Du Pont Company. (Incidentally, that move brought a chorus of protest from Washington friends who could not understand how I could sell out in such fashion. Their reaction said a lot about the sour climate of business-government relations at the time [1951], and was my preview to what was in store for business in the years to come.)

The process of "going public" carried both personal and corporate shocks. Most executives of the 1970s had been trained to abide by a narrow set of ground rules: Stick to business, keep your nose clean, play golf with your customers, and don't talk to reporters. That bygone era had its charms, but business leaders learned that it takes a different lifestyle to operate effectively in the political world. Top executives had to delegate many of the internal management duties to others, to free themselves for governmental and community affairs. Putting in twelve-hour days chained to a desk no longer meant an executive was doing the right thing; it only meant that he was working hard at part of his job.

Executives who ventured into the outside world found themselves giving up their anonymity, a good bit of their privacy, and most of their weekends. There were obvious merits in efforts to put names and faces on big corporations—and a bit of glamour in jetting into National Airport for meetings with the high and mighty on the Hill—but executives found there was another side to the coin. Corporate external affairs, when added to other duties, make executive life a seven-days-a-week proposition. It takes hard work to become conversant with relevant facts and different positions on national issues. Sundays are for studying the briefing papers. Golf scores suffer accordingly.

The glitter fades fast. Reporters telephone in the middle of the night. Political neophytes discovered that "working Washington" means tuna-on-rye at a stand-up counter more often than receptions at the Cosmos Club. They also found that it can be a great ego-deflator. One of Du Pont's executive vice presidents tells the story on himself of meeting with Senator Russell Long, thinking as he left that he had handled his presentation well and made an impression on one of the more powerful men of Washington. Then he overheard a voice, he thinks the Senator's, saying, "Who did that guy say he was?"

Businessmen learned that, important as it is to have the facts, arguments based solely on economic efficiency, technological imperatives, and statistical probabilities (these are supposed to win every time with rational executives) have limited power to predict outcomes in Washington. Politicians are less likely to ask "Is it true?" than "Will it sell back home?" and "Does it sound fair?" Those questions have enormous political leverage and account for what would otherwise be entirely mystifying decisions of government. On one issue, cold facts do carry the day and the governmental process seems to make eminently good sense. The next time around, an equally convincing set of facts seems to get lost and a vast illogic takes over. The much-vaunted "balanced view" never surfaces, and the side with the weightiest stack of charts leaves the forum shaking its head in defeat. Often when that happens, it is because people making the decision "just didn't think it was fair" to side with the losers.

Executives learned that there is a big difference between talking at Congressmen and talking with them, and that politesse is not as common in political arenas as in corporate boardrooms. As the Roundtable hit stride, several of its leaders were given an opportunity to meet in the offices of the Speaker of the House with him and his key lieutenants, to talk about the interests of specific Roundtable task forces. The first such meeting was intended to last about one hour, but it stretched into an all-afternoon session, with the people on both sides wanting to talk more rather than less. The only hitch came when one of the corporate leaders, instead of talking informally as the other task-group leaders had done, read from a paper and, what was worse, a paper obviously prepared by somebody else. There was a painful silence at the time, and a more explicit message later came back from O'Neill's office: Don't do that again. The executive learned his lesson. He attended a later meeting of the same group and did not commit that offense a second time, but spoke from his own head and reestablished his credibility. He has since become an effective public-policy advocate for business, proving that the Roundtable's founders were not wrong in thinking that the organization might help its own members as much as anyone else.

A common experience for executives submitted to this introductory course in politics was to find themselves on the hot seat in committee hearings, being grilled by regulatory-agency staff aides half their age, fresh out of law school and bristling with zeal, but not long on good manners. These were young people, as the saying has it, who might sometimes be in error but never in doubt. To add to the executive trauma, lessons in political survival often were administered in front of microphones and in the presence of critics who may not have been without malice. The first time under fire, with the television lights on, is an experience not many people forget.

Learning to live with a few bruises is just part of the game, though, and my experience is that business people in Washington generally have been treated no differently from the way government people treat everybody, including each other. Politics American-style is a noisy process, and as executives became accustomed to it during the Seventies, they learned that some of what sounded like deep hostility was no more than people shouting for attention on the six-o'clock news or using the proverbial two-by-four to get the mule's attention. The most important lesson learned by the Roundtable members was not how to handle themselves on TV—in truth, many executives dislike being on stage, no matter how much practice they get—but how to deal with people in government on their terms. Once past the opening rounds, business executives found that many people in government are at least as open-minded and willing to listen as their colleagues in commerce, and sympathetic to the problems faced by private-sector companies.

There is no better way to document this than to recount the story of the Roundtable and Jimmy Carter. As I look back on the chain of events, it strikes me as a textbook case of people from different backgrounds learning bit by bit that they can narrow their differences and identify common objectives where they can comfortably help each other. That the man in question is a Democrat is probably of key importance. Representing "the party of the people" rather than "the party of business," to echo the tired and persistent stereotypes, Carter was in a better position than his campaign opponent, Gerald Ford, to fraternize with corporate leaders. A Democrat could even side with businessmen on some issues without seeming to be in their pocket, a posture that would be difficult for a Republican. (I would go further and say that business, or at least big business, generally has done better on narrow issues with the Democrats than with the Republicans. If Democrats do something for industry, they at least are given a chance to explain themselves. Republicans doing the same are immediately accused of giving away the store—by Democrats, of course. This was true to a great extent in the Kennedy, Johnson, and Ford administrations as well as in Carter's, though in fairness to President Ford it needs to be added that he and his staff had an open, accessible attitude toward business.)

When the campaign for the election of 1976 began to take shape, it slowly dawned on everyone that the former Georgia governor, though a dark horse, had a real shot at the nomination. The Roundtable's Policy Committee, in a move that struck some members as fairly radical, invited Governor Carter to address the group on issues that interested us. Contending that he had so many invitations that he could not respond to them all and did not want to play favorites, Carter declined; but he did not forget. After the Democratic Convention had nominated him and Walter Mondale, an invitation was extended to about twenty business people to meet with Carter in Atlanta. It turned out that each of us on the guest list previously had invited Carter to some event and had been turned down. This was Carter's way of repaying the courtesy and hearing us out.

At the Atlanta meeting, each of us was given three minutes to talk about any subject we wanted to bring to Governor Carter's attention. My chance came about midway through, and I used the opportunity to tell him about the Roundtable. I emphasized its interest not in immediate issues alone but in public-policy problems more broadly, and said the organization was willing to create position papers for him on any subject where he had an interest and we had competence. He accepted the offer on the spot and directed his staff to work out with me a process for identifying topics and getting the papers done promptly. Nine topics were picked. Within a few weeks, Roundtable companies produced papers laying out the issues, describing alternatives, and recommending positions. To maintain an even-handed stance, the Roundtable extended the same offer to President Ford, via James Baker of his staff, but that offer was not accepted. Our inference in the Roundtable was that the Republican team felt they already knew how business saw the issues and needed no further contact at that time. Whatever the explanation, no papers were submitted to Ford's team.

Whether Carter took time to read our papers I do not know. It is fairly clear that some of his staff read them, and even more clear that his team began to look upon the Roundtable as one of the organizations willing to devote serious attention to issues, in terms that recognized political realities. Following Carter's victory, people he had met from business were asked to help with the transition and to submit names of candidates for the cabinet and other key slots. I participated in several other meetings with Carter before and after he took office. One was in Plains, Georgia, to talk about the state of the nation and to look over some potential appointees. Most of the people who wound up in cabinet posts were there that day. Another was at Blair House in Washington, where the President-elect stayed before the inauguration. The purpose of that one was to sound out businessmen on public-policy questions that would land on his desk as soon as he was sworn in.

I believe I was included in the first of those two meetings because my name had been floated for a possible cabinet position, but in Plains I made it clear to the Vice President-elect and others that I was not interested. The point I made to them was that whatever contribution I was qualified to make could best be delivered in my roles in the Roundtable and in Du Pont. They could count on my candor because I was not looking for a job. Apparently they took me at my word because they invited me to the Blair House meeting, and to some other gatherings in the next four years.

Perhaps the most unusual of these meetings, and one that gives a measure of President Carter's openness, was convened after he had been in office a year or so. He invited four of us, with me as the only person from business, to give him a performance review on his administration to date. Carter opened the meeting with words to this effect: "I want you gentlemen to forget that I'm President of the United State and be completely candid with me." Then we went at it, with a spirited exchange on everything from major economic-policy issues down to some problems so small they amounted to distractions on which Presidents of the United States should not waste their time (which is the message we gave him).

As a footnote to that event, about a year after Carter was defeated by Reagan, I received a phone call from the former President with some questions about a project he was interested in. After he had finished with that business, he asked, "Irving, do you have any advice you want to give me?" I replied: "Mr. President, I am not in the habit of giving advice to former Presidents of the United States," to which he quickly responded, "Well, you weren't reluctant when I was President."

The contacts between business executives and President Carter cannot be said to have made sudden and dramatic differences in administration policies. That could not have been expected, given the chasms we had to bridge and the political moods of the times. What the meetings did accomplish was the building of trust between a President who had had little contact with large corporations, their people and problems, and big-business representatives who had had little contact with political leaders, Democrats even less than Republicans, at anything other than the local level. The consensus among business leaders who met with President Carter early in his administration was that this was a man of considerable intellectual ability, dedicated to doing his job, limited in his perspective on broad economic issues and their ramifications, but willing to listen. He and selected members of the White House staff, notably Lloyd Cutler, Stuart Eizenstat, Robert Strauss and Anne Wexler, developed and maintained a genuine interest in an exchange of views with industry, and the White House doors remained open throughout Carter's term even to some businessmen who opposed his decisions time and again.

Business did score some direct hits. For example, when one of Carter's state-of-the-Union addresses was being drafted, some liberal staff members pushed for a strongly worded statement favoring harsh, anti-industry, antitrust policies. Those were the days when Senator Ted Kennedy and some others thought it would be a good idea to break up the big oil companies, and make bigness alone a *per se* antitrust offense. Some of us in business argued to another White House staffer that President Carter might well speak in favor of the principles of antitrust, but that he ought not send a signal that his administration was setting forth on a "get business" campaign, especially when the nation needed the help of large corporations to resolve such pressing problems as energy supply and rising international competition. That argument reached the President, and the message he took to Capitol Hill contained only a brief and temperate comment on antitrust.

There were also some indirect results of our contacts, in what might be called less-worse developments. As one illustration, Carter's wage-and-price-control program was opposed by industry, on the grounds that such controls in a peacetime economy invariably do more harm than good, and forestall needed changes that are going to come sooner or later. However, once it was clear that the administration was committed to controls and had the support to impose them, people from business worked to soften the impact and make the guidelines flexible. As a result, the harmful effects were at least limited. Cutting your losses is as important in governmental affairs as in business.

The Roundtable members quickly learned that facts are most persuasive when they are most persuasively sold. Doing the selling means going easy on ideology and putting the energy into demonstrating practical answers to current public issues. As newspaper columnist David Broder has said, government is not an exercise in applied theology, but is instead a process of struggle and accommodation. He who would succeed in this arena must get into the struggle and learn to accommodate.

Lectures on mom and apple pie are not needed. Government officials know that the public endorses in principle the economic system as it stands: that is, a system characterized by competition among privately owned enterprises. It follows that attempts to lecture Congressmen on first principles are likely to backfire. They irritate people ("I already know all that") and arouse suspicions ("Why the Fourth of July speech? What's this guy really want?").

The Roundtable members also learned, or should have, that businessmen can be effective in government only if they leave their personal political preferences on the company plane. It has never been secret that most leaders of big companies are more comfortable with Republicans than with Democrats, but the Roundtable would have been doomed if it had made its pitch along party lines. Anyone who can count can count votes. The obvious fact is that even if all Republicans in government had stuck together through the 1970s, which they declined to do, and even if all of them had been certified boosters of big business, which not all of them were, the Republicans would not have had the votes to control the political outcomes.

Since World War II, control of the White House, the Senate, or the House of Representatives, or all three, has been in the hands of Democrats (who, it must be added, also have declined with increasing frequency to vote with their leaders). The same is true at the state level. Had the Roundtable founders confused their personal hopes with political realities, the organization would have sunk without a trace. In that circumstance, it would have been just as well, for few issues of concern to business lend themselves to division along party lines. In addressing the largest issues—America's competitive position in world trade, for example—partisanship is simply irrelevant; even the liberal-versus-conservative division offers only a slightly better cutting device.

I do not suggest that Republicans and Democrats are interchangeable, only that the differences have to be examined against specific issues, and it is best to take your friends wherever you can find them. Historically, Democrats have been more regulation-prone than Republicans, but it was Republican as well as Democratic votes that put into effect the most stringent and costly regulations imposed on business during the 1970s. By the same token, when the countercurrent began to flow and the idea took root that regulation had gone too far, support for reform came from both sides of the aisle. The movement to reregulate and deregulate was launched with White House backing during a Republican administration, Ford's, continued under a Democrat, Carter, and given a third push when Republican Ronald Reagan came into office. Through it all, there was a steady increase in the compliance costs as the regulations on the books reached their due dates, though there was a loss of momentum.

If there is a moral in the regulatory story, it is to avoid making "enemies" lists. As the Roundtable's experience has demonstrated many times over, the person who opposes you on one issue may change his mind on that one later, or at least be on your side on some other issue. Further, one learns to go slow on the generalizations. At the time support was declining for continued regulation of air transit, it was holding steady for continued regulation of natural-gas prices and was building for stricter regulation of health and safety. Thus, when someone argues that the trend in government has been pro- or antiregulation, the proper questions are "When?" and "What kind of regulation did you have in mind?"

While the Roundtable did not start the backfires against regulation, it did work hard on specific cases with government people from both parties, and perhaps that made some difference. Among its activities, the Roundtable produced a multicompany study of actual regulatory costs, compiling the data under the gaze of independent accountants, and eliminating much of the "off-the-wall" estimating that had surrounded the topic. That study, coordinated by Frank Cary of IBM, provided Washington with the most credible picture it had ever had of the financial load imposed by regulation, over and above the costs business would have incurred for other reasons.

In its early years, the Roundtable tried to keep itself out of the public eye. The original leaders felt that fanfare about the organization would make people in public life wary. Their thought was that a Congressman would see no great political risk in letting a CEO make his pitch in person, but that it might be another matter to appear to be cozy with a whole organization of such moguls. So it seemed at the outset, at any rate.

That feeling was soon reversed by events. The organization drew attention anyway, by virtue of some of its successes. Moreover, as its people built reputations as trustworthy sources, some of the fears about motives began to ease. At the time I joined the Roundtable's Policy Committee, it was clear that the organization could only raise new doubts if it attempted to shroud its work in secrecy. Everybody knew about the work of the Chamber of Commerce. There were thousands of trade and industry associations working the political territory, open to public view if anyone cared to know about them. Why should the Roundtable draw a cloak of mystery around itself? It had nothing to hide. The trends encouraged it to go the other way, toward openness. The public was demanding more information, not less, about the inner workings of organizations. Government was under its self-imposed Freedom of Information Act, a 1967 law that had been brought about by public fear of behind-the-scenes manipulation in Washington. Watergate was still fresh in mind. Thus, by 1976, when I became chairman of the Roundtable, we had no trouble gaining membership support for a more open policy: If anybody wanted to know what the Roundtable hoped to accomplish and why it was formed, we would tell them.

To my way of thinking, then and now, the best principles to guide such an organization are the ones that work well for individual dealings: Never lie to people; don't try to use them; and don't do or say anything you would not be willing to see reported on the front page of the *Washington Post,* given a fair chance to tell your side of the story. If you decide to have lunch with a regulatory official, make no secret of it. Be prepared to present the same data and views to others who may want to know what went on. As Justice Louis Brandeis said, sunlight is the best disinfectant.

How successful has the Roundtable's approach been? One way to evaluate that is to look at specific issues on which the Roundtable has taken stands and see how it fared. The Roundtable (and others) opposed a bill that would have created a new independent consumer-protection agency, and the bill was soundly defeated in Congress. That was an interesting example because the Roundtable followed the rules to the letter and made its case to Congressmen of all persuasions. As a result, even some of the liberals sympathetic to the consumer movement failed to vote for the bill.

The Roundtable's argument was that there already was enough regulation covering consumers and suppliers. More than twenty Federal agencies and departments had responsibilities in this area. They were backed by more than 100 pieces of legislation, more than forty-five of which had been added within the previous ten years. If all of that Federal oversight was failing to protect consumers' interests, there was no logic to say that another law and still more bureaucracy would do the trick. The step to take, the Roundtable counseled, was to forget the new agency and find out what if anything was wrong with the existing ones.

Another victory concerned a bill to allow members of craft unions to picket all of a construction site, including subcontractors for whom they were not working, and thus shut down the entire project. There were two issues there. One was simply the question of power. The law would have permitted a handful of sheet-metal workers to stop construction of a new industrial plant or office-buildings complex, where the costs of delays could run millions of dollars per month. Presumably, the mere threat of such losses would be enough to make a contractor knuckle under. Then the next craft union, the electricians or masons, could step to the plate for its time at bat. The other issue was of equity. On what basis is it right for one group of workers to stop the work and the paychecks of their fellow workers when they share no grievance and have taken no strike vote?

The Common Situs bill was defeated in a Democratic Congress under a Democratic administration, to the astonishment of the labor unions pushing for it. A labor lobbyist was quoted later as saying, "We didn't do our homework. We had relaxed. We thought we did the job in November [the Carter election]." It was a telling admission.

For the Roundtable, it was a shared victory. The Chamber of Commerce, NAM, several contractors' associations, and individual companies acting on their own all campaigned vigorously against the Common Situs bill. Such coalitions often surround issues of interest to the Roundtable, which is what makes it impossible for the Roundtable to claim singular triumphs.

There is no difficulty, though, in pointing to some lost causes and long-delayed gains. Some of the most thorough work done by the Roundtable in its early years was in the area of capital formation, taxation, and incentives for risk-taking. The effort was headed by Reginald Jones of GE, who made himself an expert on the topic. He devoted countless hours to the task of persuading policymakers that the way to create jobs and make the economy stronger was to encourage savings over consumption spending, liberalize depreciation allowances, and stimulate capital investment in productive facilities. Yet, for years he and his fellow believers were unable to win more than a handful of converts. The typical political response was to pass such bills as the Humphrey-Hawkins Full Employment Act, a law glowing with good intentions but completely lacking in practical means.

There is some comfort in the fact that most of what Jones and company were saying in the early 1970s became the conventional wisdom for Democrats and Republicans alike a decade later. The discomfort lies in the knowledge that good, solidly-documented advice was available long before. Had it been heeded, the nation might have been spared much of the economic agony of the early 1980s.

There was similar experience in other broadly important areas, including energy policy and the old bugaboo, inflation. Representatives of the Roundtable were among the many people who argued for years in favor of policies that would have expanded domestic energy supplies and provided incentives to conservation. Meanwhile, government continued to pursue policies that increased national dependence on foreign sources for oil and maintained price controls on oil and gas, thereby stimulating consumption and creating additional pressure for more imports. Business' complaints about Federal deficit spending and the inflationary consequences were heard so often that they became background noise in Washington, always there but not registering in the Congressional consciousness. Again, there was no shortage of documentation or analysis. The problem was excruciatingly clear. What was missing was the political will or courage to do something about it.

The won-lost record is only one way to keep score on the new breed, however. Only rarely do issues swing entirely to one side or the other, and the Roundtable's report card probably should say "Partial Credit" more often than anything else.

Over a decade or more, the Roundtable's refreshing approach may have permitted it to make the most headway in the very areas where it seemed to have the least day-to-day success. Environmental policy is the best case in point. As of 1970, when amendments were made to tighten the provisions of the Clean Air Act, Congress chose to keep in its own hands the timetables for meeting standards, instead of turning such decisions over to the newly formed Environmental Protection Agency. Congress then elected to set standards based not on the technology available at the time but on what it thought might be developed in the future. Next, it compressed some of the timetables. On auto emissions, for example, it declared that the carmakers had to reduce hydrocarbon and carbon-monoxide emissions 90 percent by the target date of 1975, rather than by 1980 as earlier intended.

Such was the low level of trust in industry's credibility that Congress chose to follow a hunch that industry could meet the goal if it cared to try. Senator Edmund Muskie's argument at the time was, "The deadline . . . is based not . . . on economic and technological feasibility, but on consideration of public health."

A decade later, the climate was markedly different. The head of EPA, Douglas Costle, was telling audiences in his speeches that more than 90 percent of compliance with environmental regulations was on a voluntary basis, without EPA having to exercise its muscle. Privately, he remarked that hardly any knock-down, drag-out fights were taking place with industry over particular issues. With few exceptions, he

said, people from industry, from EPA, and on occasion from environmental activist groups were sitting down together to resolve problems
and develop compromises.

The environmental issue had not gone away. Clean air and clean
water had remained on the legislative agenda, and the control of toxic
substances and wastes had since been added. The difference was that
people from different factions had begun to trust one another at least
to the degree of looking at evidence on its merits and not being blinded
by its source. Some of this change was due to the fact that the climate
was better (no pun intended). Improvements in air and water quality
could be measured. Beyond that, however, the shift in attitudes must
partly have reflected the change in approach by some industry leaders.
In the environmental-policy area and elsewhere, the willingness to
look realistically at government, and not oppose it in a knee-jerk re-
flex, was what made it possible for business to obtain amendments
that could not otherwise have been won, and to avoid regulations
more harsh than were imposed.

Experience shows that it sometimes pays to stay in the debate even
when you know the deck is stacked against you. John deButts of
AT&T and I had that role to play as members of what Senator Howard Metzenbaum, an Ohio Democrat, called his "blue-ribbon advisory
committee." The desired advice was on corporate governance, and the
committee included labor leaders, a representative of the Nader
Group, and a professor who at one time had chaired the Securities and
Exchange Commission. From the first meeting, it was clear that what
was wanted was endorsement for new Federal legislation on the composition and actions of corporate boards. Needed reforms, our report
was supposed to convince the Senate Committee on the Judiciary,
would come from added Federal regulation.

DeButts and I disappointed our colleagues. We did not agree that
the problems of corporate governance were as the others saw them;
and in our view, putting more Federal governance into corporate
boardrooms was the last, worst step to take. We argued that boards
already were subject to outside forces, were changing in desirable
ways, and had strong incentives to continue to do so. We did not turn
the committee our way or expect to. We participated because the alternative was worse: not to have any influence at all on the outcome.
You cannot score points with no team on the field. By being there and
trying to deal with the concerns that surfaced, we were at least able to

block release of a one-sided report. Perhaps the fact that deButts and I were two people on the scene with personal experience as directors of large corporations made a difference in the way the report was received. At any rate, new legislation did not move forward.

The development of personal relationships between business and government leaders has had unforeseen but welcome results. An example was the response of the U.S. government to the Arab boycott of Israel. It came in 1977, at the height of U.S. dependence on oil imports from OPEC nations, many of which are Arab. The Arabs said they would not do business with any company doing business with Israel.

American businesses and government were caught in the middle. The boycott outraged the American Jewish community, which put pressure on the government to retaliate against the Arabs. Many U.S. companies, though, were doing business with both the Arabs and the Israelis. Some had major construction projects under way in Middle Eastern nations, including the one with the most oil, Saudi Arabia.

The U.S. Congress and the White House staff saw the need for compromise but were unable to bring it about, and it fell to a small Roundtable group to work out compromises one inch at a time. Working with Jewish leaders and corporate heads, we were able to get agreement on a legislative response, one that forbade companies in the U.S. to comply with the boycott but still fell short of the extreme position originally sought by some of the Jewish organizations. The agreement was hammered into a bill and passed into law by Congress, and the issue was defused.

I was involved in this instance not only because I am a Jew and was then head of the Roundtable, but also because contacts and trust had been built up with people in the Carter White House. It is worth asking whether ten or twenty years earlier it would have been politically possible for any President to have a corporate executive serve as private negotiator on an issue with such overtones. It is conceivable, but barely.

As a follow-up to the Arab-boycott legislation, I was invited to visit Saudi Arabia with George Shultz, whose company was one of those with construction contracts there. I agreed on the condition that the two of us would also visit Israel, a country he knew less well. Five years later, there was some comfort in the thought that the new Secretary of State was a man with firsthand exposure to Israel as well as to the Arab world, and therefore could understand the full range of emotions behind the gut issues in the Middle East.

While the Arab boycott was an unusual situation, it is only one bit of evidence of a narrowing of differences and a breakdown of old stereotypes. Another sign of that is the Labor-Management Group, mentioned earlier. Also a creature of the 1970s, it was organized by John Dunlop, former Secretary of Labor, and given quasi-official standing as an advisory body to the government. Later, with a change in administrations, it lost that sanction and became strictly a private group, though its missions remained the same: to bring management and labor together to consider issues of national importance and try to devise joint recommendations that would help the country.

Declared out of bounds were any topics that might land on the bargaining table in unionized companies. This is what made it possible for me to attend meetings of the group which also included the head of the United Steelworkers, a union that at the time was trying to organize employees of Du Pont.

The Labor-Management Group was set up as a club of thirteen: six corporate leaders, six leaders of national unions, and (by now Professor) Dunlop. On paper, it was an unlikely combination. Union leaders ran the gamut from moderates to hard-liners of the old school. George Meany and Lane Kirkland of the AFL/CIO, William Winpisinger of the machinists' union, and Irving Bluestone and Douglas Fraser of the UAW were all members at one time or another. On the business side were people from heavily unionized companies such as General Electric and General Motors, and the leaders of firms with few if any employees enrolled in national unions, such as Du Pont and Citicorp.

In practice, the Labor-Management Group found more grounds for agreement than disagreement, though its meetings were peppered with plenty of the latter. As with the Metzenbaum advisory committee, there was no thought of turning opponents into chums. There are fundamental differences in world view, not to mention tactical approaches, between a Winpisinger and Reg Jones. What the Labor-Management Group lacked in harmony, though, it made up in educational value. I never attended one of its meetings without learning something worth knowing about business, labor, and governance. There also have been useful side effects. Learning to work with someone in one setting makes it easier to work with him or her in another. As but one example, Lane Kirkland and I have since been asked to cochair several organizations. One was a council on renewing the nation's industrial base, a project of President Carter's that went down with him in the 1980 election. The other was a study on present and prospective Federal policies regarding industry. That project, sponsored by an independent private group, was headed by a troika of Kirkland; Felix Rohatyn, a partner in the investment house of Lazard Frères and a pivot man in the effort to keep New York City from going bankrupt a few years ago; and myself.

All of this may sound too neat, as though the gladiators had agreed to meet in the forum for disarmament. Obviously, nothing of the sort has happened. Labor and management continue to quarrel. Distrust continues to discolor relationships between the public and private sectors. There are fumbled chances on all sides, and it will take some more years before a lasting structure can be built on the foundations that exist. One Congressman, asked whether he thought business was doing a better job in its relationships with government, summarized it only too well: "You fellows have come a good distance . . . but you still have a long way to go!" I accept that. As has been said by Richard Munro of Time Inc., the public is still given too many reasons to be disappointed with the narrowness of perspective so often seen in the private sector—the self-pleading, the aversion to risk, and the denigration of the public-policy process.

Business still has not outgrown its well-known ability to shoot itself in the foot. An example of that came during the crisis in Poland, when the Communist government moved against Lech Walesa's Solidarity movement and imposed martial law. During those tense times, when the world was watching to see whether the flickering light of freedom might be able to survive behind the Iron Curtain, a question arose about the Polish government's ability to continue payments on its international debts. A senior-level executive of one of the largest banks in the U.S. was quoted in the press as saying that no one really knows what system of government works best; what bankers care about is whether governments can make good on their debts. Totalitarian regimes, some financial people maintained, are better credit risks than weak democratic ones.

It is perhaps unfair to dust off that story. The banker claims he was misquoted. Assume that he was; whatever he did say, the public was left with the impression that business executives are monumentally insensitive to the plight of people, and think only of profit. Of such small cuts, multiplied a thousand times over, is negative public opinion made.

The 1980 election was an important shift in national politics, in some ways the most significant change since Roosevelt's election in 1932. In the months that followed Reagan's victory, though, business did not turn in one of its better performances. Instead of looking broadly at the change in administrations as an opportunity to work for reasoned policies that could help the whole economy and nation, some businessmen used the election as an excuse to revert to the narrowest kind of partisanship. They celebrated the arrival of the conservatives to power in exactly the wrong way, by adopting a do-nothing line on problems and squaring off for a take-no-prisoners battle with their old tormentors. Reagan had consistently maintained, in the campaign and before, that the Federal government ought to do less for people and private resources ought to do more. Taking him at his word, one would expect that his victory would increase the responsibilities falling to the private sector; but an unfortunate portion of the nation's business leadership read the election returns the other way, taking the results to mean that its obligations were reduced. The idea that floated to the surface was that "Our team is in (at last). They will take care of things (and us)."

In fact, nothing of the sort was about to happen. Big business held few IOU's from Ronald Reagan. He owed little of his success to any of them except his California friends. Most corporate executives had favored one of his opponents for the nomination, some having been for George Bush and more for John Connally. More importantly, the national problems that existed the night before the election were still there the day after, and Reagan could no more walk away from them than Carter could.

A fine example was the political storm surrounding the health hazards from toxic wastes that had been discarded in years gone by. Abandoned dumpsites had been found, and before the election one question before Congress was whether legislation could be passed to clean up those dumps. A bill tagged as "Superfund" had been drafted, under which industry would put up an initial sum of money to get the effort started, with the proviso that the fund would be replenished when and if the companies responsible for the dumping could be identified and presented with the overdue bill. Estimates on the ante required for the Superfund kitty ranged up to $6 billion.

With numbers that big in mind, some corporate leaders concluded after the election that the thing to do was to bury Superfund once and for all. It was assumed that the Democrats would have a hard time pushing a bill through the lame-duck session of Congress, and that once a new administration was in office such legislation would have even less of a chance. Even if the democratic majority in the House pressed for action, the election had left the Senate in control of the Republicans, friends of business. So the scenario went.

Those who believed it fooled no one but themselves. The election removed the Carter administration, not the dumpsites. Nor had it diminished public fears about toxic chemicals. The incoming chairman of the key committee in the Senate, Environment and Public Works, was Robert Stafford of Vermont, who happens to be a strong advocate of environmental-protection programs, as are most of the fifteen other Senators on his committee. Those are facts which any Washington-watcher ought to have known. Whatever the true extent of the health risks from toxic-waste dumps—and that was and still is in dispute—in 1981 there was a rapidly increasing public concern that these dumps represented a serious hazard. That is another fact anyone could confirm by reading the newspapers and opinion polls. It would have taken wild leaps of fantasy to suppose that the Reagan mandate included instructions to walk away from an issue like this one.

The sensible bet was that legislation would come. The only question was when and how much, and some of us in business were convinced that the price of stonewalling would be high indeed. Any incident might trigger explosive public feeling. If, for instance, another disposal site were uncovered that was on a par with Love Canal in New York State, there surely would be another round of congressional hearings, with public charges that industry had put the community at risk and walked away from its responsibilities. Thinking about this at the time, I could almost hear Commodore Vanderbilt's words being thrown back at us with embellishment: "The public *health* be damned."

The obvious national need was for a program to clean up the dumpsites as soon as possible, beginning with the ones that, based on the best evidence available, appeared most likely to pose serious health hazards. It seemed to me that the sooner a bill could be passed, the better, and that the place to begin was with an amended version of the Superfund bill still in the hopper. I said that to Phil Shabecoff of the *New York Times,* and added that if Washington was interested, some of us in industry could show them in about two hours how to write a bill that might pass before Carter left office. A day later, Union Carbide took the same position. The word by then had reached the White House staff that people it knew in the chemical industry were willing to lobby for a bill that was going to cost industry money. Within weeks, a modified Superfund had been passed by Congress and signed into law by President Carter.

It was not an ideal piece of legislation. There was more politics than hard science behind it. Several years later, we still do not have good evidence to show that this law is predicated on a proper definition of the problem or that it leads to the best solution to it. The cost to industry, though smaller than it would have been under some earlier proposals, is still in the billions, a cost ultimately to be reflected in the prices people pay for manufactured goods. The point of all this, though, is that it was industry's responsibility to step up to the toxic-waste problem and work for a practical approach to resolve it, not to use the changing of the guard at the White House as an excuse for inaction.

There are some nonpartisan lessons in this story. Action came because government and the media had learned to take some people in industry at their word. The comment relayed by the *New York Times* would not have made a difference had it not come from someone the White House staff knew and trusted, and had it not been supported by others in industry in whom they had confidence. The bridges had been built properly, not on a foundation of party politics but on the basis of concern with public issues. As a minor addendum under the heading of "Strange Bedfellows," as I write this the Chemical Manufacturers Association and the Environmental Defense Fund, a leading activist group, are joined in a suit against EPA and the Department of Health and Human Services. Government has not pursued the objectives of Superfund as aggressively as we think they should, and the suit is an effort to force a speed-up in the collection of data on the effects of toxic chemical wastes on health.

If this episode has anything to teach us, it is that business leaders have to look beyond the election returns and force themselves to ask the "What if" questions. The public is not willing to allow the enterprise system to decide by itself when the open market will be used as the only device for monitoring or modifying actions, or cleaning up problems such as toxic wastes. The notion that right-thinking politicians will do away with codes that offend business, or block such codes in the future when business believes them wrong, simply brands an individual as someone who has not been paying attention to what has been happening in this country for the past fifty years.

The more optimistic side of this, equally supported by evidence, is that there has been substantial progress in bringing business and its leaders into the public-policy process in desirable ways, and that the initiative for this change has come mostly from businessmen themselves. They have tried to raise the level of discussion within government and the private sector, and stand on higher ground than they occupied in the past. They have attempted to demonstrate that business is no more a monolith than government, and that there are some people in both institutions who are willing to work on points of convergence instead of concentrating on differences.

It is hardly necessary to add that my view is far from unanimous within business. Some in the ranks continue to regard compromise as a loss of principle. There remains an instinct to charge up San Juan Hill, give as good as you get, and never yield turf. The simple answer to those people is that business tried that and it did not work. All business got in return was more belligerence from government, no worthwhile change in the outcomes, and frequent reminders about the arithmetic of politics: Corporations have no vote, and all the CEOs of the Fortune 500 companies have among them just 500 votes.

Following the hard line of no compromise creates a national politics consisting solely of factions, each asserting claims it regards as nonnegotiable. No free society can govern itself under that condition. It is a prescription for chaos, and, as the next chapter tries to show, the nation already has come closer to that Balkanized status than is healthy or safe. Business ought not make the situation worse. To return to David Broder's comment, it is not just government that has to operate through a process of accommodation, but the private sector as well. It is not a neat or always satisfactory process, but it is the best we have, and leaders in business as much as people in other kinds of institutions have to recognize that if they are not willing to work within the process, they are left with no basis for the system at all.

3

Getting In and Getting On

ONE OF James Stewart's most memorable movies was *Mr. Smith Goes to Washington,* circa 1939. Stewart starred as a naïve idealist who finds himself in Washington as a short-term Senator and is nearly undone by the evil around him. His special tormentor is a corrupt Congressman trying to save his own unworthy hide by framing our hero and having him expelled. Virtue triumphs in the end, though, amid patriotic cheers and tears.

In 1982, another novice, this one a real person, was posted to Washington. Nicholas Brady was plucked from the pleasures of executive living to fill the remaining eight months of the term of Senator Harrison Williams, who resigned because of the Abscam scandal. Brady had been a managing director of Dillon, Read & Company and chairman of Purolator, Inc. He returned to business after completing his stint in the Senate, and later was appointed by President Reagan to serve on his commission to study U.S.–Latin American relations. Brady did not want to be a candidate for the New Jersey Senatorial seat in the November election, and therefore his only mission during his months in Foggy Bottom was to look, listen, and do whatever a neophyte could for the cause of good government. Brady's career as a United States Senator was, by his own admission, a revelation. His observations challenge people in both the private and the public sectors to rethink their objectives and responsibilities.

Where Jefferson Smith had encountered graft and comic-opera characters, Mr. Brady encountered a Senate more marked by confusion, misuse of time, and a chronic inability of legislators to focus on significant matters. Individual Senators, far from being bumblers, impressed Brady as being high-caliber, committed people. Some displayed enormous capability and prodigious work habits, and Brady found among them people as bright as or brighter than any he had known on Wall Street. Yet Brady concluded, as he said in an exit interview with the *Wall Street Journal,* that, despite the talent, "the place doesn't work very well. It is very frustrating. . . . We waste a lot of time." Unimportant or peripheral issues crowded the agenda. Brady was called upon to vote more than 300 times—a number ten times larger than he thought appropriate. A Senator might be expected to do justice to twenty or thirty votes per year, in his opinion.

Incredible energy was consumed by campaigning or planning for it, despite the fact that the body in question was the Senate, where only one-third of the members stand for office in any election year, rather than the House of Representatives, where the rollover is 100 percent every two years.

No surprise but nonetheless an outrage to Brady was the pay scale for members of Congress, then about $60,000 to $70,000 per annum (at this time, the House had voted itself a salary increase, but the Senate had not: hence the spread). A newly minted broker or lawyer would have expected to make that much or more on Wall Street a few years after leaving school. The major-league baseball teams, whose total roster is about the size of the U.S. Congress, paid substantially more than this to utility infielders, and a high multiple of it to heavy hitters. Brady's comment was that, unless there was change, the U.S. could expect future Congresses made up entirely of millionaires or people who could not get other jobs.

Equally dismaying to a man of his background was the realization of how little politicians understood about businessmen, and vice versa. At a time when interest rates were far too high, he recalled Senators asking him why Wall Street did not deal with the problem by simply lowering rates, as though the New York Stock Exchange and investment bankers controlled that. His Wall Street friends, concerned as always about deficit spending, asked Brady why the Senate did not simply balance the Federal budget. Perhaps they thought this could be done by resolution.

Conceding that eight months does not make a Washington expert, Brady came away from his experience with a few suggestions. One, perhaps obvious, was that business and political leaders ought to learn more about each other. Other recommendations included a hefty pay increase for Congress; a top limit on the number of years a member can stay; major reforms in the election process, with limits on campaign spending; and changes in legislative-committee structures, workloads, and procedures to encourage better use of time. Brady recalled that at one point several weeks went by while the Senate debated abortion and school-prayer issues—when the business before the body was the national debt limit.

What is interesting about Senator Brady's list is what he left off as much as what he put on it: He offered no nostrum, no quick fix or formula for reform, and not a single step that is politically easy to sell. Brady's experience reflects a dilemma that has been with us for many years: The kinds of reforms most easily imagined in government—that is, those for which support could readily be rallied—have proven inadequate to solve underlying problems, while the kinds of change most needed are immensely difficult to put in place. Proposals for serious reforms suffer from a double whammy: They carry immediate downside political risks offset only by long-term payoffs. Few elected officials rate that as good percentage politics.

The fact remains, though, that only through drastic change can we achieve improvements of consequence in American governance. The prescription has to be written not, per Mr. Smith, on the premise that all we need to do is replace rascals with bright, honorable servants. Rascals there still may be, but they are the least of the problem. There is no evidence that the people being elected to office now are any worse than the rest of us and, as Mr. Brady suggested, they may well be better. Rather, the medication to be prescribed has to attack infection in the basic organs of the body politic.

As Brady and some others have suggested (he is far from alone), we need better ways of running and financing elections as well as an overhaul of the way in which administrative and legislative work is done. What is to be sought, and what I regard as the proper objective for governmental reform, is a reversal of incentives and rewards. A system that now drives legislators and administrators to expedient, patchwork decisions—and, in fact, tends to punish more statesmanlike behavior—has to be turned so that it favors the placing of emphasis on economic and social policies responsive to long-term needs.

Such a turnaround will not be easy to engineer. It is not work for the timid or impatient, nor is it a task that can be carried out by government alone. While sympathizers will be found there, I take it as a given that no step of consequence will be taken or even seriously debated unless the private sector puts on the pressure and generates support for what is now a minority view in government. Government will not abandon the status quo until people in office sense that by protecting it they are losing more outside support than they are retaining. If that sort of pressure has not yet been felt within government, it is because there has not been a sufficient head of steam within the private sector.

That brings us full circle. Almost any group, outside government as much as inside, can find some short-range reason to defend the status quo, which keeps public policy in the inglorious state it is in, even though in the long range almost everybody stands to lose by doing so. This is the primary reason that special-interest politics reigns. If we are to have better government, it will be necessary for people in the private sector, no less than the public, to review their own conduct and re-examine the return of their participation in the public-policy process.

We need to look at the whole package: the ways people are picked for office, the ways they do their jobs once they are insiders, and the relationships they build up with the private sector as they go about the business of getting in and getting on. In Column One, I would argue for shorter, less expensive election campaigns; Federal funding for Congressional as well as Presidential candidates; direct election of the President and Vice President in place of the Electoral College system; a substantial pay raise for Senators and Representatives; and limits on the number of terms they may serve. That done, it would be possible and wise to abolish the political-action committees and displace some of those donated dollars into the political parties.

Under the present system, all trends lead in the wrong direction. Campaigns are becoming longer. A winning Congressman, unless privately wealthy, usually is driven to post-election fund-raisers to cover his campaign deficit, and then to the lecture circuit to make extra money to cover Washington's living costs.

Once in office, legislators see little incentive to try to be accountable to a constituency any larger than is necessary to get reelected. Given the fragmentation of power, the first advice given to a new member arriving in Washington is to angle for a seat on those committees in which he or she has the greatest interest, meaning the largest political stake. It is in the committees that the work gets done and reputations are made. Most novices heed the advice. Thus the House and Senate end up being served not by committees designed to provide the full body of the membership with counsel that is as broad and objective as possible, but by committees so constructed as to amount to interest groups themselves. This ordains that Congress almost always begins from narrow positions and muddles through. This gives the public small reason to believe that Congress truly understands the dimensions of national problems or has a clear sense of legislative intent.

Meanwhile, the price goes up. If it costs more to run government than ever before, it also costs vastly more to win elective office. In 1970, a campaign for a seat in the House of Representatives cost as little as $12,000 in some districts, and a $100,000 campaign was a big one. In the 1982 election, $12,000 was not enough to cover the races for some seats in state legislatures. Candidates for Federal offices who spent ten times that much were pikers. Total spending for U.S. congressional election campaigns, including the primaries, was close to $350 million. On average, it cost $284,000 to win a House seat in 1982 and $2.1 million for a Senate seat. Some candidates for governor or U.S. Senator spent more than $5 million each.

It is only money, but the dangers that go with it are real. The quest for contributions drives incumbents and challengers to concentrate on narrow interests, where the hearts of many potential donors are to be found, rather than on broader public issues, which do less to loosen purse-strings. Then too, there is the question of the type of person attracted to office. Years ago, when frontier politics and big-city party machines were the rule, the fear was that people would come into political life to make their bundle at the public's expense. Now the worry is that the only people able to come into politics and stay will be those who have already made the bundle, or those willing to do the bidding of those prepared to finance them.

People who do not have it made financially have two jobs instead of one in public office: raising money and doing the public's work. Winning candidates used to tell their supporters at election-night victory parties that they would "hit the ground running" as soon as they got to the capital. They still say so, but today that means running to restore the campaign coffers, as much as anything else. For a nonrich Congressman, fund-raising for the next campaign begins as soon as the returns are in. One-third of the 1982 winners at the national level finished their election runs in the red.

The obvious question is whether officials who have two jobs do keep them separate. Blatantly or subtly, does the money steer the vote? There is no way to answer that. As one study from the California branch of the Common Cause organization put it, there are concerns and fears, there are cases where the pattern of votes and the flow of campaign contributions seem more than accidental, but there is no smoking gun. There are charges of conflict of interest and protestations of innocence in return, but there is little hard evidence. For the defense, the argument is usually that the money is given freely by people who already agree for the most part with the recipient. The most that anyone is buying is "access." One Washington lobbyist, Robert McCandless, has been quoted as saying, "You're not going to get in the door of Congressman X, you're not going to get a full and complete hearing, unless you have attended to his most pressing interest, and that is his reelection." That does not resolve the matter, though. It only raises the question of why an individual or group on a legitimate mission should have to put a coin in a turnstile to get into a Congressman's office. To make a bad pun, there is the suspicion that "access" makes the heart grow fonder; and that is the prosecution's case.

Explanations for giant increases in campaign budgets are easily found. With political power dispersed, supporters of different views see the need to spread their bets in many places. It is not enough to make one contribution to a party on the theory that after the election, win or lose, events will follow predictable courses.

The modern tools of communication and political organization make it easy to spend money. A single TV commercial distributed in a metropolitan area can cost $50,000 or more. Political-action committees have undeniable attractions as vehicles for rounding up such big amounts. While an individual is permitted by law to give no more than $1,000 to a single candidate, a PAC can give $5,000. Further, a PAC gift has a concrete quality that appeals to many donors. In trying to sell an argument through a lobbyist, it is never certain how much headway is made, but in delivering a check to a candidate, the action is visible. The help to the recipient is tangible.

A private corporation cannot offer such help directly. U.S. law prohibits use of corporate funds in national elections, but permits companies and associations to form committees to which individuals may donate voluntarily. The limits on disbursements are liberal enough to allow a single PAC to distribute hundreds of thousands of dollars in one campaign year. In 1982, labor-union PACs put $20 million into the Congressional campaign; corporate PACs, $27 million; professional and trade associations (physicians, realtors, trial lawyers, and so forth) another $22 million. The estimated total of PAC spending at all levels of government was $240 million.

There is no agreement on what ought to be done about this, if anything. All that is clear is that the higher the price tag on public office goes, and the more time candidates are obliged to spend building war chests, the greater the chance that political decisions will be skewed to the side with the deepest pocket. There is always a possibility that the money will cancel itself out (that seems to have happened in some election campaigns), in which case the big winners will be those who sell advertising space and air time; but that still leaves the spectacle of a nation being governed by elected officials who work only part-time for the public, and who are required always to be on guard lest they be compromised by the election process.

If the public-policy process has become overly expensive and frustrating to outsiders, it has also pushed many insiders past their limits of patience. A number of veteran politicians, instead of tossing their hats into the ring for another term, have tossed in the towel instead. Following the election of 1982, eighty-one newcomers took seats in the House of Representatives: twenty-two had dropped out because of redistricting changes in the wake of the 1980 U.S. Census. Interestingly, one of those who elected to go was Richard Bolling, a thirty-four-year veteran from Missouri and an intellectual father of the reform movement that swept aside the seniority system for picking Congressional leaders. At age sixty-six, which is far from old for public servants, he was one of the group who had had enough.

Exodus is a still greater phenomenon at the state and local levels. One-fourth to one-third of all state legislators are neophytes. In a few states, anyone with ten years or more of service is regarded as a Grand Old Man in the legislature. There is something to be said for new blood; but it is one thing to displace hacks who never should have been entrusted with public office in the first place, and another to see seasoned, skilled, and dedicated individuals burn out or give up.

Apart from the sad consequences to them as individuals, it leaves the rest of us worse off. There is a growing need in state affairs for competence fortified by experience, and when the able veterans leave, legislatures lose their institutional memory. The political system then begins repeating its past mistakes.

Nominally, election campaigns begin with the state primaries. In fact, they begin whenever candidates put together their campaign committees. Some Presidential hopefuls for 1984 were handshaking through New Hampshire, the leadoff primary state, even before the 1983 calendar year started, more than twenty-two months ahead of the election. Jimmy Carter began his march from Georgia to the White House with a similarly long lead time. Largely as a reaction against the outpouring of money for Richard Nixon in 1972 (one man gave him $2 million), a law was passed in 1974 which included a cap on contributions in Federal elections (this is the source of the limit of $1,000 from an individual donor and $5,000 from a PAC). This did not stop giving and spending from rising astronomically. The average expenditure to win a seat in the House of Representatives about quadrupled between 1974 and 1982. The $1 million-plus figure for a Senate seat was just the average. In some states, the amount was much higher. In Texas, Minnesota, and California, spending by the two rivals for each seat topped $10 million. That also was the combined campaign budget of the two men running for governor in New York.

It is hard to find good reasons for all this money to be spent. Most incumbents win anyway. In the House, in a given election year an average of forty to forty-five members are not renominated or choose not to stand for reelection; of the remainder, about 90 percent win back their seats. That percentage has not changed much since 1950. There is more turnover in the Senate, but there, too, a majority of the incumbents who stand for reelection win it.

Why does it cost so much to help voters choose between Lloyd Bentsen and James Collins in Texas, Dave Durenberger and Mark Dayton in Minnesota, Pete Wilson and Edmund Brown in California (at nearly $14 million, the most costly Senate race ever), or Mario Cuomo and Lewis Lehrman for the job in Albany? (Let it be added that in the cases of Dayton and Lehrman, the fortunes spent in losing causes were mostly their own, from department stores and drugstores, respectively.) The standard answer has two parts: You have to start early and you have to use the media to win recognition, especially in large states where whistle-stop, back-of-the-train campaigns cannot hope to reach the public. This means big budgets for advertising in print, radio, and especially TV.

There are ways around this. The game can be made shorter while keeping the playing field level. Less money can be spent without inequity. National campaigns do not have to begin two years before election day. Other nations manage to select national leaders more expeditiously, and we could learn to do so.

In West Germany, though the candidates have previously been selected, the period of intensive campaigning is restricted to about six weeks prior to the election. In France, in one election the candidates for the National Assembly began serious campaigning in the middle of February and the race was over and done with soon after the middle of March. In Great Britain, Prime Minister Margaret Thatcher called in 1983 for national Parliamentary elections. The Queen dissolved Parliament on May 13, the campaigns took place, the election was held June 9, and the new Parliament convened on June 15 with Mrs. Thatcher reaffirmed as PM. Elapsed time: thirty-three days. Despite the short campaign periods in such countries, the voters turn out just the same, in far larger proportions than is true in the U.S. Among leading nations, the average voter turnout is about 80 percent. The U.S., with a turnout that has declined to 53 percent (as compared to 78 percent a century ago), is at the bottom of the list. This surely does not suggest that dragging out the process encourages people to vote.

In most other political democracies, as in the U.S., television and the press are major factors. Only in a few instances (Israel, the Netherlands) are the populations and distances small enough for shoe-leather national campaigns to succeed. Vital as the modern communication tools may be, however, few countries other than the U.S. allow paid political advertising on TV. Instead, parties and candidates are allotted free air time, and there are rules about fairness and balance in political programming. The only limit in the U.S. is that, after the midsummer national conventions, Presidential candidates can appear on TV only in party-sponsored programs, in arranged debates (Nixon-Kennedy, Carter-Ford), or on the news programs. Otherwise, it is a free-for-all.

For the 1982 elections in the U.S., the bill for TV advertising was $117 million, according to the Television Bureau of Advertising. The forecast was for a 50 percent increase in the 1984 campaign. In allowing such spending, the U.S. is unique. Yet the other democracies, large and small, manage to provide their populations with enough exposure to candidates to staff national offices with representatives who seem to be equal in quality to those we send to Washington.

To permit candidates in the U.S. (especially challengers) to make themselves known to the public, some national funding of Congressional elections is in order. This is commonplace elsewhere. Only France and the U.S. do not provide public funds to candidates for national office (other than President), to slates of candidates, or to party organizations. Also needed here is a requirement that television and radio stations provide air time to candidates, in addition to whatever journalistic coverage their news departments find appropriate. Many newspapers already open up their editorial pages as well as advertising space during the political high season. The electronic media could do the same, as is the practice in other countries.

There are these differences: A newspaper can add pages to accommodate more words, while no radio or television station has more than 1,440 minutes of air time per day. Further, TV stations in almost all other countries are publicly funded. Giving away air time does not sacrifice profits, as it would for the commercial stations of the U.S. Still, I side with those U.S. newspaper-owners and others who look upon ownership of a major communication artery as largely a public trust. As a way of paying their dues to society, owners of commercial stations should be obliged to provide blocks of time. It would not be an unconscionable burden if the campaigns were short enough.

While leaving the door open to individual contributions to parties and candidates, I would slam it on the political-action committees. In a true spirit of nonpartisanship, we should put them all out of business— the labor-union PACs and the corporate PACs, the trade-association PACs and the professionals' PACs, the nonconnected PACs which are usually ideological (the National Conservative Political Action Committee, for instance) and those which are not just nonallied but fully independent, meaning that they spend money for (or against) candidates without those candidates or their campaign organizations asking or being consulted.

It is not that any PAC, individually, has less right to survive than any other; collectively, they are becoming a monstrosity. The straightforward way to handle this is to say, "A PAC on all your houses," dismantle the lot of them, and restructure the national election financing system through a mixture of public funding and limited gifts from individuals. If suitable changes are made elsewhere, that can be done. We got along without PACs for 150 years and can do so again.

While the money should come down in the campaign column, it ought to go up in the salary scale. Members of Congress are obliged to maintain two residences, one in D.C. and one in the home district, and face other expenses that inevitably go with the job. At the present rates, they do not break even. We penalize them financially for representing us, and tempt them to find friends to put them into "sure thing" investments—a real-estate deal for which buyers are already lined up, for instance—so that they can put their children through college. What is needed is not a salary increase of a few percentage points but a massive raise, pushing Congressional salaries to at least $100,000 in 1984 dollars.

The *quid pro quo* would be that Congressmen would be permitted to accept no more than token sums of money for outside activities such as speeches or articles. Many now net $20,000 to $45,000 or more per year from such honoraria ("dishonoraria," they have been labeled by one Congressman, Mike Synar, an Oklahoma Democrat). Fully one-quarter of the members of the Senate take in fees of more than $25,000 a year from such activities—in effect, giving themselves a pay boost of 40 percent. One of those who declined on principle to accept such fees is Millicent Fenwick, a maverick Republican and, to be sure, a wealthy woman, who served in the House until 1983 and was the model for one of the characters in the *Doonesbury* cartoons. As she argued, if a speech relates to the government's business, it should be covered by the member's salary and expense allowances. It is wrong to be paid twice for doing the same work. If the event is not in the line of duty, then it is a distraction that ought to be questioned and, if done at all, be done on volunteer time.

Mrs. Fenwick had the right idea. We do not allow Federal judges to practice law on the side. Why should Congressmen be allowed to moonlight? The answer is that a lot of them do it to make ends meet. Probably the best example is Utah Senator Jake Garn. With homes to maintain in Utah and Washington, D.C., and three of his seven children in college, Senator Garn was frank in saying that without the honoraria ($48,000 in one year) he could not remain in the Senate.

What would be the effects of the sorts of changes suggested here in picking and paying elected officials? A number of them come to mind.

In what I regard as a roughly ascending order of importance, these steps might bring recession in what has become a growth industry for campaign consultants and candidate packagers, bring state and local party organizations (which in effect have been elbowed aside in the new politics) back into the picture, place a greater reliance and more responsibility on the shoulders of journalists, make elective office a practical possibility for many people now able to run only at great sacrifice to their families, and restore the reputation of politics as something more than an avenue for people on the make. Most important, by downgrading the importance of the money factor, these changes would improve the environment of the public-policy process. There would be a better chance for legislative and administrative programs that are both responsive (admittedly, they now are—but often to the wrong stimuli) and also productive (which they too rarely are). We might reach a stage, going back to Brady's remarks, where Congress could focus on significant matters without first having to have a crisis command its attention.

This is a large lump to swallow. Anyone with political street-smarts knows that even under the best imaginable circumstances only a fraction of those good effects (and I regard even the first of them as good) would come to pass. The last of those outcomes being as important as it is, though, it makes sense to work for what may have to be partial gains.

There are stumbling blocks, some easy to deal with, some not. The Supreme Court in 1976, in *Buckley v. Valeo,* held it unconstitutional to limit the amount most Federal candidates may spend on themselves. Independent spending may not be stopped or capped. First Amendment rights extend to political freedom of speech and association as much as any other kind, said the Court. In effect, then, it is legal for the Moral Majority to buy every billboard in North Carolina to back its favorites. Equally, a man of inherited wealth may spend a fortune to defeat a rival who has to pass the hat on the streetcorner.

Any serious reform of the election process requires the amendment of that view, and many legal scholars believe such a move is in order. The Supreme Court left the door open: The *Buckley* decision says that a limit on outside funding is permissible for Presidential candidates because this limit is a condition for their receipt of public funds. As long as candidates are free to reject money from either source, such limits are constitutional. Presumably, this would apply if Congressional campaigns were allotted public funds.

What impedes a much higher pay scale for Congress is not dollars but political sensitivity. Not many incumbents wish to hand their opponents the chance to accuse them of having four feet and the snout in the public trough. A campaign for higher salaries therefore would have to be pressed by outsiders, with inside help from lame ducks who could not benefit personally. What would the total cost be? The raise proposed would cost about $20 million per year. For comparison, the C-5B military transport plane, of which the Pentagon plans to buy fifty, costs more than $200 million per copy. That is to say, by reducing the fleet from fifty to forty-nine planes, government would save enough to pay the additional costs of $100,000 Congressional salaries for about a decade. If the objective were understood, that trade-off might even draw citizens' support in Marietta, Georgia, where the C-5Bs are built, and Dover, Delaware, where many of them may be based.

If the power of privately-financed campaigns were curtailed, candidates might well look in two other directions for aid and comfort: to the state and local political parties, which in days gone by provided the bulk of the support, and to people on the editorial side of the press, radio, and television, as distinct from the space salesmen. In effect, we would be restoring power, relatively speaking, to the parties and the press. Neither is an unmixed blessing. The blotched history of political-party organizations is too well known to need recounting here, and some of the present state and local examples seem determined to maintain the worst of that tradition. The press, for all the sacred noise made about its striving for objectivity, still gets the story wrong a fair amount of the time. Bias is no more extinct among journalists than among the rest of us. Candidates who trust the media to tell their story may find themselves in the hands of people who not only have favorites but play them.

Nonetheless, the trend goes in the right direction. Local political organizations have been elbowed aside in national politics largely because elected officials have become less dependent upon them for money. That is a negative in that it weakens discipline throughout the governmental process. The objective should not be to keep party organizations impotent because they sinned so much in the past, but to restore their authority while drawing higher-quality people into their service and illuminating their activities more brightly, so that the parties will behave more responsibly in the future. To the extent that the governmental balance of responsibilities shifts in the years to come, with more services undertaken at the local level and fewer at the Federal level, there will be further reasons to put priority on the strengthening of local party organizations: The folks at home will need strong, well-run party structures as much as these are needed by the folks in Washington.

It is hard to find harm in a move that would place greater responsibility on the shoulders of journalists and their publishers or producers. This would encourage the efforts, already under way and showing some success, to upgrade the quality of the journalistic product (a point developed in more detail in Chapter Seven). It also might raise the level of political conversation in this country, or at least one may hope so. All things considered, the journalists are more likely to give us a measure of the people intending to represent us, and the issues of concern, than is likely to come out of thirty- and sixty-second commercials. The TV evening news and the morning paper at least try to show how politicians think and work, while the "media blitz" approach mostly shows us how well candidates handle microphones and slogans, and whether they have dogs and children.

The proposal for licensed broadcasters to provide air time during elections would evoke an "of course" reaction in most countries. It is already the way of life in practically all nations in which radio and TV are important communication vehicles. Selling the idea in the U.S. is another matter. Elsewhere, stations are usually government-owned. Here, they are mostly private, for-profit businesses, and the station owners make money out of political ads. (This is, in fact, the largest single use of PAC funds.) A free-time requirement would smack of a move to take private property without compensation, and that is against the law. Splinter-party candidates would demand equal time: That objection has come up many times before.

The request still seems equitable, though. TV and radio stations are awarded exclusive regional rights to their frequencies. The available number is limited and the licenses have value, as anyone can prove by trying to buy a TV station in any city of size. Yet the owners pay no rent for these frequencies. They ought to put something back into the system through public service, and if the election process is not "public service," what is? Broadcasters have found ways to cope with the equal-time rule. They could adapt to this requirement. If the distribution of the costs is a problem, the game can be played with Chinese dollars: Charge a fee to each station for its use of a frequency, and use that revenue to cover the station's campaign "contributions."

Direct election of the President and Vice President is a perennial proposal. My interest in it lies not in the possible dollar savings but in the change it would bring in the political atmosphere. The early state primaries would be downgraded. Candidates would still need state delegates for the national conventions, but we would not be picking nominees and running mates with an eye on the number of electoral votes in their home state. No voter would be more important than another, and that is the central point. The principle of one man, one vote is now honored in the breach by the winner-take-all recording of votes by state. If you vote with the side that wins 49 percent in your state, your Presidential vote counts zero; if you side with the 51 percent, you have in effect two votes: your own plus the one the other fellow did not get.

With direct elections, the final outcome would only rarely be different. Only three times in American history has a President been selected who did not draw a larger popular vote than any opponent (John Adams, Rutherford Hayes, Benjamin Harrison). The reason to shift to direct election of Presidents, other than to serve principle, is not to put different people in office but to put a new perspective around those who seek to serve in the White House. As with so much of what is proposed here, the goal is to give general and national interests as much chance as possible to prevail over particular interests.

Another commonplace proposal for reform is to extend the terms of elective office and limit the rights of succession. For example, members of the House of Representatives might serve four years, but be allowed no more than four or five terms. Senators would serve six years, as now, but with a three- or four-term limit. The Presidential term would be six years with no second term. The thrust of these proposals and variations of them is to encourage elected officials to concentrate more on their work and less on reelection. Whether this would be the result is a matter of opinion. Some point with favor to states which have a single-term rule for governors. Some argue the other way, insisting that, instead of being more effective, the final-term officeholders, including the President by definition, would be long-term lame ducks whom their colleagues would not take seriously.

Why is a Lyndon Johnson in the Senate or a Tip O'Neill in the House always taken seriously? Because, it is contended, both friend and foe know that this power-broker is likely to be around as long as he cares to stay.

There is a lot to that point of view, but, as an offset, consideration might at least be given to an extended term for House members and to a length-of-service cutoff for both House and Senate. Imposing a top limit would help circumvent an obvious problem that would be created in the Senate if there were a four-year House term: The problem is that in each election year some House members would not have to defend their turf but would be free to run for other offices, most obviously seats in the Senate. If they lost, they still would be Congressmen for two more years. It strains belief to think that Senators would concur in a Constitutional amendment that exposed their flanks in this matter. The two-year House term is likely to remain until a length-of-service rule opens up seats incumbents are not allowed to defend.

A bit of arithmetic: About one-fourth of the members of the Senate have more than twelve years of service and an equal fraction of House members have more than fourteen. Typically, eight to twelve Senators retire in an election year or lose in the primaries. Under a three-term-maximum rule, another five seats would open up. Thus, we could expect a total of about fifteen Senate seats to be undefended by incumbents, and open to bids by, among all others, members of the House who are ambitious to move up, or who are obliged by service to leave the House, or both. Nothing in that seems to work against the public interest, except possibly the forced loss of a few senior Senators with impressive records of public service.

As for the PACs, their demise might not be as traumatic as it perhaps would appear on the surface. The staunchness of support for them is entirely a function of money—they have nothing else to bring to the political forum—and the other cuts proposed here would more than erase the funding gap left by the PACs. In 1982, PACs contributed about one-fourth of the money spent on Congressional campaigns: $83 million of a total of $344 million spent. Much more than $83 million could be removed from the total account through other reforms. Not all of the PAC dollars would stay out of the game completely, though. Some givers might personally turn toward the parties, or make gifts to candidates. Most people who give money to PACs do not come close to reaching the legal maximums that, as individuals, they would be permitted to donate through non-PAC channels.

The move would be timely. Neither Democrats nor Republicans would have grounds to claim foul, for PAC money now gives neither side an overwhelming advantage. At last report, the PAC dollars flowed in favor of Democrats, 54:46. On the basis of the total spent on the national campaigns, from PACs and all other sources, those PAC dollars gave Democrats an edge of about 2 percent. Were the PACs outlawed, each party would stand to lose (if that is the word) more or less equally.

Labor unions ought not mourn the passing. While the PACs were their idea (the AFL/CIO had the first PAC, and for a time organized labor had the field to itself), in recent years labor PACs have been outspent by business-related PACs. In each election, the union funds have fallen further behind, and it should be plain to union leaders that they cannot hope to play a deep-pocket game with realtors, physicians, lawyers, corporate managers, and others in the higher income strata, all of whom have PACs.

Big business on first thought might see advantage in staying with its PACs, but on reflection may conclude that the PACs are not all they are cracked up to be. There is no denying they have been a popular item with corporate officers. The number of corporate PACs grew from a few dozen to more than 1,200 in less than a decade. (At this writing the total number of PACs of all kinds is about 3,500.) However, the basis for this popularity eludes me. Most campaign money, by a three-to-two margin, is spent to support incumbents, and the ratio is that high largely because of the PACs: In the 1982 election, the PACs gave nearly four dollars to incumbents for each dollar to challengers. One may ask whether, with a Congress that has been in Democratic control for most of a half-century, a funding system that backs so many incumbents is what usually-Republican business executives really have in mind. While corporate PACs do put employees' dollars behind Republicans (nearly two-to-one), the net result of the PAC system is to give the edge to Democrats. Perhaps executives are not really partisans at all in their secret selves, but only incumbent-boosters: The devil you know is better than the other kind.

With that, the PACs are also lightning rods for criticism of big business. The uncomfortable fact is that most people in this country believe that big business (meaning its management) exerts undue influence on government. Opinion polls are very clear on that point.

The PACs only make the corporate role in government look worse. A businessman pleading a case is one thing; pleading while delivering a sack of money is another, and looks pernicious. Corporate leaders may find this unfair, and it is—after all, other PACs do no differently— but you cannot ride part of a horse. An antibusiness reaction is predictable, it goes with the PACs, and it has a cost. That negative has to be factored into the pro-PAC strategy.

Congressmen are angered by the charge that campaign gifts extract a *quid pro quo:* one check, one favor. Yet it is Senators and House members themselves who indict the system. Some sample comments: "When these PACs give money, they expect something in return other than good government" (Robert Dole, Kansas). "PAC money is not free; it has strings attached" (William Proxmire, Wisconsin). "You can't buy a Congressman for $5,000, but you can buy his vote. It's done on a regular basis" (Thomas Downey, New York). "I got sick of feeling indebted to PACs. There is no reason they give money except in the expectation of votes" (William Brodhead, Michigan, explaining why he quit Congress in 1982). "It's like getting addicted by a pusher" (Andrew Jacobs, Indiana). "It used to be that lobbyists lobbied Congress. Now Congressmen lobby lobbyists—for money" (Mike Synar, Oklahoma). "I'm scared . . . these new PACs not only buy incumbents but affect legislation" (Barber Conable, New York, another who decided not to run again).

"There is," as Richard Gephardt of Missouri has said, "a growing sense that the system is getting out of hand." To this, James Leach of Iowa has added the following: "The fabric of American democracy is being stretched thin by the money. On the budget debate, Democrats are indebted to advocates of social programs and Republicans to advocates of special-interest tax breaks. It should be no surprise we have a huge Federal deficit." "No one should be so naïve or so foolish," concludes Charles Mathias of Maryland, "as to think that the public isn't already paying . . ." (in terms of misdirected legislation).

Would that the problems of government could be traced to something as simple as Congressmen being beholden to donors, but Congressman Leach has his finger on an essential issue. In a less money-driven system, Senators and Representatives might be less inclined to showboat for friends sitting in the high-priced seats, and might find it easier to arrive at compromises drawn from perceptions of national needs.

The law of diminishing returns has already set in. PAC dollars are beginning to cancel each other out just as, in the main, the too-brief, uninformative campaign commercials tend to cancel each other out. It does not strain credulity to suggest that the future payout may actually be negative: If criticism of PAC money makes politicians uncomfortable enough, they may seek visible ways to put some distance between themselves and big donors. I am not cynical enough to believe that a Senator would deliberately change his vote, against his own convictions, simply to prove that he is not in a PACs pocket. On the other hand, if the cause is not one he holds dear, and the PAC people need him for other reasons . . . well, maybe. I think this is already happening.

The backlash is bound to have some negative effect on the relationship between politicians and private-sector donors. Even the people in political life most sympathetic to business may in time decide it is wise not to appear to be too cozy with corporations. At minimum, one must say that when corporations and industry associations joined the PAC brigade with such enthusiasm, they were asking for trouble. It would be in their interest if there were less PAC money in the system, and more financial support from other sources.

Nicholas Brady may have been an amateur as a U.S. Senator, but there is a lot of wisdom in what he had to say about the state of the political arts today. By one device or another—public funding, more reasonable salaries, a cutoff on length of service—we need to move the center of gravity of national politics away from its overweening concern with electioneering, toward a greater concern with governing. To that end, business organizations as well as other parts of the private sector ought to redefine what they mean when they say they are "contributing" to the public-policy process.

4

Governance—American Style

JOSH BILLINGS once wrote that "the trouble with most folks isn't so much their ignorance as knowing so many things that ain't so." To that a Columbia professor, Wallace Sayre, added that the public and private sectors in America are "fundamentally alike in all unimportant respects." Those two bits of folk wisdom say volumes about the problems of the public and private sectors in this country, and what it will take to make them work together more effectively.

A tour of duty in both sectors convinces me that each side cherishes its myths about the other, and that the best of intentions and the most careful attention to national needs will avail us little unless both sides disabuse themselves of the more serious of these fictions. Perhaps of the two the private sector has the greater distance to travel, with business facing an especially great re-educational task. Business would be a more constructive force in society, and go far in reducing the defensiveness of its relationships with government, if it shed its Number One myth, which is that government is just a business being run badly. In truth, government is a different sort of enterprise from private commerce altogether. It hears a different drummer. The priority list for government is not the same in content or rank-order as the list that makes commercial organizations tick. Where business deals in the hard coin of efficiency, government revolves around such softer notions as equity, fairness, and consent. Where people engaged in private enterprise usually can agree without difficulty on a short list of organizational objectives, and are prepared to follow their leaders in those directions, people in government must contend with a full spectrum of goals, while trying to keep peace in a national family whose members by no means agree on the direction in which lies the promised land.

These sorts of differences seem to be understood as they apply to the workings of local government. It may be that all of us expect less of local than national government and, thinking there is not much at stake, forgive what we take to be the folly of the folks on the other side of the street. The better explanation, I believe, is that many people in the private and public sectors at the local level know one another and have learned to work together. The same cannot be said as confidently with reference to national government. There, the points of contact are fewer, and perhaps that is why the fallacies seem to persist.

It is useful to examine the myths and I intend to do so here, but first some further comment is needed on the problems of governance, as a frame of reference. Running the country is not just a different task but a tougher one than running a corporation or university. At least at the Federal level (and this applies to some states as well) the jobs of key people in government are more difficult to begin with, made so by the complexity of the issues and of the negotiations required to resolve them. To complicate government's work, the individuals in senior spots, up to and including the President, often come to their assignments with little or no practice in handling issues of the dimensions they must face. Not many cabinet officers or agency directors have had an opportunity for a staged, step-by-step exposure to the responsibilities they are sworn to undertake. For most, it is baptism by total immersion. That rarely happens in the private sector.

A further factor, and at this point the most important of all, is that there has been a loss of discipline and of the sense of order throughout the national political structure. A pattern of disintegration began several decades ago, and now makes it all but impossible for even the most dedicated public servant to deliver in the spirit and letter of the oath of office. There are many reasons for this, not least among them the activities of the private sector. Business no less than other types of organizations shares in the blame for compounding the disorder of government, and bears some of the responsibility for reconstruction.

At the national level, it is disarray that most cripples government today, not the inefficiency and bloat about which we so often complain, with justification. In the past two decades, in a well-meant effort to make government more democratic, we have managed as a nation to fragment it to a point where it is strongly biased toward expedients and has lost most of its capacity to think in terms of durable policies. As discipline has waned, government has fallen back on a strategy, if that is the word for it, of patching together coalitions to paste over clusters of problems. Having lost sight of broader responsibilities, government has bought short-term accord without counting the long-term costs. This style of governance, undesirable in any circumstance, might do minimal harm if the nation were facing no great economic or social challenges. However, in times as troubled and competitive as these, it is another story. Chaos is a luxury we cannot afford.

We are close to it. Neither political party has been able for years to hold a dependable national majority. The power needed to govern has been dispersed around Washington among duchies by the dozens—there are now no less than 310 committees and subcommittees of the Senate and House. The process of political negotiation is being drowned in a sea of interest groups, which have rushed in to fill the power vacuum left by the decline of party organizations. The worst of these interest groups live by a creed of rule or ruin. They have little stomach for compromise. Even the best of them are preoccupied with narrow goals and are rarely concerned with the public good in a broad sense. This is where business comes in, along with other private-sector organizations. Many groups representing commercial interests—trade associations and lobbyists—are no different from other types of interest groups in that they focus to a fault on day-to-day goals. Business rates some criticism for that, no less than other institutions.

In the midst of this stand the legislators and regulators who are supposed to try to identify the public good, which of course each faction claims to represent. While government officials may honestly claim lofty purposes, what most of them spend much of their time doing is greasing squeaky wheels and trying to strengthen their own power bases. As has been said by John Brademas, formerly the Democratic whip in the House of Representatives and more recently a university president, "Congress is more and more becoming a place of independent contractors, each member intent on constructing his own record in a manner most pleasing to the eye of his constituents or special interests but without regard to his responsibility to serve the national well-being. This is more than a question of aesthetics; it is a fundamental structural problem that raises the question of whether representative democracy functions effectively in the twentieth century."

I think he is correct. There is only a slim mathematical chance that out of the Tower of Babel will emerge a clear leadership voice, one that most citizens, were they polled in a referendum, would feel does indeed speak to the general "public interest," however that might be defined. The more likely products are social divisiveness, the loss of anchor points for the body politic, and what the editors of the *National Journal* call interest-group gridlock, a condition in which quarrelsome factions become so entangled in defending their pieces of turf and pitting their PACs against one another that nothing gets done.

The questions I extract from this, questions that are unanswered but deserving of the highest status on the political agenda, are these: Can government learn to discipline itself? Will the private sector push government in that direction, or the other way? Can the sanctity of democratic process be preserved amid such a confusion of self-interests? As organized at present, the system not only fails to address such questions in an intelligent way, it cannot even make clear assignments of responsibility for handling ordinary, day-by-day issues that come before government. Frequently, the Federal solution to a problem is to keep everybody happy by letting the decisions be made everywhere—policymaking by the sum-of-the-parts—as a result of which, good decisions are made nowhere.

What makes the decline of process so worrisome is the fact that, in the public arena, process is all we have. Within the private sector and as consumers, people vote every day for products and services, but remain free to take the results or leave them alone. In the public sector and as citizens, people vote, but then must abide by whatever results the process delivers. If they do not like what "the system" is selling today, they have no other vendor to turn to. Hence a well-placed concern, shared by thoughtful individuals in and out of government, about the growing inability of government to distill varied points of view into a durable consensus. Hence, too, my contention that we must try to rebuild the system into one in which respect for the process again stands above ideology.

Compromise has been given a bad name, undeservedly so. From our history, we conjure up images of old-style party machines run by venal bosses. No one wishes to return to that, but what is needed is a nonvenal version of that spirit of compromise to replace the certitude and inflexibility that so often characterize the politics of the day. It has to be understood that it is not a sign of weakness or lost integrity to "give a little to get a little." As Dr. Brademas has pointed out, in a representative government the role of elected officials, of necessity, is to reconcile and conciliate: "It's the only way to get anything done, to make the system work," he has said, adding, "Frankly, there's too much ideology around, and not enough civility."

Is all of this mere theory, as a pragmatist might say? Is this an issue that troubles no one but parliamentarians and a rare ex-Congressman with a Ph.D. and a reflective mind? Far from it. Political disorder has real, direct consequences, and we live with these every day. They are reflected in the goods and services, good and bad, that we all buy with tax dollars. Washington's monument to the diffusion of decisions and the failure to face the costs is not an abstruse article in an economics journal, but annual budget deficits and a growing national debt now at $1.25 trillion. At about $20,000 per family, this is the biggest debt most families ever see, next to the mortgage on the house. The fact that government has for years been playing musical chairs with spending and revenues takes on a painful reality for tens of millions when they look at such problems as the chronic anemia in the financing of the Social Security and Medicare programs.

It costs all of us heavily to have a government that hears but does not heed warnings about long-term economic problems. The industrial arena is witness to that. For most of two decades government ignored the signs of decay in important industrial sectors. There were repeated efforts to convince Washington that its policies were partly to blame, but only after the U.S. had suffered serious losses in competitive position versus other industrialized nations, and after workers had lost jobs, did the government begin to act on the facts. Only then did it make needed policy changes, primarily in the form of incentives to encourage the private investment that is required to maintain a strong productive base for the economy.

The governmental process of today is one our high-school civics books never described, and one no President before Franklin Roosevelt would have recognized. The scaling factor astonishes even people who are used to bigness, and the very fact of size speaks to the need for a strong sense of order and internal discipline in Federal government. The once-small office of the President has become a full-blown bureaucracy, with a White House phone book that contains more than 2,000 listings. It takes experience just to find the right person to call. (Whether the calls are returned is another question entirely, going to

the issue of the Washington pecking order.) The Congressional establishment employs more than 100 times as many people as it did in the
days of Mark Hanna and Henry Cabot Lodge. At the time of World
War I, the typical Senator had one personal staff member and a Congressman had none. Today, the Senate Budget Committee has more
employees (eighty-two) than the entire Senate had in 1914. The personal and committee staffs for the Senate and House number more
than 17,000 employees, not counting another 10,000 in support agencies such as the General Accounting Office and Congressional Budget
Office.

In a two-year session, a Congress will be asked to consider 12,000
bills, and will pass 1,000. There will be 10,000 meetings of committees, which works out to an average of more than thirty for each day
the Senate and House are in session. Legislation proceeds through
these committees and through what might properly be called the Congress of Changing Coalitions. Together with the traditional party cau-
cuses, there is a constant coming and going of groups, each with its
hands on the levers of power on some specific issues. Among the
recent examples are the Black Coalition, the Boll Weevils (Southern
Democrats who carried the balance of power that permitted President
Reagan to put through his tax and spending cuts in 1981), the Gypsy
Moths (junior Northern Republicans who wanted cuts in the defense
budget instead of in domestic programs), and the Northeast-Midwest
Alliance (Congressmen from districts hard hit by industrial deterioration and unemployment).

The fourth branch of government, the regulatory and administrative agencies, has steadily increased in staff and budget. Its emergent
power is not news. Thirty years ago, Supreme Court Justice Robert H.
Jackson wrote in an opinion on a Federal Trade Commission case that
the rise of administrative bodies was the most significant legal trend
of the past century. He said that the fourth branch "has deranged our
three-branch legal theories much as the concept of a fourth dimension
unsettles our three-dimensional thinking."

Justice Jackson's generation, though, did not envision the size to
which this instrument would grow, or the zeal with which mission-
oriented agencies would travel far from home, like Marco Polo, to
reach the distant corners of the economic and social world. As of 1950
and before, most regulation was in the hands of industry-specific agencies. The Food and Drug Administration and the Federal Aviation

Administration are examples. If you happened not to be involved with pharmaceuticals or flying, you had little reason to be concerned with their work. The laminate added since that time is a thick layer of agencies with authority over all lines of commerce and all kinds of institutions. Examples include the Environmental Protection Agency, the Occupational Safety and Health Administration, and the Consumer Products Safety Commission. They regulate not only manufacturers but also hospitals, shopping centers, colleges and universities, and retirement villages. No one is unregulated by them, directly or indirectly.

At the state level, there has been a similar increase in scale, and there, too, there has been diffusion of responsibility when the scale of activity would seem to call for order and organization. State and local units have expanded more rapidly than the Federal branch in staffs, committee structures, and regulatory agencies. Because numerous problems drift across state borders—air pollution, water rights, and welfare recipients being examples—governors and state legislators have formed regional and national associations that meet on a regular basis. The National Conference of State Legislatures draws more than 2,500 legislators and staff members to its meetings.

For the private sector, keeping track of and staying in touch with state activities are full-time jobs. In a typical year, 250,000 bills go into the legislative hoppers of the fifty states; 50,000 of them become law, and a few more are added by a wrinkle called "R&R," the process of referendum and recall in which the voters bypass the legislature and make law directly at the ballot box. Lobbyists are as commonplace in the state capitals as in Washington. There is now a national body, called the State Government Affairs Council, with more than 100 corporations and trade associations as members.

Surrounding the formal institutions of government is a Milky Way of professional societies, consultants, unions, think tanks, and interest groups. They are so numerous that there is even an association of the executives of associations, headquartered, of course, in Washington. It has been estimated that there are 10,000 lobbyists and "Washington representatives."

This is certainly not all bad. There is a lot to be said for a sharing of powers within the executive and legislative branches, and for people of all persuasions lobbying for their views with elected officials. As a practical matter, it is necessary for individuals and organizations to federate to keep an eye on government; few constituents have the time and resources to thread the mazes for themselves, or keep track of what is in the hopper. An abundance of groups on the fringes of government also means that seekers of wisdom and truth will have access to enormous amounts of information and analysis, some of it of high quality, generated by private or semi-private organizations and there for the taking.

Open government has a democratic ring. It gives us a picture of fresh air being let into Congressional hearing rooms once dominated by dictatorial chairmen. It suggests that power is being remanded to states and localities, in keeping with Jeffersonian principles. That is hard to oppose, especially since this process of sharing is bringing forth a new quality of regional leadership. Beginning to disappear from state, county, and city governments are the amateurish politicians who captured office with no visible credentials and remained in power mostly because no one thought it important enough to take the trouble to drive them out. Coming onto the scene are newcomers who are energetic and usually young, and who bring credentials of intelligence to make up for what they lack in experience. They have sensed that there is more at stake than was previously supposed, and they are welcome arrivals.

All of that notwithstanding, it remains that the system is not working well. The swing of the pendulum has taken us from a process too closed to one that has become a free-for-all. We have Balkanized the structure to a point where insiders and outsiders alike find it difficult to accomplish anything worthwhile. In subdividing responsibility we have fragmented the intelligence of government. Knowledge of the technology is in one place; economic perspective, somewhere else. Domestic and international impacts are appraised in different offices, as though State had no reason to care how Commerce is doing. The world is messier than that, though. It does not allow such neat compartmentalization. To take but one example, U.S.-Mexico relations involve (inseparably) such matters as hemisphere security, energy supply (because of Mexico's large oil reserves), water rights for agriculture, the treatment of illegal migrants who compete for jobs in the U.S. (eight million thus far, by one estimate), the business interests of companies involved with Mexico as traders and investors, and the problems Mexico faces in paying its debts, most of which it owes to U.S. banks. Where in the U.S. government do thoughtful people meet to sort out the facets of that problem and consider what policies make the best sense, all things considered, as they say? The answer, most often, is that they do not meet at all.

The staffs try. There are interagency and interdepartmental committees. The White House encourages State to consider Labor's position and Commerce's. Yet the people in the Congress and cabinet departments who are most knowledgeable about different parts of the issue work in different places and owe their loyalty to different heads. There are few opportunities for those heads to think through the problems in terms of what ought to be the primary interest—namely, the appropriate U.S. policy toward Mexico.

In situations of this kind, what often happens is that the major pieces are fitted together and compromise agreements are made whenever and wherever the key people can find a few minutes to talk. That might be in the last few minutes on board Air Force One en route to Mexico City. It might also be at a Washington cocktail party, where power brokers past and present gather with officeholders of large or moderate reputation. This is not a comforting thought, but some portion of America's political history is being written on a scratch pad on final approach, and on the guest lists for the salons of Georgetown.

What Washington honors, the nation gets. Administrators have few incentives to run a tight ship, take risks, and cancel experiments that fail. Therefore, they do not often do so. Department heads are given awards not for keeping expenses under budget and eliminating deadwood, but for advancing the chief executive's projects. Status and scale go hand in hand. The more groups an agency is trying to please, the more projects it administers, the more departments with which it must interact, then the higher its standing. Given such a reward system, it is hardly surprising that administrators maneuver for larger staffs and bigger budgets, and are not known to boast, as corporation heads sometimes do, about how "mean and lean" they have made their organizations.

In the private sector, there is no need to apologize for projects that are losers. Taking chances is part of the game, and any large, old company has at least one giant failure in its closet: Ford's Edsel; Du Pont's Corfam poromeric material, a substitute for leather; Polaroid's instant color movies; GM's developmental project on rotary engines. Is is hardly a feather in an executive's cap to be the patron of a corporate flop, but neither is it invariably fatal. In the public sector, though, errors far more modest than these can lead to exposés, Congressional investigations, and ruined careers. Open admission of error is thus to be avoided at all costs. He who tries something new and fails incurs greater punishment than he who does not try at all. Sins of omission therefore outnumber the other kind by a large margin. Moreover, it is rarely easy for a government official to retreat gracefully from any project, because most Federal-program dollars go to pay people, and what one man calls waste another man calls his paycheck. Thus, the temptation in the public sector is to let sleeping dogs lie. Thus, we are governed by people programmed to be less concerned with being right than with not being found wrong, and by agencies locked into old programs, however outdated the rationale. Alexander Pope's lines are modified by government to read: Be not the first by whom the new is tried, but be sure to be the last to lay the old aside.

The myths that surround the public-policy process have little to do with such substantive problems. If running this tangent serves no other purpose, it shows how much energy we all waste arguing about "things that ain't so," and suggests how unlikely good governance is when disorder is compounded by fiction. Over the years, private business has harbored various theoretical constructs, mostly wrong, about the workings of government. One is the Fallacy of Riddles, which holds that people in government must be remarkably dense because problems stare them in the face, often problems that could be analyzed with no great difficulty by an ordinarily intelligent teenager, yet government officials charged with solving them seem to be unable to work out even simple riddles.

A corollary of that is the Optimizing Fallacy: Out there somewhere lies the one best answer to the question, the one best program to pursue. Government ought to try to find that optimal solution. The efficiency-minded in the private sector have trouble understanding why government has so much difficulty grasping this simple point. Derived from that one is the Bull's-eye Fallacy, which works from the premise that government will never become efficient, or close to it, until it starts using rifles instead of shotguns. It scatters its shots too much, firing in the general vicinity of targets but scoring few bull's-eyes. Most of the buckshot is wasted, and innocent victims are sometimes hit by stray lead.

All of these are reinforced by the Myth of Precision, which rests on the massive assumption that what counts the most, or ought to, is what can most readily be counted. As with many myths, there is a touch of truth in this one. Measuring usually is better than guessing. However, not all decisions can be illuminated by numbers, and the type least susceptible to a countinghouse approach is the set that deals with social choices, which is much of the business of government. Moreover, as accountants and engineers have long known, the precision claimed for a number is no measure of its accuracy. A badly made forecast does not become a good one simply because the calculations are carried out to two places behind the decimal point. What it probably becomes is more misleading.

Instruction on the truth of that was offered early in Ronald Reagan's administration by David Stockman, head of the Office of Management and Budget. The executive branch forecasts for Federal revenues and spending showed with apparent precision that the budget could be balanced, when in fact the nation was facing record deficits. As Stockman conceded to a journalist friend, who took it all down and published the confession in the *Atlantic,* some of the numbers in the projection seem to have come off the wall. The forecast of a balanced budget rested on assumptions about national economic growth and governmental spending cuts, assumptions made in haste and soon proven to be wrong. For this memorable display of candor for which the public should be grateful, Mr. Stockman was taken to the woodshed and given a spanking by the President, a man who for years had pledged allegiance to balanced budgets. Neither the President nor anyone else, though, should have been surprised by the flaws in those numbers. Any forecast that requires everything to work out for the best ought to be suspect, if for no better reason than that it violates Murphy's Law: If anything can go wrong, it will.

If there is any one doctrine that pervades the decision-making process in government, and does for the public sector what the idea of efficiency does for industry, it is the doctrine of fairness. The notion has enormous political leverage. It is often the hub around which policy revolves. When the Reagan administration soon after its election pushed aggressively for cuts in social programs at the same time it was increasing defense spending, it was quickly stung with charges of being uncaring, even cruel. The proposals, it was said, were not "fair," because in the give-and-take one group was doing all the giving while the other was doing the taking. This accusation hurt to a point where, a year later, the President's own people at OMB urged him to speak out forcefully on the theme that the administration was indeed concerned with "fairness," "compassion," and "decency," and that the Democrats had no "moral monopoly" on social issues. In the 1982 Congressional elections, the Democrats had a field day attacking their opponents' presumed deficiencies in the equity column. It was nearly the only point on which a diverse band of Democratic candidates agreed, and they got good mileage out of it at the polls.

When Congress voted to reduce taxes in 1981, there was less concern with questions of economic efficiency—how much revenue would be lost, with what stimulus or other consequences to the economy—than with the question of equity in distribution of the cuts: Would everybody get a fair share? The following year, when it was decided that Congress had overdone it and ought to move immediately to restore nearly $100 billion in lost revenues, the question again turned on equity. The first place Congress looked was at businesses that paid little or no taxes, and at the cuts it had only recently enacted that favored corporations, including accelerated tax write-offs, tax reductions for certain research and development expenditures, and reductions in taxes on some of the profits oil companies earned outside the U.S. The last of those items provided some language that is instructive:

"We were looking for areas that did not fit with our ideas of equity and fairness, and this [treatment of foreign earnings] stuck out like a sore thumb." What is significant is the identity of the speaker—not an opponent of the administration, not a doctrinaire critic of big business, but Republican Robert Dole, chairman of the Senate Finance Committee and one of the architects of the tax revisions being proposed. "Fairness" is a universal touchstone in politics, one of the few.

Misreading that can be costly. It can easily bury a case built strictly on the merits. On the same tax-restoration issue, an oil-company executive, Jack Bennett of Exxon, contended that the proposed shift in the rule about taxing foreign earnings would make U.S. firms less competitive and probably lead to greater dependence on foreign oil and perhaps to higher oil prices, exactly the results the U.S. did not want. On a broader basis, some private companies and organizations, the Business Roundtable included, tried to sell the argument that the nation would gain in the long run if the cuts in taxes on business and higher-income individuals were kept intact and the extra revenues were raised entirely from other sources, mostly middle-income families.

Technically these arguments may have been right, but politically they had no chance. As Treasury Secretary Donald Regan, an ex-business-man himself, remarked at the time, it was ironic to hear $200,000-a-year executives saying that $20,000-a-year workers should bear all of the pain. *Fortune* magazine quoted Regan as saying to a delegation of executives in the Oval Office, "Tell me which Congressman is going to vote to take a tax cut away from the little guys and let you keep everything."

Government is not immune to its own flights of fancy. In its rela-tionships with business, it often succumbs to the notion that business executives have essentially unlimited power, like Louis XIV, and that when the private sector fails to do government's bidding, it is proba-bly because the leaders do not want to cooperate or do not care. Be-hind this Sun King Myth is the assumption that a private power elite not only exists but also has all the clout that Hollywood scriptwriters think it has. That myth has been debunked countless times, but, like the celluloid soldier bleeding from a dozen wounds, it keeps staggering around the movie set refusing to go down. Myths die hard on Sunset Strip or Capitol Hill.

Government also has given itself over to the Myth of the Conven-tional Wisdom, and founded more than one of its programs on the Fallacy of Moral Outcomes. The first holds that if all the smart money says something is so, it is so. The second is that if the motives be pure and the results promise to be popular, then the evidence in defense of a program or policy ought to carry the day. The conventional wisdom, however, is not always right. All the smart money said airplanes could not sink capital ships and Harry S Truman could not sink Thomas E. Dewey in the Presidential campaign of 1948, but both General Billy Mitchell and Harry Truman came up winners. From Ecclesiastes on, each generation has been reminded anew that the race is not always to the swift nor the battle to the mighty. That may be the way to bet, but not with the rent money. Purity of motives will not justify govern-mental programs if other arguments for them are unconvincing and there are alternative, perhaps more urgent calls on the same budget dollars. Surely one test ought to be the level of demonstrated public need. Not every claim has substance, most crises do not happen, and a little research is usually a good thing. As an old adage has it, "Some-body went outside and looked, and found it ain't so."

We should not criticize government because it fails to solve riddles. That is the least of its problems. Its greatest difficulty is in carrying its basket of answers through the political minefields. It was an open secret for years that the Social Security system was headed for a financial crisis, and it would be nonsense to claim that the inaction of Congress and the White House was based solely on ignorance. Washington procrastinated because of an absence of politically painless correctives: Every proposed answer promised either to reduce benefits for the retired or to increase taxes for the rest of the population, and to embrace either course of action seemed politically suicidal. True or not, that was the reading of the political waters at the time. So it was as well with the problems of inadequate capital investment. Government heard what business leaders and economists were saying, but to do something about it meant favoring savers and investors over spenders, and at the time, spending seemed to have more votes. Conveniently, there were a few economic seers prepared to argue that consumption would continue to pull the economy along indefinitely. They told us that prosperity would be assured if only wages stayed high so the public could keep flocking to the shopping malls and auto showrooms to spend the cash. The advice was comforting, and wrong.

Government comes up with plenty of good ideas. On the Social Security problem, any one of three or four plans would have restored the system to financial health. Amid all the hand-wringing about declining growth rates for productivity and technological innovation in America, one thing that has never been lacking is an abundance of specific correctives, including some which have worked before. On productivity growth, one consultant to the government came forth with a paper providing no less than ninety-nine recommendations. On another occasion, the Joint Economic Committee of Congress was given some 514 recommendations on what could be done to help technological innovation.

Congress has neither the time nor the patience to find out which of those ideas would certifiably be the best, but that is not necessarily important. All we might hope Congress would do is accept a few from the list that will do an adequate job and, as a Congressman would add, be politically salable. As government defines "optimize," then, the word has nothing to do with the kinds of neat answers that please engineers, and a great deal to do with the wish to garner maximum votes with minimum complaints.

Whether government even ought to look for optimal solutions in a technical sense is moot. It is not going to happen. Efficiency, as the private sector uses the word, ranks too low in government's priorities. There is a sensible reason for this, going back to the fundamental risks associated with unchecked power. Only when authority is subdivided can a republic be made safe for people. As Justice Brandeis pointed out long ago, the proper Constitutional objective of government is not to promote efficiency but to prevent the concentration of power. That view reflects an even earlier caution offered by James Madison, who wrote in *The Federalist Papers* that while it was first necessary for government to control the governed, government was obliged in the second instance to control itself. In democracies, one might say, it is necessary to trade away some efficiency for security.

It is not an accident, nor a sign of stupidity of the people in charge, that Congress will set the stage for the regulation of some component of daily life—let us say, the movement of goods in interstate commerce—and then leave the decision on the precise rules for compliance to a regulatory agency, which leaves the interpretation of those rules to an administrative law judge, whose decisions may be overruled by the full regulatory commission, whose members in turn may be challenged in a Federal Court of Appeals, whose decisions may be reviewed by the Supreme Court. The system is set up that way, to prevent an unwanted congregation of power.

No one needs to be reminded that such a system can be expensive, inconsistent, and maddeningly bureaucratic. Its decisions are sure to be uneven in quality; its procedures, cumbersome. Any management consultant worth his salt will find plenty of room for improvement. Further, the system cannot even claim to be entirely "safe," democratically. There are obvious possibilities for abuse because some of the agencies making the rules also are licensed to enforce and adjudicate them, at least up to the stage where appellate-court review begins.

It is wrong, though, to take any of this as justification for reforms that would press government operations into the mold of a private corporation. The difference in accountability has not yet been factored in. If too much power collects in the executive offices of Exxon, or if Hewlett-Packard runs amok and imperils the well-being of the citizens of Silicon Valley, there are outside, higher authorities with the power to put the corporations in their places. If you do not like Du Pont's products, you can change brands. If Allstate sells you a bill of goods, you can go to another insurance company and at the same time seek redress through a state insurance commissioner or, if necessary, a court. These are not always easy pathways to follow, but they are there. In the public sector and especially at the Federal level, there are not the same options. When government violates the civil rights of individuals or comes up with a lemon in economic policy, recourse can be found only within the confines of the same government that created the problem in the first place. Thus, we lean over backward with government, applying checks and balances and dividing authority in ways that would never make sense for the private sector. Thus, the political apparatus moves forward only by a complicated process of brokerage and compromise. Thus, every government program born is bound to fail a pure efficiency test.

A flaw in our political thinking is that there should be no more than two positions on controversial problems, with its implication that each of us must choose a black hat or a white hat. In practical fact, except on a few Constitutional issues such as separation of church and state, there are numerous options and plausible compromises, most of them more sensible than the action at either pole. The nation is not obliged to choose between a cold-logic conservatism and a warm-puppy liberalism as its political coda, between supply-side and demand-pull as its economic religion, between efficient production and environmental protection as its resource-use policy, between soft-path technologies versus nuclear energy as its power source, or between better schools versus better health care for the aged as the outlet for social spending. To the question "Which do you want?" the appropriate political answer almost always is "Some of both." That makes it possible for the political machine to creak along.

We can and should do better, but there is no point in getting our hopes too high. Nothing suggests that we can sensibly look to some distant date when our society will be so close to perfection that the lions will lie down with the lambs. The Peaceable Kingdom is a utopian picture, and just another myth for people trapped in the real world. All that can be said in defense of this myth is that it is more pleasant to behold than its opposite number, which holds to the paranoid conviction that all the other animals in the jungle are out to get you and the thing to do is to get them first. Appealing as the Peaceable Kingdom is, though, it is not an innocent vision. It steers people away from a reality that has to be faced: namely, that our society contains significantly different world views, differences that are more than tactical, differences that cannot be reconciled by argument, however polite and patient we all might be.

People disagree, often in fundamental ways, on what is right and wrong with the world as it is and what it will take to put things right. Senators Jesse Helms and Lowell Weicker cannot see eye to eye, except possibly on the conclusion that Congressman Tip O'Neill has poor ideas on how to run the country. Yet all three read the newspapers and have access to the same data and research services. It was ever thus. Alexander Hamilton and Thomas Jefferson frequently agreed to disagree, based on more or less the same evidence. Two of the most influential Senators and Presidential candidates of this century, men who did much to focus issues around political philosophies, were Hubert Humphrey and Robert Taft. After a lifetime of public service, Senator Humphrey went to his grave convinced that the Federal government had to be a direct and often decisive force in social affairs, "for the good of the country." Senator Taft, a man of equally distinguished standing, went to his grave believing nearly the opposite. They worked from the same set of facts.

Not only does this demolish the myth that if we were more charitably disposed toward one another, "the public will" would be done: More importantly, it reinforces the singular importance of process to the preservation of the democratic order. It says that, precisely because people are not going to agree on the decisions, they must agree to honor the process by which decisions are reached. The system absolutely depends on it. Hence the statement that the sanctity of process must be preserved above self-interest.

The best chance for that happening is to build on the national scene a sense of collaboration between public and private sectors that is analogous to the relationship that already exists, in the best of cases, at the local level. At the beginning of the chapter, there is a passing remark to the effect that the people from government and business who have worked together on local issues harbor fewer myths than are often displayed by their counterparts at the national level. To me, this is significant. Often (not always, to be sure), familiarity has bred cooperation, not contempt. In communities where individuals from all sorts of organizations have sweated out together the hospital fund drives, the municipal sewage-plant bond bills, and master plans for urban renewal, and done so under the right conditions, those individuals have lost their illusions about themselves and each other. Having avoided the worst flights of fancy, they have preserved a chance of working together productively on community problems none of them could have handled alone. There has been no guarantee of success— some of the urban problems have overwhelmed everyone—but there have been enough happy endings to force us to ask whether the experience can be broadcast and transposed to the national scene. Can we not hope that more of this public-and-private-sector collaboration would help restore a needed sense of order and common purpose within government, and thus lead to better governance? I think we can.

The climate has to be right. The local experience makes that clear. The best examples (at least, the ones where the case record is most readily available) come from the area of economic development and urban renewal. Among the cities in which there have been strong private-and-public initiatives are Baltimore, Bridgeport, Chicago, Kansas City, Oakland, Philadelphia, Dayton, Albuquerque, and Minneapolis-St. Paul. In each, either the private sector has been involved from the start, often providing the initial push, or the publicly sponsored programs have begun to pay off more impressively after the private sector has added its support.

The programs that at this juncture appear to be most successful have a number of common characteristics. One is that they deal with objectives that are relatively clear-cut. Government, business, and other slices of the community are trying not just to "build a better town," which could mean all things to all people, but to reach such limited, identifiable goals as expanding the economic base, reducing unemployment, improving health-care facilities, or rebuilding a stated number of decaying downtown city blocks. If they succeed, they will know it.

A second component of success is for the private sector to provide resources and ideas but not to try to dominate. The business executives who have been most effective in this area have not made the mistake of trying to give orders to City Hall or talk down to state legislators. People in government need help, not lectures. Many of them are part-time public servants and most of them have no staff. Few of them have ready access to solid data. The most valuable contribution the private sector can make is to bring them an unbiased presentation of facts on current issues, with their own views drawn from those facts. Community programs begin to move off dead center when representatives of the private sector come before a public council or assembly and say words to this effect: "Here are as many of the facts as we can get. Here are the alternative courses of action. Here is what we think you should do. Here is what the opposition has to say, and here are the answers we make to those arguments." Often, people in the public sector have a terrible time getting issues to a point where they can be analyzed that way.

Third, success seems to grow when the actors come to know one another personally, and this is often the pivotal element. A long-established custom in business calls for management people to take an interest in community affairs, and some of them have built high reputations as worthwhile contributors. When their communities tackle new programs, it is routine for the town fathers to turn to these people for help. The community is dealing not with anonymous "corporate spokesmen" but with individuals with familiar names and faces, who have shown that they can be trusted to keep their word.

How large a difference that can make is suggested by the experience of the state of Delaware in digging its way out of a deep hole in which it found itself a decade ago. Because Delaware is small in size and population (its 600,000 population would fill only one corner of the city of Philadelphia, a few miles to the north), one would expect state problems in Delaware to be approached much like local problems in many other places, and so they are. People know their elected representatives. An astonishing number know the governor, the state's U.S. Senators, and its lone Congressman. State legislators, cabinet officers, and people from the private sector are willing to work on details, and do not find this demeaning. They recognize, as Mayor Marion Barry of Washington, D.C., once said, that a lot of "urban government is potholes, not policy," and that potholes count.

Delaware's economy had been built on a sound foundation, balancing agriculture, manufacturing, and services, but by the early 1970s it had slipped into an unenviable position. Economic growth had stalled. Rising personal tax rates, undisciplined state spending, and some other negatives had made the state unattractive as a place to locate new companies or expand old ones. From 1953 to 1973, Delaware led the nation in the amount of increase in state and local tax burdens, to more than 12 percent of all personal income. High-bracket earners were obliged to pay the state a top tax rate of nearly 20 percent. Not surprisingly, few out-of-state executives were intrigued by the thought of putting Delaware into their expansion plans, or themselves in that tax jurisdiction. The management of one German chemical company visited the state with the thought of building a plant there, but found the climate so hostile and state officials so indifferent that the company ended up 800 miles away, in Alabama.

A group of Delaware business and community leaders decided this situation was unacceptable and they sought to help change it. The man who was then chief executive of Du Pont, Charles B. McCoy, made a state-of-the-state address, analyzing the problems and proposing correctives. Later, a Delaware Roundtable, patterned on the national organization, came into being. People stopped ducking issues and began calling a spade a spade. At one point, with a new governor, Pierre S. du Pont, in office, I was interviewed by the *Wall Street Journal* and said that the business climate in Delaware was so bad I would not recommend to any of my friends in business that they move their operations to Delaware. The newspaper ran that story weeks after the interview was conducted but, by chance, on a day when the governor was on the West Coast, making speeches to encourage economic development. Needless to say, the timing did not help his cause.

By this time, though, there was broad enough support to turn the situation around. With strong private-sector lobbying and backing from both parties in the legislature, personal income tax rates were cut, a balanced-budget rule was imposed, and the delivery of governmental services was improved. Development offices came into being or were strengthened at the state and local levels. Additional changes were made in state law over a period of several more years, including a pivotal Financial Center Development Act that encouraged banks and other financial institutions to locate in Delaware. The upshot of all this is a revitalized economy. Financial service corporations have been persuaded to locate new facilities in Delaware—fourteen companies in a period of less than three years. Unemployment has fallen below the national average. State finances have gradually been put in much better shape than average, and Delaware was able to weather the 1979–82 recession with less difficulty than its neighbors.

When Delawarians tell this story, they often face the counterargument that the state's good fortune is mostly due to luck and location. They point out that Delaware has all the wherewithal for growth: a choice location on the East Coast; good farmland, a deepwater port, rail lines, interstate highways and airports, all close to one another; a population with above-average education; and an array of vocational schools and colleges, with a large university near its principal city. That is all true, but another state which can boast the same features, and is similarly small, has languished during the same period. That is Rhode Island. It lost population in the 1970s (only one other state, New York, did so). Rhode Island has suffered from above-average unemployment, and as of 1983 was ranked near the bottom of the states in its business climate by the Conference of State Manufacturers' Associations. What the comparison says is that demographics and infrastructure will not do it by themselves. What has made the difference in Delaware is the willingness of business and government leaders to work together on a bipartisan basis to face problems and to build legislative and popular support for positive action.

More of this at the national level might not be a miracle cure, but it surely could help an ailing patient, and the need is there. In national affairs, we have passed the point where it can be argued that all we see before us is a healthy pluralism that proves the diversity of the democratic process. What we see is difference run rampant, and disorder far beyond the amount we have to accept in the name of checks and balances. The more fragmented political power has become, the less flexible the government and the weaker its instincts for self-restraint.

The Catch 22 in government is that those who can see problems in the round cannot get them addressed politically except in bits and pieces, while those who have the political levers to deal with the bits and pieces lack the vision to assemble them into a whole. Government sometimes claims to have broad policies, but nobody trusts these to endure. Time and again, this scenario has been played out: Government launches a program with a high sense of mission and much rhetoric, but some of the promised results do not appear on schedule; criticism then begins to grow and to erode support. Other issues capture attention, new advocates clamor for attention, new coalitions are formed and some of them become more powerful than the old. "Enduring," "firm" commitments are then traded in for shinier new models.

The myths tell us that there is more divisiveness in the national system than is warranted by the facts, and perhaps more than the system can stand. The surfeit of interest groups is at best a sign that leadership with courage is lacking. At worst it is a symptom that many groups, impatient with the democratic process or never much impressed by it in the first place, have wrapped themselves in the cloaks of vigilantes and elected themselves as protectors of the moral order. Either their views will prevail or the democratic process will, but not both.

As I am trying to suggest throughout this book, people in the private sector have eminently good reasons to be concerned with this. Practical men and women of commerce, if they really are practical, should have a long list of reasons for not indulging in behavior that makes their organizations just another "special interest" tugging at the sleeve of Congress, pleading for favors. For the National Rifle Association or the Environmental Defense Fund, it may be enough to win skirmishes in the thicket of the Capitol cloakroom, but if business is to win the victories that mean the most to its future success, it will have to fight on higher ground. What commerce needs is not governmental indulgences but policies that encourage long-range capital commitments and stimulate domestic as well as international economic growth. Those are the policies that most affect jobs and national competitiveness, and to be effective they must be consistent and relatively predictable. Only national governments can make them so.

It is a given condition of our society—and not a failing of our system of governance—that the American public holds no single world view and therefore cannot give government one clear set of instructions on what "we the people" want. We have to settle for three more modest goals: agreement on a few basic principles regarding ends; agreement on the means that will be allowed or prohibited in pursuit of those ends; and agreement throughout the public and private sectors that all of us will submit to enough discipline to make those means effective. The first test is met, but the nation has been wavering on the second and going backward on the third. The private sector has to help change that.

5

Managing the Public's Business

ONE MAN I admire greatly is Nathaniel Wyeth, a retired engineer and inventor who had a long and distinguished career in the Du Pont Company. His ability to cut through problems and find novel solutions was such that management let him operate as a free spirit. Mostly they let him think up projects on his own or choose among those brought to him by others. "Ask Nat" was one of the Engineering Department's most successful strategies. It was also very cost-effective because frequently his response to a challenge, instead of calling for thousands of dollars' worth of black-box electronics, was a simple device he mocked up in wood at home over the weekend.

Nat tells this story on himself: When he was a young man beginning in his profession, he struggled for months trying to make a new machine work properly. He added controls, then gauges to monitor the controls, then controls for the gauges, until he had a Rube Goldberg contraption in which nothing worked unless everything did. It occurred to Nat that this condition rarely applied, and that his whole approach was wrong. The problem was that the machine was already too complicated, and the road to success lay in making it simpler. He stripped away the parts he had added, and concocted a simple, inexpensive way of eliminating the original flaw. Thus began his lifelong adherence to a principle of creativity: Keep it simple. Don't give a system capabilities it does not need.

Nat comes from a family of artists. His father and brother, N.C. and Andrew, became famous as painters. The world does not usually pay similar attention to engineers unless they take up a different line of work, as, for instance, Herbert Hoover did. Yet Nat the engineer deserves no less honorable mention than Andrew the painter or, for that matter, mining engineer Hoover. Nat's wisdom ought to apply beyond engineering, to social as well as mechanical systems, to governance and politics: Ask first what you are trying to accomplish; do not complicate needlessly; look at what others have done and see if there is a simpler way to do it. Perhaps it is not too late to borrow from that counsel and improve the operations of government, though this task may be even more difficult than changing the election process, and will call for the unbolting of many gauges and controls.

Much attention has been given to managing the public's business in those government agencies the public sees at first hand. That is where people encounter the bureaucracy moored across the channels, our "permanent government." Unfortunately, the problem here is more symptom than cause; unfortunate, because answers would be relatively easy if the bureaucracy were the central problem; only a symptom, in that the failings of departments and agencies are rarely of their own making, but commonly have another source. Most of the problems go back to headquarters, to the executive offices of government as represented by the White House and state governors' offices, and to the legislative branch as represented by Congress and the statehouses. If the process of government is to be managed better, this will call for a different mind-set at the top, a shorter menu of tasks, and more discipline and accountability in the system.

One of the questions in the executive branch is whether the senior officials, the President and state governors, will be allowed enough authority so that they can manage properly and the public can legitimately hold them responsible for results. What executives in government need is not more subordinates or a reworking of the organization chart, but, in the blunt language of business, more kickable fannies. An executive cannot be blamed for what he cannot control, and in the present circumstances, that includes many of the offices and agencies that are nominally part of the administrative branch. The rules governing their work were created by legislation and can be changed only by joint administrative and legislative effort. The key questions for state and Federal legislative bodies, to use a tight summary suggested by David Broder, are those of choosing between individual autonomy and party loyalty, fragmented decisions and integrated policies, and representation on a parochial basis as versus representation that recognizes broader interests. The question for both branches is whether leaders are prepared to meet the responsibilities of governing.

This chapter explores those questions in some detail, and ends with a look at the private sector's role. Are its leaders, equally with those in government, willing to deal with policy issues and not merely immediate interests, and will they pay the price required to move the nation away from a "command" economy and social order toward a style of governance that leaves more decisions to private initiative? We will not move far down the path to a good answer, I believe, unless the private sector applies to its governmental relations the same management precepts that guide its internal affairs, and accepts the same responsibilities of leadership it wants to see in the public sector.

Both sectors have to tackle public problems in a logical sequence: first, purpose; next, structure; then, details for action. The common-sense leadoff is to ask, "What's the problem? Is it serious enough to demand action?" Then come the secondaries: "What will it take to do the job? How much of the answer should come from the private sector, and how much from government?" Only then does procedure belong on the agenda: "Do we need a new box on government's organization chart? How do we set up the lines of reporting and the timetables to measure progress?" Finally, dead last: "Do we play hardball, or try this one with incentives?"

Government often inverts that order, and the private sector, at least in its relationships with government, often does the same. Before a Congressional committee sees a bill, its sponsors have chosen a course of action, picked an agency (or created a new one) to carry it out, and made up a list of "thou shalts" for an administrator yet to be picked. The unstated premise, often shaky, is that general questions about needs and priorities have been adequately considered, and alternative approaches examined and found wanting. Where private business enters the fray, it frequently does so at a late date, after someone has decided that action is definitely in order. Business then concentrates its arguments on its particular interests and wonders later why the debate never got back to the general questions.

A call for leadership is easy to sound, but leadership to accomplish what? In recent years, at both Federal and state levels, and always in the name of better governance, there have been all manner of efforts to fix the engine. Leaders in both the public and the private sectors have called at different times for sunset laws, zero-based budgeting, abolition or restructuring of departments and agencies, regulatory reform, cost-benefit analyses, economic-impact statements, legislative vetoes, referenda and recall petitions, and Constitutional amendments requiring that budgets be balanced, the last having been imposed in some states and more recently proposed for the Federal government. The U.S. Congress has changed its rules to elect committee chairmen more on merit and less on seniority. It has created the Congressional Budget Office and the Office of Technology Assessment. The Federal executive has set up its Office of Management and Budget. A Senior Executive Service has been created, to attract more competent people to government by offering above-scale pay.

In the hope of encouraging economic progress and allying themselves with it, officials in government have responded to outside urging and called for programs to foster innovation, productivity improvement, and job training and retraining. There have been calls for a new energy policy, an incomes policy (read wage and price controls), supply-side economics, a new federalism, and a new industrial policy. Most of these recommendations have been tried at least in some measure, with mixed results, but not even the most promising among them has lived up to its advance billing.

One may assume the best of intentions. Many of these causes have been backed by dedicated people. They gave it their best shot. If they failed, any of the rest of us probably would have done no better. Peter Drucker used to argue that if most people outside government were obliged to trade places with the insiders, they would soon be behaving in all the same ways. He is probably right. A few people in public life deserve to be cast into the outer darkness for mental or moral incapacity, but they are the least of the problem. What is of concern here is that well-meaning and often very intelligent people have led trials at reform, netting little at best, and bringing us nostrums at worst.

There may be as many explanations for that as there have been reform proposals, but at least two reasons call for attention here. One was suggested by Charles L. Schultze, an economist, former Federal budget director, and former chairman of the President's Council of Economic Advisers, in a wise and knowing book, *The Public Use of Private Interest*. The center of his argument is that the approach government has chosen foredooms its programs to failure. Government manages not wisely but too much.

Schultze grants that government must intervene to some degree in decisions that used to be regarded as strictly the private business of citizens—the complexity of affairs now requires this—but he adds that "as a society we are going about the job in a systematically bad way. . . ." Programs are constructed to deal in exquisite detail with all manner of social and economic problems, and require the supervision of the activities of hundreds of millions of people; but people in government do not and cannot know enough to do this successfully. Whether they are politically motivated or are supposedly apolitical experts, Schultze contends, the problem stands: The system is arranged in such a way that mortals are trying to act omnisciently. Inevitably, they are failing.

The second key source of difficulty is that important principles of management, the most crucial being accountability for results, are often honored in the breach in the government. Again the caveat: Government is not a business and is not meant to be run as such. Nevertheless, some essentials of management pertain as much to the public sector as to the private, and citizens have as much right to ask for performance by those who manage their business as stockholders have to demand the same of a corporate management. The principles in question are not mysterious, esoteric, or numerous. They are few and simple:

• The goals of administrative and regulatory offices ought to be set forth in clear language. A reasonable test is to ask if an individual put in the job could tell from his charter what he ought to begin doing tomorrow morning. There is not much point, for instance, in telling the OSHA administrator to think about health and safety. That is not a goal but a state of mind. What he needs to be told is that his job is to reduce the frequency rate of certain kinds of accidents by a given amount within a given period of time. An unreasonable assignment? No so. Corporate managers are given precisely that kind of objective in the companies which have built the best safety records. It is the way to get the job done.

• There should be clear lines of authority. This implies a unity of command and some mechanism for resolving conflicts within the organization. If you see separate divisions riding off in different directions, as often happens in government (and in the private sector, too), you are looking at an organization in trouble.

• There should be accountability for performance, and with that goes the need for rewards and penalties to be distributed according to contribution. The ratings may have to be subjective, but government cannot hide behind that façade. Other kinds of organizations face this problem and have found ways to handle it. Universities somehow manage to decide which junior professors will become full professors, committees somehow decide which journalists will win Pulitzer Prizes and which will not, and corporate managers find ways of picking their successors. It ought not to be more difficult to decide that one regional administrator is miscast and ought to be replaced, while another is an outstanding performer deserving of promotion.

• There should be oversight. No one should have power without someone looking over his shoulder. No program should go unaudited. This implies a planning and analytical function, with priorities being reviewed from time to time and alarm bells sounding when programs jump the track or results are overdue.

Government at the senior executive and legislative levels fails all four of those tests. For the most part, it does not set clear goals, delegate authority, demand accountability, or monitor performance. It is a polite fiction that the various agencies of government report to the President or, in the case of the states, to the governors, if "report" is meant to denote managerial control. As a practical matter, the President has only limited power over the agencies within the cabinet departments (as, for example, OSHA, which is housed in the Department of Labor), and hardly any over the agencies chartered independently (such as the Interstate Commerce Commission and the Federal Trade Commission).

One general guideline if you are a manager is not to get involved in programs you have no power to change. The nation's senior executive and his staff thus stay away from the work of many agencies even though these need more administrative oversight. Usually, the executive's only true power over the independent agencies is his ability to appoint people to them, and once there they remain in office for periods of five years or more, answering, as it were, to their own consciences or to such outside voices as they choose to heed. In some cases, this means that interest groups have more effective power over agencies than the President of the United States does. If the President disapproves of his Secretary of the Treasury, he can remove him and name another with the advice and consent of the Senate. In practical terms, all he can do about the head of the ICC is outwait him, and given the trend in our country toward one-term Presidents, there is a question of who will outlast whom. "Independent" is a well-chosen word. The reasons for establishing such agencies go back in time, but cannot go unchallenged now. It is time for those agencies to lose some of their independence, a point to which I will return.

The mandate of many units of government is unclear. One can rarely be sure that an agency is carrying out the mission Congress or the White House had in mind because the initial intent is often debatable. Do not assume this is accidental. Legislators are in the habit of investing agencies with high-minded charters vague on particulars, and administrators are in no hurry to protest. They see advantages in the fuzz theory of governance: If your duty isn't clear, you can be flexible about what you do without being blamed for the results.

Inside the agencies, lines of responsibility are sketchy and standards of expected performance are loosely stated. Results tests are not specified, so effectiveness will always be difficult to measure. Poor performance is rarely punished. Discharge or demotion for cause is so rare as to be a news story when it occurs. In the year 1980, two years after President Carter launched a movement to reform the civil service, one-tenth of one percent of employees were dismissed for poor performance. In the Senior Executive Service, a bonus system was arranged in 1978 under which excellence could be honored for as many as one-half of the members, through additional pay of up to 20 percent of salaries (these already being on a par with Congressmen's). In 1979, one agency went almost to the limit: NASA decided that 46 percent of its SES corps had done bonus-quality work. An embarrassed Congress stepped in and reset the limit at 25 percent. The *quid pro quo* for the SES salary scale is that nonperformers can be bumped back into the regular civil service. So it is said, but in the first three years of SES's existence, that happened to but one person—not quite two-tenths of one percent of the corps. *E pluribus unum.* Any organization that claims 99.9 percent acceptable-or-better performance on the part of its employees invites doubt about its judgment or its management system. By this standard, a retail store with 100 employees would find cause to dismiss only one employee every ten years.

Matters fall between the chairs. Even instructions that would appear to be clear may not be followed. When a new chairman took over the Federal Trade Commission in 1981, he found sixteen trade regulations, some dating from 1975, trapped in the review system. Ordinarily,

120 days is considered a reasonable lag time. When the Airline Deregulation Act of 1978 was before Congress, it was predicted that some carriers would be bankrupted or badly hurt. Congress thus set up a safety net for airline employees who might be put out of work. The Civil Aeronautics Board was told to report on airlines suffering "major contractions" due to deregulation. The Labor Department was instructed to produce rules as needed to set up financial-aid programs and help laid-off workers find new jobs. The time allowed was six months. Five years later, some airlines were belly up and most of the rest were in distress, perhaps to some degree because of deregulation; but no former employee had received any of the mandated special aid. The rules had not been issued.

When effective control systems and policy leadership are missing, government sins by omission and commission. It fails to arrive at coherent policies where needed and stumbles forward on programs that even its best friends have trouble defending. No one seems to be clearly in charge, or to have defined limits of authority.

Energy policy is an example. It offers evidence for almost any criticism one might want to level at the Federal establishment or the private sector's relationships with it. The nation has lurched along on energy policy not because policymakers have been kept in the dark—the White House and Congress have been reminded of the basics dozens of times—but because there has been no constancy of direction, no organized constituency beyond those concerned with particular fuels or users, and no administrative or Congressional leadership committed to a policy that has been at once national in its interest and objective in its contents.

The importance of energy supplies to the nation is all but self-evident. Along with crucial raw materials, an adequate supply of energy is the essence of production and commerce, and of national defense. Oil, natural gas, and coal not only are needed as fuels for transportation, power generation, and home heating; they also feed the boilers and power the tools of industry and agriculture, and are in themselves the raw materials synthesized into most of the products made by the chemical industry, ranging from man-made fibers to pharmaceuticals. No hydrocarbons, no nylon.

The private sector brings the hydrocarbons to the market and generates most of the power used in the U.S. The diverse parts of the energy industry have their own missions, but no sector is concerned with the needs of the nation as a whole. There is thus need for an overarching policy coordinated by the Federal government. It can be said in summary, then, that in the name of both national defense and domestic economic order, government should have a comprehensive energy policy, one that considers as a package various raw materials and all of the important uses, one that encourages conservation and efficient use of nonrenewable resources (or at least does not penalize frugality), one that discourages overdependence on supplies coming from troubled areas abroad, one that thinks ahead to stockpiles and to research and development of alternative sources, and one that "manages" the Federal participation at least to the extent of coordinating the work of whatever government agencies have energy or raw materials in their missions.

This sounds like motherhood and apple pie, and readers with long memories may recognize it for what it is. It is a lightly disguised summation of the recommendations of the Paley Commission report of 1952. That report, named for the commission chairman, William Paley of CBS, was widely publicized in its time and still makes good reading today. More than twenty years before the Organization of Petroleum Exporting Countries created the "energy crisis" of the mid-1970s, with much unwitting help from the nations outside OPEC, the Paley Commission read the storm warnings correctly and urged the U.S. government to provide appropriate leadership on a range of resource questions.

It goes without saying that government did not follow the advice. The pleas for "a comprehensive energy policy" (the commission's words) were soaked up, like water in the desert sand, by a policymaking system programmed not to respond to such broad imperatives. Despite the Paley report and numerous other calls to arms before and since, the U.S. has had not one but many energy policies, on-again, off-again, ad hoc, and fuel-by-fuel. These have been implemented by about a dozen different Federal agencies or departments, under the guidance of a Congress and a White House responsive to a moving parade of interest groups carrying their own banners.

The Paley report and its successors might have had a better chance if the private sector had rallied behind them, but business was as divided as Washington on the response. Coal had one position; oil, another. Big refiners and small refiners sought different action. Over the years, conservationists, Interior Department officials, economic developers, miners trying to protect their jobs, consumer groups thinking about home-heating costs, admirals worried about oil for the fleet—all these and more have had interests on the line and lobbyists in the hall. There have been countless conferences and numberless Washington seminars to outline "the big picture," but at no time has government found a way to coordinate disparate views or overlay these with a national policy.

What we have seen instead is price controls imposed at one time because government decided this was the way to keep down consumers' costs, and removal of controls at other times because government saw shortages and wanted to stimulate development of additional supplies. The dependence of the U.S. on foreign supplies of oil has ranged from a few percent of total consumption to more than half of it. Prices have gone from $2 per barrel for Middle Eastern oil (in 1973) to a high of $42 per barrel (in late 1980). There have been high tax allowances for depletion to offset some of the risks of exploration and development, and low allowances plus windfall-profits taxes to take away the gains. There have been natural-gas shortages, with a message from utility companies to consumers, "Save gas." Industrial plants have been put on rationing and utilities have refused to sign up new customers for gas heating. There have been other times when natural gas supplies were abundant, and utilities have urged homeowners, "Choose gas." Gasoline shortages and fears of same were at one time severe enough to create long lines at the gas pumps. Less than two years later, headlines spoke of an oil glut, with a drop in consumption and selling prices severe enough to create financial crises in countries which depend on money from the sale of oil to pay back their debts to banks in other nations. Synthetic-fuel R&D projects (the Paley Commission saw those coming, too) were elevated during President Carter's term by a crash mentality. They were part of a program that was "the moral equivalent of war." A few years later, under President Reagan, synfuels were on the back burner. They retreated to a "not yet" status because private industry was unable to see a market to justify the multibillion-dollar investments required, and the U.S. government was unable to make up its mind on what it would and would not support across a time frame of ten years or more.

Energy has never lacked for spokesmen, though the voices have often cried in a wilderness. In each decade in modern times, people have tried to provoke government to proper action. Before World

War II, an Energy Resources Committee advised government that the important energy sources are interrelated, and urged national and international policies recognizing this fact. In the postwar and Korean War periods, that line of thought was promoted by the National Security Resources Board and the Office of Defense Mobilization. Under President Dwight Eisenhower, the Bureau of Mines and the White House economic advisers looked with concern at the future and pushed (without much success) for technical programs to make new uses of coal and to develop synthetic liquids. Under President John Kennedy, an Interdepartmental Energy Study Group kept alive the notion that the nation was vulnerable to shortages in the future and that these could limit economic growth. In the 1960 campaign, in a speech in West Virginia, Kennedy called for a "national fuels policy," but, under his administration as much as others', the U.S. developed no such policy.

There has of course been a politics of energy. It could not be otherwise. Usually, it has followed predictable lines. Senators from coal-producing states could be counted on to support efforts to restrict imports of oil, that being a move to give coal a shot at more of the domestic market. Jennings Randolph of West Virginia, where there is lots of coal, was for years one of the standardbearers for that cause. Senators from New England states, John Pastore of Rhode Island being an example, long stood against such restrictions, reasoning that if more oil were allowed into the U.S. market, the price would remain low (foreign oil was then lower in cost than U.S. suppliers'), to the pleasure of voters whose homes were heated with oil. Most New England homes have oil furnaces.

With the politics, there is an overlay of energy ideology. America has a love-hate relationship with Big Oil. People love the products, but hate their dependence on the companies, and are particularly angered by the presumed power of the six to ten largest oil companies. To knee-jerk liberals, the proper label for rising oil-company earnings has been "obscene profits." In votes on questions that affect oil producers, the best correlation is not between a Congressman and the mail from his constituents, or with his party, or with the region from which he comes. It is the Congressman's voting record on a conservative-to-liberal spectrum, as measured by such scorekeepers as Americans for Democratic Action. The more "liberal" the Congressman, the more likely an anti-Big Oil vote, whatever Big Oil might stand for.

For all the efforts to integrate government's role, we continue to address energy problems in that "systematically bad way." Layers of rules are added to correct errors caused by other rules, and authority is parceled out among departments and agencies no less than before. The Federal government at last count was dealing with natural gas (one molecular structure) in twenty-seven categories, setting the market price according to the location, depth, and age of the wells, with prices varying by a multiple of ten. Regulatory overlap is still the rule. Following the inverse logic of a command economy, the market response to decades of price regulation has been a labyrinth of contracts with lock-in provisions that make the most expensive gas move to market first, and the cheapest gas last. Individual and commercial users pay for that. Overlaps persist as always among the independent agencies and executive-branch offices. The Interstate Commerce Commission, Federal Maritime Board, Department of Interior, Corps of Army Engineers, Tennessee Valley Authority, Atomic Energy Commission, and Department of State all were in the energy business in the 1950s and were in it still in the 1980s, allowing only for reorganizations and some changes of names.

If departments and agencies seem bent on conquering problems by subdividing them, it is because Congress itself has set the pattern. An enterprising journalist who works the Washington beat for the *Atlantic* has counted the Congressional groups with jurisdiction over one segment of energy affairs, power generated by hydroelectric dams. In the House, he came up with eleven subcommittees reporting to these nine committees: Energy, Science, Interior, Public Works, Agriculture, Appropriations, Budget, Government Operations, and Small Business (that one's entry has the catchall title of Subcommittee on Energy, Environment, and Safety Issues Affecting Small Businesses). In the Senate, the list included ten subcommittees, six of which report to the Energy Committee, the other four to committees on Environment and Public Works, Agriculture, Government Affairs, and Appropriations.

Such jurisdictional disorder is the rule in Congress, not the exception. Federal departments have not one but many masters. National-defense issues, for example, are handled in the House not only by the Armed Services Committee, which holds most of the power, but also by more than a half-dozen other committees ranging from Interior to Education and Labor. Federal agencies must make their peace with the authorizing and appropriations committees, with the Committee on Government Operations, which has overall jurisdiction, and with whatever subcommittees choose to make an issue of their performance. When EPA became the hot political button in Washington in 1983, in the squabble over the probity of its leaders and their diligence in enforcing the law, six different subcommittees of the House launched separate investigations. They were all clawing for pieces of the prey. The Senate restrained itself and settled for a single investigating committee.

As long as Congress is a victim of self-imposed disorder and the executive branch is the victim of imposed impotence, we are not likely to see a more rational approach to the management of public problems. Nor can we expect the fourth branch to reform itself. Look at what has happened in recent years in the regulation of commerce at the Federal level. There has been a rising tide of protest, first from business and then from an increasingly dissatisfied public, against both the style and the penetration of regulation in daily life and commerce. "Overregulation," once popularly regarded as defensive rhetoric on the part of corporations, has become a complaint throughout the private sector. As a result, there have been serious efforts within government to restrain the regulators. Yet the fact is that there are more regulations on the books in the U.S. today than ever before, and it costs more than ever to comply with them.

Today, though hardly anyone disputes a continuing need for regulation in some areas (health and safety are prime examples), hardly anyone can be found who supports the regulatory process as it stands. It so offends common sense that even the people who devised it have finally agreed that it defies rational defense. Polls taken in the early 1980s showed that two-thirds of Washington's opinion leaders (a label denoting selected Congressmen, officials, journalists, and assorted movers and shakers, including numerous architects of the regulatory system) believe that the nation's economic health would be better if regulations were cut back. Nonetheless, the fortress stands.

Even the weapon of humor has not been enough to bring much change. Government regulation has become the butt of jokes. It is said of the rules in different countries that in Britain everything not expressly forbidden is allowed, in Germany everything not expressly allowed is forbidden, in France everything is forbidden but anything can be arranged, and in America everything not prohibited by one regulation is mandated by another.

Collectors of horror stories have had a field day with the regulators. What is mandated often leaves everyone shaking his head. The Interstate Commerce Commission once told a trucking company that it could haul freight between Olympia and Chehalis, communities in Washington that are twenty-one miles apart, only if the trucks were routed through Aberdeen. That makes the trip 120 miles long. Dartmouth College in Hanover, New Hampshire, was told it ought to convert its heating plant from oil to coal, despite the fact that there is no rail line to the town to deliver the coal. In Florida, one electric-power company was instructed by the Federal Energy Administration to make the oil-to-coal switch, while another utility across the bay was told by EPA to convert the other way, from coal to oil.

The regulatory process not only moves slowly but also goes around more than once. A producer of agricultural chemicals was informed that one of his most successful products, a fungicide approved almost a decade earlier and in widespread use, was being challenged under something called a Rebuttable Presumption Against Registration—an "R-Par" for short. The product had been extensively tested for safety and efficacy, but it had to go around again. In effect, an R-Par says, "We have a complaint against the product, but you are free to try to rebut it." In this case, the company tried and succeeded. EPA finally ruled that the product, in the registered uses, handled as the label said it should be handled, presented no undue risk to man or environment. That is what the clearance process had shown the first time. The R-Par consumed five years.

Regulation has been fully democratic: Its weight has fallen on all sorts of organizations, small and large. To open a beer-and-pizza parlor in the state of New York takes eighteen permits. The owner of Blackie's Boatyard in Newport Beach, California, was fined by OSHA because he did not have a ladder reaching into the water on a pier, the better to save anyone falling in. "Blackie," Arsene Gadarian, chose to fight and eventually won in a hearing before a Federal examiner, the heart of the appeal being that the water along the pier was three feet deep and a man overboard could walk ashore. The Du Pont Company, to build a new plant in De Lisle, Mississippi, had to obtain more than two dozen permits, one of which required an Environmental Impact Statement that took fourteen months to prepare. This is not an unusual number of permits for a new industrial plant or major expansion. It is about par for the course. What made this plant different was that a rail line had to be built to get raw materials in and finished products out. That required authority from the ICC, three permits from the Army Corps of Engineers to cross streams and rivers, a permit from the Coast Guard to put a bridge across a navigable river, and months of negotiations on where to put embankments, trestles, and culverts. There was even concern about impeding alligator traffic. Nearly a dozen Federal and state agencies were involved in transportation planning. All of that is exclusive of contact with the agencies on matters related to the construction of the plant itself.

Money has seemed no more precious than time to the regulators. Estimates of the nation's costs of regulation run to $100 billion per year and more, but in fact nobody knows exactly what the total is and to calculate it is impracticable. In the most precise study ever done, one group of fifty large corporations tried to get a handle on their regulatory costs. Working under common rules and the direction of an independent accounting firm, they counted up the dollars required by regulations in stated areas, excluding the sums they would have dispensed anyway for other purposes such as improving production yield or promoting safety. The "regulatory extras" came to more than $2 billion. That study cost millions of dollars and required thousands of man-years of work. To calculate a net figure for the nation, accurately weighing all of the regulatory gains and losses, is an all but impossible task.

Whatever the sum, the parts are too big to be comforting. The government practices "flat of the curve" regulation: The curve of benefits to society flattens while the price of attainment goes up geometrically. In reducing water pollution, for instance, to go from 95 percent purity to 97 or 98 percent may cost as much as to go from a "no control" level to 95 percent. At issue is the public benefit of the two-to-three-point difference. We are not buying much for the extra billions of dollars.

Experience shows that regulators are prone to require the more expensive options when the less expensive are at hand. As an example, to reduce the possibility that machinery noise will damage the hearing of industrial workers, regulatory authorities told companies to install noise-shielding equipment and rebuild or replace noisy machines. Some companies, the Continental Group and Du Pont among them, countered with the argument that in many plant settings, protective equipment worn by employees would net the same health and safety results at cost savings in the tens of millions of dollars. Evidence was brought forward: medical records on large numbers of employees who had been protected in this fashion. The data showed no job-related loss of hearing over many years of exposure. A study commissioned by OSHA showed that the ear-muff solution would cost industry $43 million per year, while the cost of rebuilding machinery to make it quieter would be $18.5 billion. The results to workers would be about the same, the study concluded. Regulators continued to press for the high-priced solution just the same. It took years to persuade them otherwise.

Even when the ultimate goal of regulation may be beyond dispute, the pathway to follow depends on the map the regulators are given. The effectiveness of action is forever colored by that. The goal for OSHA, one might assume, would have been to make the workplace safer and healthier, with the administrator invited to take whatever routes would most quickly help the most people. Whatever OSHA's creators had in mind, the agency went about its task in a manner more suggestive of politics than well-thought-out policy. The results, more than a decade later, are not impressive.

OSHA's first effort was to compile rules for working conditions in factories, shops, and offices, and to mandate the apparatus that ought to be in place, down to the specifications for building wooden stepladders (there were about 140 standards covering that). After the first sets of rules were ready, OSHA inspectors fanned out among employment points in search of violations. Citations were handed out. Fines were levied. More rules were drafted.

The model of OSHA as a police force had something to be said for it. No doubt some accidents and occupational illnesses were prevented. Some machines were caged that had not been properly guarded before. Hard hats and safety glasses appeared in plants where they had not been seen before. This must have done some good. Equally, OSHA met a political test: Under a "do something" imperative, it could be seen to be doing something. Citations can be counted and put in news stories.

Yet it is worth asking whether a different approach might not have better served the public. Suppose that OSHA had begun by identifying employers with the best and worst safety and health records, and tried to extract from their experience an understanding of the conditions associated with such performance. Then it could have nailed the poorer performers, brought together their labor and management representatives, set forth achievable targets for improvement, given them staged time limits, and held the club of law over their heads.

OSHA also might have tried to carve up the problem into pieces, looking at both severity and breadth of risks, and asking as well about the need for more than one approach. Some occupational hazards are nearly ubiquitous and threaten large numbers of workers with severe harm. These deserve priority. Other hazards affect few people or do not threaten irremediable harm. Those risks also may call for corrective action, but to pursue the second kind at the neglect of the first is no public service. Still other hazards are masked or wholly unrecognized, and the task with these is not to punish wrongdoers *post facto* but to encourage the research and engineering to find the hidden problems and prevent tragedies in the future.

Anyone with political sensitivity can see shortcomings in this approach. Had OSHA gone this route, it would have used its early months gathering data, months when it was on public view. Its administrators probably would have been accused of not moving aggressively to protect workers against callous employers, or perhaps of doing nothing at all. OSHA would surely have opened itself to attack by any people who hoped to see the guilty punished even more than safety and health promoted. An approach built on "carrots now, sticks later" would have implied that gross offenders might go free awhile longer. For all that, however, an approach based on priorities and incentives would have given OSHA a record of accomplishment far better than the one it earned in its first decade. At the end of this time period, the companies with the best records were much the same ones which had been in the front row in 1970. The foot-draggers were still bringing up the rear, and OSHA could point to few places where it had improved safety records nearly as much as had voluntary action by private employers.

It was politics and the style of policymaking, and not an absence of information, that led OSHA down the path it took. Already in existence before OSHA was born was a vast body of safety and health standards, assembled by universities, industries, and government laboratories and available in engineering and medical libraries. The private sector and government had been sharing data and ideas for decades, through such organizations as the National Bureau of Standards and the American Society for Testing Materials. There were safety committees and foundations galore, and a growing network of private as well as governmental laboratories concerned with toxicology and occupational health. Most of the serious hazards of the workplace were well known, as were the steps that could be most effective in reducing or eliminating those hazards.

Instead of reinventing the wheel so that it could show off its own set of hubcaps, OSHA might better have started with these questions: "How do the safest and healthiest companies do it? How can we get others to do the same?" Again, most of the information was there for the asking. Safety data on various occupations have been kept for years, and the patterns in them are clear. The data show that some lines of work are safer than others by factors of five or ten to one. The numbers are also kept within specific industries, and show even wider variation. Among firms making similar products, there may be one firm with twenty or more lost-workday accidents for every million hours its employees work, and another firm with a rate of zero to one such accident per million man-hours. To cite one particularly dramatic example, the Du Pont Company for many years operated a plant in Leominster, Massachusetts, making consumer products such as combs and toothbrushes. The building, bought by Du Pont from another company, was old, poorly designed, and had wooden floors. It was hardly a first choice for a safety supervisor intent on showing a good record. Yet the employees at that plant worked for twenty-seven years without a single lost-time injury: 17.4 million worker-hours.

Had government done an analysis, it would have found that the message from Leominster is supported by a great deal of evidence. There is a clear record that the inherent hazards of a production location or product are among the worst predictors of accidents and occupationally related illnesses. Clerical work is not very dangerous, but some clerical offices are. Meanwhile, out in the production area, some of the lowest accident rates are found in areas where people work with materials that are explosive, flammable, corrosive, or toxic. Some work groups have vastly better records than others, almost, one might say, in spite of the kind of work they do. For instance, some research and development laboratories in industry which handle highly toxic substances have operated for ten to twenty years without any employee suffering a job-related accident or illness. Few steno pools can match that record.

The inference is correctly drawn: The difference between safe and sorry is not the type of job one has, or how thick the safety manual is, or whether the floors are wood or concrete, or how high the fire extinguishers are mounted off the floor (which was one of OSHA's concerns). It is instead the attitudes and incentives that prevail in the workplace, and the priority attached to measurable results. Employers with the best safety records are the ones with managements committed to that goal, with review systems that provide visible rewards and sanctions. These are companies which have no room on the payroll for people who simply will not take safety seriously, who think taking chances is macho, or who operate on the notion that some accidents are going to happen anyway, "when your number comes up." One of the first things I was told after joining an industrial company was not to tip back a straight chair but to keep all four of its feet on the floor. The chance of the chair toppling over is small, but it is there. Of such "risk management" attentions, multiplied thousands of times over, is that company's safety record built. It is one of the best in the world.

Doesn't your number come up though? Are there not high-risk jobs—sandhogs, miners, workers putting up high steel—where some accidents are regarded as inevitable? With all the new products coming into the marketplace, it is not practical to "test everything for everything," so that no worker or consumer need fear injury. What about the "surprises"—the chemical compounds that have been found to cause cancer, with the disease appearing twenty years or more after the first exposure? The answer, of course, is that there are differential risks and some surprises. In dealing with them we find no simple answers except those that are simplistic. The regulatory process moves toward an ethical thicket, where all the questions are normative: How many injuries or deaths should society be prepared to suffer to get its work done? Is it worth it to have one person killed to build a high-rise office building? Is the Brooklyn Bridge worth the twenty-eight lives it cost? If not twenty-eight, then ten? Five? How do you calculate how much a human life is worth? This all has the grisly sound of human sacrifice. Even to debate it, as the regulators and regulated do, offends.

Yet there are factors here that ease the problem. Some of the questions as framed are flawed by false premises. The fact is that people do not have to die in order to get bridges built and ore mined. It is entirely possible to do those jobs without injury, and wherever the hazards are known, the ethical answer to the question of a "socially acceptable" death rate is simple: "Zero." With rare exceptions, the conditions that cause occupational harm, and the properties of products that spell "danger," are foreseeable, controllable, and manageable by ordinary people. There is no economic reason why any worker in the private sector (it may have to be different for the military and police) should have to do a job where it is known that the job cannot be done safely.

What about those exceptions, though—the "surprises"? Some of them must give us pause. At different times in the history of industry, it has been discovered that various materials can cause cancer: Radium and other radiation-emitters, beryllium metal dust, and various organic chemicals are among them. The amounts required are comparatively small and the appearance of the disease, long delayed. In some instances, there has been a gradual awakening of understanding as cause-and-effect data have come in, followed by a phasing in of controls. The organic coal-tar chemicals began to be suspected early in the development of the modern chemical industry. Research focused on this, found at least some of the culprits, and avoided what could have been tragedies far worse than those that did occur (though, sadly, not before hundreds of workers had been exposed, some of whom later developed cancer from that cause).

The effort to raise the right questions does not always yield enough of the right answers. A case in point is vinyl-chloride monomer, an intermediate used in the production of a widely used plastic. While vinyl-chloride plastic is benign, the monomer from which it is polymerized is indisputably a human carcinogen. That discovery was made only through medical experience, though. Previously, toxicologists had looked at the structure of VCM and concluded that it was unlike other organic molecules associated with cancer. VCM therefore was not on the suspect list of scientists and medical professionals, until cancer cases appeared. Then, retrospectively, the cause was tracked down.

This does not ease the tragedy, but it is a fact worth noting that such events are not daily occurrences, and when they happen they usually involve small numbers of people. One of the reasons is that chemicals such as VCM often have other, well-known risks attached to them. They are often highly flammable, for instance. They are thus treated with many precautions. (An exception is asbestos. It was long considered harmless, but it is now known that exposure can cause disability and death.) Generally speaking, though, it is not the "surprises" of the industrial environment that place most workers at risk. What affects the overwhelming majority are commonplace hazards mapped long ago and still susceptible to vast reduction.

The issue of occupational safety and health as a matter for government intervention turns primarily on the need for a diversity of approaches and a scaling of known risks, and only secondarily on a search for unexpected hazards. No number of OSHA inspectors and regulations could have prevented the vinyl-chloride tragedy. Only research might have done so. No blizzard of citations for unsafe work practices can bring a large improvement in occupational safety and health records unless the focus of enforcement is on places where large numbers of people face serious hazards.

The trouble with the "do something" response, to return to that point, is that it is satisfied by almost any kind of action. For government to do something effective, however, requires much more. It requires a regulatory process pointed toward objectives that have been screened for their probable public value. The first step in that journey is to draw upon whatever lessons experience has already taught. With OSHA, the Federal government spent the start-up years doing other things, not only reinventing wheels but spinning them.

Efforts at pollution control provide other examples of government doing the expedient instead of the logical. The need for action was real when the Federal government moved into this area aggressively in 1970. Air and water quality had deteriorated badly as a result of industrialization, urbanization, and expansion of agricultural output. It was clear from the beginning of the clean-up effort, though, that the sensible way to attack waste-disposal problems was through an integrated approach. Otherwise, pollutants might simply be converted from one form to another. To prevent liquid wastes from going into a river, they would be reduced to solids, only to become a problem on land. Solid wastes would be incinerated, potentially creating air-pollution problems, or they might be trucked to other locations, leaving the problem in somebody else's backyard. This is known in environmental parlance as "passing the cookie," and EPA was set up by Congress in a way that encourages just that. Air, water, and solid-waste problems were placed in different parts of the agency, administered under separate codes. EPA had no integrated approach.

Consider in a bit more detail one piece of this, the effort to reduce air pollution. The Clean Air Act and its amendments are among the most important pieces of environmental legislation in existence, as well as the most expensive. Regulations stemming from the law have brought steady gains. According to the Council on Environmental Quality, air quality nationwide has improved since 1974 and the amounts of most pollutants have declined. Reductions are noted in particular in two pollutants currently regarded as the ones of greatest concern to health, oxides of sulfur and suspended particles. With this for a measure of performance, one might conclude that the Clean Air Act ought to be held up as a model of government doing what needs to be done.

In point of fact, no piece of environmental legislation has been more controversial, more politicized, or more criticized by outsiders. When the act came up for renewal in 1981, Congress could agree on nothing except to grant it an extension. Through the regular session of Congress and its lame-duck period, and despite rounds of hearings and uncounted efforts at compromise, no action came. "Clean Air" went into the next Congress, the 98th, unresolved.

At the heart of the dispute was the question of cost. The dollars are not small. Using numbers from the CEQ, the Clean Air Act was costing a typical family of four $500 per year by 1980. By 1988, due to additional requirements being phased in, that bill was expected to rise to $800 per family (in dollars as valued at the time of this writing). The price tag per family unit is a reasonable way to look at this because pollution-control costs are passed on to the public in higher charges for electric power, autos, and other manufactured goods. Clean air is not free, and in the long run the only place the bill can fall is on the public.

Is it worth what it is costing, though? That has been a pivotal point of debate. Critics campaigning for an amended law, including many manufacturing corporations, have taken the position that the nation has long since passed the point of optimal yield on its air-pollution investment, and that tens of billions of dollars are being spent each year for benefits so small as to be marginal, if not infinitesimal. The money could better be spent, they have maintained, in more productive investments, some of which would help create more new jobs than will ever be generated by pollution-control spending. In reply, those who wanted the old legislation kept intact or made still tougher have argued that any easing of requirements would bring a decay in environmental quality, and serve to bail out corporations and municipalities that ought to clean up their act.

What is optimal in pollution control would seem to be a question subject to objective study by scientists, engineers, and economists. Those groups have studied this one, but objectivity has not been the final result. Clean air has become an essentially political issue. It has been inflamed by interest-group politics and confused by imprecision in the language of the enabling act and EPA's regulations. Regulated industries have not been shooting at well-lighted targets. They have been told to use the "best practicable technology" or the "best available control technology" to reduce pollution in areas where air quality is unacceptable, and to "prevent significant deterioration" in areas where the quality is better. "Adequate margins of safety" are to be maintained; "unreasonable risks" avoided. This is obviously the stuff of which dispute is made. Congress knows this. In putting this language in the law, it knew that someone else would have to sort it out. Who is to say what is "reasonable," "practicable," and "significant" unless it is a hearing examiner, and then a judge, and an appellate court after that, and eventually the Supreme Court? One consequence of the regulatory process, as exemplified by the Clean Air Act, has been to turn environmental law into a growth industry and put added burdens on an already overloaded judicial system. The air has become cleaner, but the process for making it so, in the words of one think-tank scholar, Robert Crandall of The Brookings Institution, has been "staggeringly inefficient."

All is not lost on the regulatory front. There have been gains in several areas, largely through efforts led by the White House. Beginning in Gerald Ford's administration, Congress was asked to deregulate some industries including the airlines, and regulators were instructed to assess the impact of their rules on inflation. Presidents Carter and Reagan both issued Executive Orders requiring more review of costs and benefits. Interdepartmental committees were created to encourage coordination and cooperation. EPA, late in Carter's term, under Douglas Costle as administrator, began putting more emphasis on voluntary compliance, and sought meetings with employers, labor leaders, and environmental activists to resolve problems cooperatively. OSHA under Reagan stopped measuring performance by counting inspections and citations, and started counting the numbers of accidents and occupational illnesses prevented, accepting credit for gains achieved through cooperation as well as coercion. Step by step, there has been reduced regulation not only of airline fares and routes, but also of trucking and of the communications and financial industries. Price controls on petroleum have gradually been removed.

There has been a change in the climate regarding trade, antitrust, and mergers, generally in the direction of leaving more discretion to the market and removing some of the "Big Brother" quality of past regulation. Several of the largest antitrust cases ever brought, including those against IBM and the biggest makers of cereals, were dropped by the government before trials were completed, each on the basis that the defendants had not been shown to be restraining trade or monopolizing markets illegally. The Federal Trade Commission, of which more later, was forcibly restrained by Congress after some of the commission's excesses became an embarrassment even to that glass-housed body. The changes were impressive, the more so considering how far the pendulum had swung the other way. Yet, as noted earlier, life in these United States is more regulated than it was at the beginning date of reform, and such gains as have been made have without exception involved long, hard fights.

Why has there not been more progress? Perhaps the answer lies in that earlier comment about people being generally unhappy with regulation. They are, but about different parts of it. There is no better example than business itself. It is the lead victim of zealous regulation, but it has been far from consistent in its own attitudes toward deregulation. Too many executives have uttered glowing words about the competitive enterprise system, while lobbying to protect some governmental regulation that has the effect of curtailing the entry of new competitors into their industries. The strongest opponents of deregulation in the motor-freight business have always been motor-freight companies themselves. The battle to deregulate the airline fares had to be won over the prone bodies of several airline executives.

So it is in many sectors of the economy. All applaud the principles for which antitrust law stands, but physicians do not want antimonopoly codes applied to them. The right of newcomers to enter markets and compete is honored everywhere, except in those cases where it is your market. Over the years, the principal "protectionist" sentiment in the U.S. has related not to international trade and the threat of imported products to domestic producers, but to the protection of domestic turf from domestic competitors.

Each piece of the private sector has to answer to that in its own way, but government is not an innocent bystander. The history of governmental economic and regulatory policy does not engender trust. Many companies tend to be "protectionist" because they long ago learned that it is risky to believe government when it promises to bring the greatest good for the greatest number, and claims to know exactly how to do so. It is a stock joke that there are three great lies in America: "Your check is in the mail," "Of course I will still respect you in the morning," and "I'm from the government and I'm here to help you." The fear has been that, instead of treating everyone equitably, government will hold an umbrella over others while letting you stand in the rain. Many companies and industries have preferred to put their trust in a few good friends, to be found in the subcommittees of Congress and, in some cases, within the regulatory agencies themselves. This process has become so deeply embedded that, sad to say, some competitors have even lost the ability to operate in an open marketplace. Like animals kept too long in the zoo, they would have to relearn how to survive in the wild. When all is said and done, then, much of the momentum of the regulatory system derives from the regulated, and from the fear that the alternative to regulation is worse.

Frustrated with the political system, reform-minded people are driven to pills and palliatives. The schemes they endorse all sound prodemocratic and some have garnered enough support to become the law of the land, or parts thereof. Yet many of these proposals are capable of much mischief, and there is in all of them the aura of defeatism. That they are popular at all is a sign that many people have abandoned hope of reaching worthwhile goals through traditional political channels.

A Constitutional amendment to balance the Federal budget was mentioned earlier. What is that but a statement that Congress and the administration have failed in their duties of stewardship, cannot balance income with outgo even as well as an average homemaker, and must be forced into fiscal prudence through this drastic step? Instead of amending the Constitution, is not the real task to amend the behavior of the nation's senior officials? The hazard in locking the budget into the Constitution is that there will be times of recession when the public interest requires the Federal government to run a deficit, just as there will be times of prosperity when government should show a surplus and use it to retire some of the national debt. (The operative word, I agree, is "should." The principle has clearly been honored in the breach.)

Proposition 13? It became law in California in 1978 through public referendum; and, again, it is an example of an effort to accomplish by one route what voters had decided they could not achieve in other ways. Property-tax burdens had climbed rapidly, and "13" told the governor and the state legislature that this source of revenue was to be rolled back and kept at a not-to-exceed rate. The quarrel with Proposition 13 is that it cut the income side of the equation without cutting the other side. It reduced revenues from property taxes by 60 percent, but the state went on spending, supplying services Californians wanted. An economic recession came, further reducing state revenues, and California found itself in a double bind. In the five years after passage of Proposition 13, the state treasury went from a $4 billion financial surplus to red ink, with California spending more than it was taking in by $4 million a day. As had to happen sooner or later, state services were cut and employees were laid off—at the most difficult of all possible times, the bottom of the recession.

New Federalism? It has all the surface marks of a noble step: Reduce the Federal government's control over the citizen's life; remand authority to state and local units, where people are more in tune with day-to-day needs. Yet what the New Federalism would do most of all is put the monkey on someone else's back. It contains no grand design for closing the gap that drove the Federal government to this political move in the first place, the gap between revenues and the costs of government services. In Russell Baker's quip, the New Federalism means that instead of the Federal government not having enough money to do the job, the states will not have enough money to do the job.

So it is with other quick fixes. The more they promise, the more likely that there is less to them than meets the eye. Local regulatory control in place of Federal? (That might work for fire-safety codes, but does anyone seriously want to propose that we have fifty separate state Clean Air Acts?) Sunset rules that kill agencies or regulations on stated dates? (If the agencies have constituents who are numerous and noisy enough, Congress will simply make the phoenix rise again from the fire.) Legislative vetoes to correct wayward decision-makers in government agencies? (Why would Congress bother itself with line-by-line votes on detailed issues most members cannot pretend to understand?

Is it because Congress does not want to make agencies answer for their work the other way, through comprehensive administrative reviews?) Easy as it is to join in a goodhearted spirit of reform, most of what we are offered has no real chance of success because the problems beneath the surface are left untouched. Unless we address the central failings of the system at the level of Congress and the White House, policy and its execution will forever lack cohesion, consistency, and efficacy.

The same shortcoming is found in the professional efforts at management reform in government. There have in the past been a mind-numbing number of academic studies, to a point where, in the parlance of the trade, management reform became a MEGO: "Mine eyes glaze over." If there are fewer calls now for more consultants to work their magic on governmental agencies and structures, perhaps it is because people remember that in the 1950s and 1960s, when the foundations were laid for many of today's problems in government, the best management experts available were giving guidance to government. Even in the most successful of cases, as for instance some of the more recent efforts by OMB and its consultants to streamline agency and departmental operations, the net gains have been small. It takes great vanity to suppose a new team could do better today; neither the problems nor the consulting arts have changed that much.

Do not shoot the piano player; he did his best. The difficulty is that the consultants were hired to introduce management principles at the wrong end of the system, at the bottom instead of the top. As a result, "managing better" was demoted and trivialized. It concentrated on such matters as the flow of work in the shop, and was not allowed to ask first-order questions challenging the organization's purpose and agenda. Maybe government agencies or departments can be better supervised, but the first question is whether some of them should be doing the things they do at all, or doing something different, or doing nothing. If the error lies in the marching orders rather than their execution, then it is beyond the ken of consultants, and all the studies can do is deliver fat files of advice to no avail. As one ex-official said of an agency that held sway for years over maritime commerce, the only proper way to have managed that organization in the public interest would have been to repeal its charter, disband the staff, raze the headquarters building in Washington, and poison the soil so that nothing could grow there for 100 years.

One precept any manager should learn is not to make decisions he does not have to make. There is chance enough for error in making the calls that are unavoidable. To increase the count deliberately does not win a manager points for being "decisive" but only proves him foolish. It is a failing of government, even more than of the private sector, that its departments and agencies make too many decisions. They are obliged to do so because they begin at the wrong end of the manager's list of questions. They are trapped there by legislators.

Moreover, the process by which Congress considers new legislation and oversees the old, often starts from conclusions and works backward toward evidence. Standard operating procedure is for committee and subcommittee heads to call hearings and take testimony. This is supposed to be the open, democratic way, but whether the proceedings actually illuminate issues and provide forums for reasoned discourse is another matter. Some do, but many clearly do not. On many occasions when I have been invited to appear, it has been evident that the committee staff had already made up its mind and drafted a position document before the elected members had taken their seats, if indeed the members even showed up. Hearings often have been *pro forma* and listless until the discussion has taken a turn, or a celebrity witness has appeared, suggesting a good chance for publicity, at which time the name players on the committee have usually put in an appearance.

People who have spent more time before Congress than I have report the same experience. Peter Barton Hutt, a lawyer now in private practice who formerly was chief counsel of the Food and Drug Administration, has said that he appeared before committees about eighty times in a four-year period, and can recall "no oversight hearing that even purported to be a balanced and objective analysis of an issue, and was constructed to help [FDA] do a better job in the future." As he reports, trivial matters often held sway, hearings were prosecutorial in nature and designed to embarrass and badger witnesses, and there was every appearance that these were no more than staged events meant to showcase Congressmen for the media.

What is most troublesome about this Congressional hearing process is not its theater-of-the-absurd quality or the penchant for publicity, but the tragedy of lost opportunities and negligence in oversight of the public's business. There are important questions facing agencies such as FDA and the private-sector organizations regulated by them. There are hard decisions to be made, affecting life and health as well as jobs and dollars. For example, pharmaceuticals can save lives, but the cost of developing a major new drug and registering it for sale in the U.S. has climbed to about $50 million, which is nearly ten times the average cost in 1960. Inflation accounts for part of the cost increase, but the principal reason for it is the large amount of testing required, stretching over a period of five years or more. No one takes exception to a very careful premarket screening of new drugs, but there is a question whether some of the U.S. requirements add measurably to safety. Some other nations with high health standards manage their approvals more quickly and at lower cost. Also, some side effects of the U.S. approach may not be so welcome. Having driven the price of entering the market so high, government has made it doubly difficult for small and medium-sized companies to do pharmaceutical research. Few of them can afford the large-scale projects. The market is thus skewed toward big companies and major drug developments. The number of New Drug Applications filed with FDA has declined in recent years, and some drugs have become "orphans." These are compounds which might be useful or even life-saving to some people, but for which the market is so small that companies see no good chance of recovering their developmental costs.

The questions of trade-offs and relative "goods" press at us constantly, and ought to be part of Congress' agenda. Are we being too careful for our own good, with agencies of government trying so hard to eliminate risk that the public is being hurt more than helped? Is Congress partly or mostly responsible for that? How can the private and public sectors define acceptable levels of risk and stay within these? What are the responsibilities of FDA, of the pharmaceutical industry, or health-care professionals, and of individuals? Whatever one's view as to the proper answers, these questions are not being dealt with effectively through the standardized process of Congressional hearings. They are the right public-policy questions, though, and we need a better way to get them aired.

Part of the solution lies in Congress empowering the executive branch to manage the departments and agencies more effectively, with authority to resolve jurisdictional fights and mediate conflicts on goals. Much of this would have to be subject to a nonobjection from Congress (otherwise, Congress would never agree to give up this power). Independent agencies should be few and far between—possibly the only exception should be the Federal Reserve Board with its control over the money supply, and some think that even that one is arguable. The rest ought to be accountable to the President. In any department or agency, there should be authority for review and discipline for people at least three or four layers down into the structure. This can be done while still leaving legislators and courts adequate checks on the executive branch. No chief executive, however clever, could exercise runaway power in the presence of an assertive Congress. The same applies at the state level, where the dangers of executive abuse are less.

Once a semblance of control is brought to government administration, agencies should be put on a lean diet and required to show proof of effectiveness in meeting their job descriptions. It is not possible to change everything at once, but I would lead with an experiment and impose what could be called the 10–5 Rule: Cut budgets 10 percent and give administrators power to discharge, in any one year, up to 5 percent of their people for nonperformance. In the "10" part of this scheme, each agency or department would be required to list the least important tenth of its programs, and face budget cuts of that amount unless it could convince the executive of the essentiality of preserving those projects. In the "5" sector, dismissal of employees would require statements of cause but not the prolonged, multistep procedures now required before employees in civil-service jobs can be demoted or moved out.

Canny bureaucrats would seize upon counterstrategies. It would immediately occur to them to bat up not their least important 10 percent, but programs backed by large, vocal constituencies which could be counted on to rally around the flag. Another ploy would be to propose cuts that would hit the weakest and most defenseless citizens, on the assumption that this will produce howls from the press that will force the budget-cutters to retreat in shame. Cuts also might be offered that could be made only with Congressional approval, in areas where the chances of obtaining it are slim. (Suggest, for example, that benefits to veterans be trimmed.) The way to handle maneuvers of those kinds is to return fire with fire: Seek maximum publicity for the review process, and assure that the outside world has a look at what the agencies propose to leave untouched as well as what they are putting on the altar for sacrifice.

There would doubtless be cries of injustice if government workers were discharged with anything less than full-dress appeals. What about their "rights"? What is to stop an agency head or subaltern from being capricious or vindictive? Would not the first to be sacked be "whistle-blowers" who have embarrassed their bosses by calling attention to incompetence or impropriety? There can of course be problems any time one person has another's career in his hands, and at least one appellate layer is always desirable. The larger question today, however, is not how to protect government employees against their bosses but how to protect the public from government employees. Public servants today are sheltered by codes that protect the servants marvelously well, but the public hardly at all. It can take one-half of a manager's time for a full year just to push one nonperformer aside. If a strongly negative judgment about a subordinate is committed to paper and seen in the wrong places, its author may end up as defendant in a lawsuit. Protecting dissidents who have a just cause is a necessary task, but that can be said of the private sector as well. There is no reason why public employees should be exempt from the discipline and performance standards that are deemed fair for, let us say, a shift supervisor in an industrial plant or the bursar of a university.

Congress and the administrative agencies surely could use more people of superior quality in staff work, but an even greater need is for experienced managers to run the departments and agencies. The people who fill the line offices often have exemplary qualities. They may show outstanding records in a professional or academic setting. Some of them have had legislative experience and many have shown their loyalty to a political leader. Those are not criticisms, but none of this demonstrates an ability to administer a departmental staff and budget. Individuals the private sector would not entrust with the management of a large manufacturing plant are given executive spots in government organizations dealing with public problems of major importance, with responsibility for billions or hundreds of millions of dollars. They are obliged to learn on the job and to make their mistakes on a large scale. This is expensive.

The pool of candidates for management posts in government would be larger if people from the private sector were considered more acceptable as public servants, but this is prevented by the way that conflict-of-interest codes are interpreted in the power centers of government. Concern about corruption of government is so great that anyone with firsthand experience acquired in the pay of a private company is disqualified for a public position of significant responsibility, or at least has a great deal of explaining to do.

Conflicts of interest are clearly bad. No one should try to serve two masters at once, and the public has a right to demand that anyone entrusted with its work is placing public duty above all else. Watchdogs are needed, for history is full of examples of public office being twisted to private gain. Congress ought to be vigilant, for there have been enough examples of cronyism among elected officials as well as in the private sector to give anyone pause. We go too far, though. "Conflict" as now defined almost amounts to "guilt by (prior) association," and this steers away from public life many individuals of high integrity who have talents that are in short supply.

Judgment tends to be harsh, swift, and preemptive. It is not "conflict" alone that is condemned, but the appearance of conflict based on circumstantial evidence, and sometimes on past circumstance at that. One of many possible examples comes from the Environmental Protection Agency, an organization that got in trouble early and often in the Reagan administration. Congress was exceedingly touchy about the doings of EPA, and one reason was that key officials put into the agency by the White House had prior commercial ties, or had records that made them otherwise unacceptable to hard-line environmentalists. I am no defender of the Environmental Protection Agency on the issue in question, which centered on the performance of those responsible for the clean-up of toxic-waste dumpsites, and I have no firsthand information on the circumstances that ultimately led to the resignation and replacement of the administrator, Ann McGill Burford, or other senior staffers. However, it is instructive to review this celebrated incident for what it says about public and governmental attitudes. The initial outcry from some of the critics in government went beyond fair limits even for politics. The class-action crime of the EPA staff was that they had worked or lobbied for Crown Zellerbach, Exxon, Aerojet General, and a group named the American Council on Science and Health, whose sin is that it takes money from industry. Mrs. Burford had as a state legislator in Colorado voted against some air-pollution control regulations. The alleged sins of her administration at EPA were that deals were made which would allow industry to escape its responsibilities. Appointment calendars showed that EPA staffers had had lunch with industry representatives, with no public-health official or representative of a private environmental group present. Many agencies have rules prohibiting such *ex parte* meetings.

Eventually, the Senate Republican leaders convinced the White

House that it could restore its credibility in environmental affairs only if EPA had a new head, someone "lily-white with no baggage, no hint of conflict." At that point, the President replaced Mrs. Burford with William Ruckelshaus, the man who had headed EPA when it was formed a decade earlier.

The question, of course, ought to be what Mrs. Burford and her staff did, not what suspicion based on association hints they might have done. Were the Colorado proposals so meritorious that no one could have voted against them in good conscience? What decisions did EPA hand down after lunch or before, and were these defensible under the law? Were favors done in violation of public trust and legislative intent? Did EPA officials tell the truth about the meetings? These are legitimate questions, but who had lunch with whom ought to be irrelevant unless we are prepared to turn the table and say that it is also wrong for people from the Environmental Defense Fund or the faculty of the Harvard School of Public Health to break bread with EPA unless the industries whose products may be discussed also are represented. What is intriguing here is the one-sided logic, not the outcome of the case.

A double standard applies. One critic particularly offended by some of EPA's staff assignments is Russell Peterson, head of the Audubon Society and a former head of the Council on Environmental Quality. In a letter to the *Washington Post,* he protested the presence of industry alumni and charged that "interest in a clean and healthy environment has been subordinated to the private, profit-making interest of the favored few. . . ." Dr. Peterson might himself be offended, though, by any suggestion that his own credentials as a protector of the environment are stained by the fact that he is a former executive of Du Pont (an ex-research director of a department), or that his personal integrity ought to be questioned because he served in a fairly high post in the Nixon White House, a place not remembered for high morality. If guilt by association is unfair for one, it is unfair for all.

Some Congressmen who would be incensed by the charge that they have been "bought" by contributors to their campaigns, have no trouble concluding that a businessman is the captive of his profit-making past and would surely protect his interest in 1,000 shares of stock before he would be swayed by the public's concerns. There is even suspicion about letting profit-makers get close to governmental problems in the role of consultants, on the premise that this just lets the camel get his nose in the tent. When the Department of Agriculture put forward a list of consultants it intended to use in a review of dietary guidelines for the nation, some of the nominations were immediately attacked by the Center for Science in the Public Interest, a Washington-based group. The problem? The nominees also consulted for (not worked for) such commercial organizations as the Cereal Institute and the American Egg Board. One of the administrators in Agriculture, Isabel Wolf, said, "It's a big jump to assume that someone who does scientific work for a food company or a group represents or speaks for that group." She added another good point, that it is bright people who usually end up consulting for industry as much as for other organizations, and if we remove all "tainted" counselors, we will be left with less competent individuals on review panels.

It is worth noting that in some respects the public appears to be far less doctrinaire about conflicts than government and some of the interest groups. During the Carter administration, a Harris poll found that two-thirds of the public believed that if expert knowledge acquired in business were brought into government deliberations, better laws and regulations would result. An even larger majority said that in regulating industry it makes sense to include some people who have some experience in the industry. What the public clearly does not want, though, is a system that simply dumps power into the hands of special interests, from business or anywhere else. That is an entirely reasonable position. Such a balanced public view provides a common-sense route to take in staffing government. The approach that best serves the public's interest is to draw into government as much talent from the private sector as is available, but to require public disclosure of all material interests that might color decisions, and, further, to make public the decisions that are made and the basis for them. The disclosure approach is the one taken by SEC to maintain an environment of honest dealing in financial markets, and it has been effective. It can be equally so in other areas if the emphasis is placed on conduct as exposed in the public record rather than on assumptions about ulterior motives.

In its internal affairs, the private sector has taken a leaf from SEC's book, and the same can be done to advantage throughout government. Employees are required to disclose to their employers any facts that may affect the businesses' interests—personal investments in suppliers to their companies, for instance—and judgments are made. Relationships that are uncomfortable have to be severed in one way or another, by removing the influences or removing the employees. It is a simple approach, a mature one, and one that would improve government's ability to attract and retain highly qualified people. Individuals of character and competence are going to avoid conflicts of interest, and with a proper chain of command plus clear-cut disclosure requirements, there will be others to double-check their judgment.

It is easier to change procedures than structures. That is why I look upon a tightening of administrative responsibilities in government as more practical than an overhaul of the organization chart of the executive branch. The same applies to Congress and state legislatures. The number of committees and subcommittees ought to be reduced, but legislators will not commit that kind of surgery on themselves willingly (though they might be less defensive about it if there were changes in the election process, as proposed earlier). We may hope for a better reception for procedural reform. Congress in the 1970s found it possible to make such changes to correct some of its shortcomings (admittedly a move that also created some of the present problems), so it is not beyond question that Congress in the 1980s might be persuaded to try another round of self-improvement.

Several approaches have been discussed at the Federal level and have found favor among some legislators, which at least means we are not starting at zero. One is for elimination of some of the overlaps in Congressional and departmental jurisdiction. The idea of dismantling agencies and subcommittees may be too traumatic for Congress to accept. In any case, it is not the place to start. The better route is to work within the existing structure, reshuffling assignments and clarifying ground rules so that the number of separate bodies tracking a given area (energy, environment, etc.) is cut by, perhaps, one-half. This is one of those instances where half a loaf is better than a whole. To maintain checks and balances, Congress and the administration oversee governmental operations on two axes at once: vertically by department (Defense, Transportation, etc.) and horizontally by issue (environment, problems of the elderly, etc.). Add politics to that matrix and you have a cat's cradle. Trying to impose complete order on this would be a mistake.

Another suggestion is for stronger direction of subcommittees by the senior committees of the House and Senate, extending to budgets, selection of subcommittee members, and review of proposals. Letting the subcommittees largely go their own ways adds the gloss of approval to an ancient but disreputable practice in which each Congressman allows his fellows their pet projects, expecting a *quid* in return. It also gets back to questions about foxes guarding henhouses.

As long as subcommittees lean to the will of their constituencies and the regional interests of their chairmen, as they are sorely tempted to do, the subcommittees will need to be constrained by a force more representative of a national view. Use as the example the House Armed Services Committee and its procurements subcommittee. At the opening of the 98th Congress in 1983, there was a fight over the chair in procurements. A Democrat from Florida tried to win it away from a Democrat from New York who had held it in three previous Congresses. Both ranked high in the pecking order. One was second in seniority in Armed Services; the other, third. Each had his own reasons for wanting the job, but prominent among them was the near-certainty that the chairman's district would get a goodly share of military spending. This subcommittee wields authority over about one-third of the military budget, that share for the year in question being between $60 and $70 billion. The New York Congressman, Samuel Stratton (for the record, he won), made no bones about the home-district factor. He was quoted as saying, "You have a battle between a guy who is doing his best to get military funds to New York versus a guy who would want to channel them to the South."

The home folks may have been cheering on their champions, but where in this picture does the public find disinterested judgment about where best to spend the public's money in the interest of something as important as national defense? Is not the likely outcome that after the right people in Congress are "taken care of" in the Pentagon budget, the military will call for whatever other spending it needs to feel comfortable about national security, thus making the budget bigger? The military is not unique in this, surely. The same process takes place elsewhere, and to the extent that it does, the present subcommittee system in Congress looks remarkably like a welfare program for Congressmen.

"I have to get reelected" is a stock political remark, but that is not good enough. There is nothing in the public interest that requires that particular Congressmen be reelected, or that Federal spending by region be a reflection of the skill of a Congressman in cutting deals for committee seats. One way to constrain this, and at the same time build public confidence in Congress and the political process, would be to consolidate some of the committees and subcommittees, rotate committee chairs more often, operate from a more rigid legislative agenda (getting to the important issues first instead of at the last minute), and tighten the oversight functions by auditing decisions that bring special benefits to districts whose Congressmen sit in high positions.

The senior committees can fill this function if they so choose, and if the system of party leadership is made strong enough to hold them to it. The committees have both the size and the geographic diversity to display the necessary detachment. Of the seventeen standing committees of the U.S. Senate, all but four have seventeen or more members, and one of the most powerful (Appropriations) includes more than one-fourth of the senators. Of the twenty-two committees in the House, all but four have twenty-five or more members. Without exception, the rosters span the nation, with representation from states small and large, agrarian and industrial, North and South. Armed Services has forty-five members, and to return to our example, it turns out that forty-one of them are not from New York or Florida.

Another option open to Congress, one that would save it grief and ridicule, is to limit the ability to amend bills moving toward votes. The Senate prides itself, unduly, on a willingness to put up with any number of amendments and any amount of debate. The House is not far behind, with a peculiar tradition that allows amendments that fail at one stage of the legislative process to be dressed in new clothes and paraded before the members once again. The door is left open by the fact that Congress goes through a two-step process to dispense money. First comes an authorization bill; it answers the "Do what?" question. Then comes an appropriation bill: "How much?" Riders can be tacked on at either stage, and are. Congress has been urged by some of its own members to change this so that amendments could be made only in the first round. Riders would be prohibited on appropriation bills, with exceptions only in cases where a majority of the full House of Representatives granted special permission and in effect reopened the authorization bill.

This may sound like a minor change in procedure, but it could make a large difference, helping Congress eliminate needless repeat business and permitting leaders to do more leading. "If at first you don't succeed . . ." may be noble advice, but it clutters the legislative agenda as almost nothing else does, and leads idealogues to play single-issue games. The riders attached late in the game to broad-ranging money bills often tell departments to do such things as withhold money for abortions, or spend no dollars on legal cases that might encourage busing of pupils for purposes of integration. Whether or not one agrees with such steps, they are obviously sidebars to the purpose of the appropriations. The riders go piggyback because their sponsors have not won their points in a straight floor vote on the merits. Rules that allow this do not encourage better decisions, only more of them, redundantly.

The objection to changing the rules is that the Congressional leaders would be awarded greater power. Perhaps they would, but is that not a blessing? The pendulum needs to swing back a little, and the public might find the change attractive for the same reasons that it might like the proposed changes in lines of reporting in the executive branch: If poor decisions came forth, the public at least would know where to place the blame. It is time to try some experiments in both the legislative and the executive branches. The possible rewards in the form of better governance are too large to be ignored, and the risks to the public are minimal. Nothing proposed need be cast in concrete. If proposals such as these lead to new and different problems, the management approach can be changed again at a later date.

No one expects people on the senior committees to be immune to all "me first" urges and pork-barrel temptations (they are, after all, the same people who sit on the subcommittees), but the presence of the full committee ought to bring forth more sensitivity to national concerns. If such a spirit does not emerge there, the public has no place to turn. The full House and Senate are too big to manage the legislative process in a useful sense of the word. That is why committees exist, and if they cannot rise to national needs, we are only an inch away from the conclusion that representative government at the Federal level cannot be made to work in this country. Dr. Brademas' concern is well placed.

Have we gone too far to turn back? Are we to be governed by "politics only" without hope of anything better? It takes faith to ward off cynicism, but I hold to the conviction that the public-policy process can be lifted out of the quagmire. I believe this is true because the people with the largest stake in this are bound to find that their self-interest will not square with a no-change philosophy. Out of a sense of the practical, rather than appeals to their idealism, people in both government and private organizations can see advantages in looking farther down the road and putting broad responsibilities ahead of parochial ones.

I count business in this process even more than any part of government. Private corporations, like government departments, may be consumed by narrowness and expediency. Their leaders also may spend too much time at the wrong end of the management list of questions, but people in the private sector at least have an ability to do something about it, and for them the alternative to change should in the future be unacceptable.

Return to the earlier question: What is it that the private business needs most from government? To echo the refrain, what it needs more than anything else is a set of cohesive, consistent policies against which to plan, invest, build, and produce. Business needs freedom from the gross distortions, for which government is often responsible, that demolish whatever well-laid plans there may be, punish the productive, or realign the economic system without rhyme or reason. There is of course the temptation in the private sector to fight for particulars and let somebody else play the statesman's role, and it has to be conceded that there is a half-good reason for this. Particulars can be expensive. To a state school superintendent or university head, legislation on the budget for education can be a life-or-death matter. By the same token, for a profit-making corporation, every day is election day in the market, and one or two votes in a Congressional committee or an agency staff can make a difference of millions of dollars and thousands of jobs. My view on this, though, is that general policies have far more leverage than any of the particulars, and deserve priority attention whenever there is a chance for the private sector to affect the outcome.

As a case in question, it makes sense for the chemical industry to work hard for an amendment to the Clean Water Act to permit a case-by-case waiver of requirements for the use of Best Available Technology wherever it can be shown that effluents going into the water pose no toxicological threat. Such exceptions would save millions for the industry, and harm no one. It makes even better sense, though, for industry to invest resources in the task of building public support for a more temperate definition of what constitutes "pollution control." A 10-percent easing of many requirements, beginning with the elimination of the BAT approach, would bring savings in the billions of dollars, with public health and safety no less protected. The first job, if it can be done at all, can be handled through persuasion in EPA and a Congressional subcommittee. The second task takes industry far out into the public arena and implies a long effort; but only if industry is willing to undertake this, and prevails, can a significant part of the burden be eased.

Consider another example of general effects outweighing particular interests. Numerous American firms have built markets in Europe for a major portion of their product lines manufactured in the U.S. This business is a source of jobs for American workers, and a positive contributor to the balance of trade. A number of the products face tariffs or other import restrictions in Europe, and U.S. firms have pressed for government help in lowering these particular barriers, making their case through the U.S. trade representative and GATT, the international General Agreement on Tariffs and Trade. Further, company forecasts and capital spending plans have been based on a few percentage points of advantage in the price or quality of U.S.-made products versus competitive articles made in Europe. A slight change in production efficiency or raw-material costs can make or break a product. The gains or losses implied by this, however, are as nothing in comparison to the money put on the line by changes in the exchange rates of national currencies. In one recent two-year period, the U.S. dollar rose by 30 percent versus European currencies and the Japanese yen. That is to say, the same handful of Deutschmarks or French francs would buy only a little over two-thirds as much American products as it had two years earlier. U.S. companies that had been hoping for a better break in the European market then found themselves, in some cases, effectively priced out of that market entirely. Their export businesses collapsed. The other side of that coin is that products being imported into the U.S. suddenly had become less expensive for American buyers—the Almighty Dollar would command more goods—and this served to worsen the U.S. deficit in international trade in goods. Whether the swing was positive or negative for specific companies, it is dramatic evidence of how easily particular interests can be overwhelmed by general changes that are heavily influenced if not absolutely controlled by governments.

The operative question is whether the private sector can affect broad governmental policies, and I think the record shows that it can if it is persistent and patient. One reason that the U.S. government turned in the early 1980s toward tax policies that encourage savings and investment, as opposed to consumption, is that private corporations, trade associations, and independent research centers had generated a steady flow of evidence that a pro-investment strategy is required for job creation and economic prosperity. It took years—and a recession—but the message finally sank in.

Another example is health care, where a lot of hard work in the private sector is finally convincing the public and the government that an ethic of open-ended entitlements, promising all possible benefits to everyone, is not medically necessary and cannot be sustained financially. What is taking shape now is a different system, stressing more cost-effective use of services, more competition among providers, more choice for consumers among health-care plans and payment schemes, and new alignments for delivery of the services of doctors, nurses, hospitals, nursing homes, and clinics. Health care in the U.S. has long been a mixed industry, with both private and public sectors deeply involved. What is new is the degree to which the private sector, through community groups, coalitions, and corporations, is producing ideas for change and the pressure to make it happen.

What is behind this is the escalating costs. The nation's bill for health care sets the world record. It has passed $300 billion per year, which is $1,300 per capita and 10 percent of the Gross National Product, a higher percentage than in other advanced nations. Spending for government-funded programs such as Medicare and Medicaid has been running out of control, as have the costs to private employers who pay for the insurance plans that cover much or all of their employees' health care. Unfortunately, there has been no one-for-one correspondence between the size of the bills and the health of people. With each passing year, it has become clearer that the nation has been practicing "flat of the curve" medicine, just as government practiced that art in its regulatory activities. The slope of health-care spending has been steeply upward, but the curve of demonstrated benefits has fallen off. The objective now is to retain the most important feature of past programs—the ability to supply necessary care to all people, including the indigent—but to draw sharper distinctions between what is necessary to health and what is luxury. It is a major shift, one calling for both public and private collaboration and for able leadership in both camps.

It takes time and practice to learn to work with policy issues of such dimensions. No one's proposals for changes in tax policy are likely to be taken seriously if all he has examined is the impact of taxes on himself. It is not the work of a few hours or days to become familiar enough with health care to understand the strengths and weaknesses of the system, and to avoid the classic bureaucratic solution, which is to move the problem rather than to resolve it. In my own experience as a health-care nonexpert, the answers seemed easy until I worked as a volunteer in a community organization providing care for the aged, headed a corporation whose employee health-care-benefit costs were rising at 15 to 25 percent per year, and became a member of the board of a company that operates hospitals in many cities. Then I found out how much background one needs to claim to be a knowledgeable layman, and to think of practical answers that do not merely take care away from Peter to cure Paul. I am now convinced that it is possible to contain health-care costs and do so with a clear conscience. Further, I believe that the way to do it is to invert the incentives, toward responsible management of the resources, and away from an ethic that says we offer everything for everybody by way of health care, with the promise that somebody else will pay the bill. There is now enough momentum behind this approach for it to be sold politically. I am also convinced, though, that to contain the costs without undercutting the quality of health care, people in the private sectors will have to spend many hours studying the numbers, lobbying, building coalitions, negotiating, reshaping plans a dozen times over, and building public support.

There are both costs and risks in public-policy immersion. To deserve to have an influence on policy in a general sense, people in the private sector have to make an investment of time greater by a high multiple than is required to lobby to amend a particular bill. Further, the effort can deflect policy in directions that may not be entirely welcome. Consider an example from recent history. For years, the private sector pleaded for reduced spending by the Federal government, but about 60 percent of that spending is for entitlement programs and projects with built-in momentum. Politically, the easiest way to save money there would be to keep the programs intact while shifting the costs to somebody else, namely, to the states or to private companies and individuals. If programs are shifted without being cut, the net result would be an extra burden on private-sector firms in such areas as health care and support for the elderly. Pension and medical-insurance costs, which already represent one-third of employees' pay in many companies, could move still higher.

Moreover, managers from the private sector are as much at risk as anyone else of tripping over their own positions. Much of the reason it takes so long to hammer out broad policy positions is that these must be shaped by putting together many smaller issues and consequences, and on the mental assembly line some of these refuse to fit together logically. Unless one is a genius or has just been very lucky, he will find that at least a few of his short-range or selfish interests do not square with the sensible long-range policy. A dutiful manager either will have to shed some fondly held views that are no longer tenable, or invent a way to carry water on both shoulders. Delving into public-policy issues can be a humbling experience, and awkward to someone who has been trying to sell a Congressional committee on the worth of the baggage he has now abandoned. A fear of embarrassment may not be the best argument to convince people they should think through policy questions thoroughly before they "go public," but perhaps it is an effective one. At the least, people in the private sector should do their homework with as much diligence as they would ask of government, and try to find the forks in the road early.

Now, as I write this, the burning question in the domestic economy is how to strengthen the nation's competitive status. The issue on the floor is industrial policy: do we need a new one, and if so, what kind? Though "industrial policy" has become a cliché and the surface arguments about it have been worn threadbare, the underlying issue remains important. It is worth exploring here because it illuminates a need and an opportunity for private-sector initiatives in support of more farsighted Federal policies. My analysis leads away from patch-work programs, many of which are driven by political pressures, toward a new process in which government uses a different approach, and we may hope a better one, to examine economic issues and weigh the options for action.

Among thoughtful people there seems to be wide agreement that government can help most by concentrating on economic policies that will strengthen the economic fundamentals, policies that for the most part are old and well-proven. I have no quarrel with that, but a general pledge of allegiance to the economic verities is not enough. We should also be seeking specific ways to solve problems that market forces alone cannot remedy, and this requires more cooperation among the leaders of government, private industry, and labor unions. One way to promote such cooperation in a non-adversarial setting is to expand on an idea that worked well in the past, and establish in the White House a Labor-Management Committee of people from the private sector as well as government, to serve in an advisory capacity to the President. It could identify emerging problems, provide the careful research and on-line advice that are required if the executive branch is to make informed decisions, and offer a broader perspective than is available from any agency of government, or from political debate. We are crippled at present because no one arm of government has broad responsibility for the economy. The proposed new process would try to fill this gap with advice based on experience.

The economic facts that provoked the pleas for a "New Industrial Policy" are familiar. In the early 1980s, the nation went through a severe recession, one that stopped growth and eliminated many jobs. What forced the questions onto the public agenda, though, was not that downturn alone—the 1979–83 recession was worldwide, and actually punished the U.S. less than some other nations. The concern emerged from a longer-term trend, in which the nation has charted a steady erosion of its position relative to other leading countries.

Partly, we have ourselves to blame for the slippage. Managerially, American-based businesses have not always been as farsighted or venturesome as hindsight says they should have been. Politically, as detailed in earlier chapters, we have wrapped loop after loop of fine wire around enterprises, restricting their mobility, limiting through taxation and other policies the very qualities of innovation and risk-taking we should have been encouraging. In some cases, when we should have been trying to improve industries, we settled for trying to protect them. However, the slide in our fortunes can be traced as much to the actions of others as to ourselves. In the 1960s and 1970s, some other countries, as a matter of deliberate policy, took steps to stimulate output per man-hour in their work force, encourage investment, expand production, upgrade the quality and variety of product portfolios, and promote export trade. Backed by their public's willingness to accept the short-term sacrifices that go along with such an effort, the governments of those countries maintained consistent, pro-growth policies and took special pains to promote good relationships between government and business. Harmony in some cases extended to a direct use of governmental resources to support private firms.

Skillful corporate managers made good use of those advantages, with the result that a number of countries gained growing shares of the markets in the U.S. and elsewhere, while U.S. producers lost market share. The declining positions of the U.S. steel and auto makers in the U.S. market are well-publicized examples of the trend, but they tell only part of the story. The portion of world merchandise trade represented by exports from the U.S. also has declined since the early 1960s. U.S. companies have not stopped selling abroad; it is just that others have done much more of it.

Almost as soon as the "industrial policy" label came into common use, discussion was polarized. Some people assumed that industrial policy meant centralized national planning, or would soon lead to it. That prospect pleased few and produced instant outrage in the private sector. Happily, the historical record relieved the nation of the need to debate that possibility at any length. A look back at the performance of societies which have tried the production-czar approach was enough to convince almost everyone that central planning has no future here. There is a self-evident absurdity in the notion that some sort of central agency could get its arms around the enormously complicated thing called the American economy, see its future, and prescribe correctly for its current ills.

After that straw man was knocked down, it occurred to many people that the U.S. already has an industrial policy, *de facto*, whether it admits it or not. Our policy is the sum of all the antitrust rules, tax requirements or tax credits, depletion allowances, tariffs, trigger prices, loan guarantees, import quotas, agricultural assistance programs (agriculture is an industry, too—and a major exporter), and other provisos that help or hinder particular competitors. The U.S. is in no way unique in this respect. Other countries routinely employ such devices. Where the U.S. policy is distinct is in its *ad hoc* quality. Our government has assembled a collection of laws and regulations from fragments, without a coherent economic viewpoint, and with little regard for the worldwide effects on our competitiveness. One sign of that habit-of-mind was the response the U.S. made to a question from the Organization for Economic Cooperation and Development. At about the time that industrial policy became a public issue, the OECD surveyed its member governments, and asked each to explain its industrial strategy. The U.S. alone replied, "We have none," adding, as though it were something to be proud of, that we take each issue as it comes.

If that answer served in the past, it does not suffice anymore. The new "industrial policy" question is not whether, but how. On that, answers have divided along "macro" and "micro" lines. Some advisors have insisted that, once the nation returns to appropriate macro-economic policies (stimulating investment, providing for gradual, orderly growth of the money supply, and so forth) the market-based system will respond and the key problems (productivity and unemployment) will be resolved. Others have challenged that, and insisted that additional, specific steps—micro-economic moves—are required. Even if the U.S. does everything right in macro-policy, they have said, market forces may doom some industries vital to the national interest. In other instances, policies of foreign governments may interfere with more beneficent market reactions, with untoward results.

What sorts of "micro" moves? There are all manner of prescriptions. Government has been urged to encourage technology with added incentives, strengthen educational programs, and do more to retrain workers bumped by competitive forces. Some people have implored the nation to go much further, restoring ailing industries even if subsidies and protectionist trade measures are required. Others have counseled going the other way, putting the subsidies, if such they are to be called, on "high tech" fields, and forgetting the smokestack industries. (Truth be known, many of these, such as textiles, have never emitted much smoke, so "core industries" was suggested as a more apt identifier.)

Business Week magazine came up with a helpful scorecard. It divided the players into five teams: the Accelerationists, who would pinpoint industries that already promise to become strong international competitors; the Adjusters, who would supply help to declining industries in return for their commitments to modernize; the Targeters, who would select a group of industries and turn these into engines for economic growth; the Central Planners (there are a few), who would staff a Pentagon-like structure with "experts" pretending to know how to plan for the many sectors of the economy; and Bankers, who would add an industrial development bank to any of the other approaches, on the theory that there is a need for "patient capital" to stand behind various development projects that need time to take root.

Some of the proposals sound remarkably like triage, the medical policy for treating battlefield casualties: Soldiers whose wounds are minor and who will survive in any event receive no help; those hurt more seriously are treated, but only if they can be restored to fight again; and those most critically injured are ignored, because they may not make it anyway, and the medics cannot afford to waste time or scarce medicine trying to save them. It is not that simple, though. The assumption behind triage is that foot-soldiers are interchangeable. The parallel here is that there are dinosaur industries the nation can do without, and that these should be left on the economic battleground to die of their wounds. To make it less cold-blooded, this comes with the suggestion that we enlarge the safety net to catch more of the "disemployed."

To make it still less simple, industry's soldiers, wounded and otherwise, have the vote, and no "winners" and "losers" game can be played unless it gives first attention to the human consequences. A major change in the industrial mix, especially if accelerated by government action, may well imply the moving and retraining of hundreds of thousands if not millions of people. The magnitude of that job, not to mention the potential for tragedy or chaos, ought to be obvious. The political problems, at a time when unemployment has hung for years far above an acceptable level, often exceeding 10 percent, are equally clear.

The sad fact is that much of the unemployment problem in the U.S. is not cyclical, and therefore does not disappear by itself when recessions end and expansion periods return. Labor economists once quoted 3 to 4 percent unemployment as the lowest practicable rate for a diversified, industrial economy such as ours, their point being that, even in the best of times, a few percent would be people changing jobs, or just coming into the labor force. Today, a "full employment" economy is thought of as one with 6 or 7 percent unemployment. This is because there is now more flux in the job market, a different age and sex composition of the labor force, and more job shifting due to technological change, along with competition, which today can bring rapid and drastic changes in the relative fortunes of companies.

Workers can be in the right place at the right time, and still not find work because they are not trained to do the jobs that exist. The individuals in question may have the innate ability to learn, but they have a long road to travel, they will need much help, and once employed they will be the workers most vulnerable to layoffs. When there are plant closings, the first casualties are usually not the most skilled and flexible of workers. They are more likely to be workers with low to middling skills who are not easily transferred to other occupations or locales, and who lack the educational background to succeed in the "retreading" courses that might turn them into computer programmers, electronics technicians, or whatever the future is expected to be employing. Further, it must be appreciated that new jobs in high technology industries may not be highly skilled, more secure, or nearly as well paid as the old jobs in the steel and auto plants. Computer parts can be assembled by moderately skilled workers in any country, as was made apparent to many workers in California when Atari began moving jobs out of that state to Hong Kong.

It is important that we be clear on objectives. Saving hard-pressed industries is one possible mission for national policy, on a case-by-case basis. Saving the people who work in those industries, or who have not been able to find work at all, is another task entirely. The two missions should not be confused. Both need to be on the national agenda, but they call for different strategies. (In passing, let one piece of good news be noted: A few distractions of the 1960s and 1970s seem to have disappeared from the national scene. No longer is there widespread oratory about the virtues of turning away from that contemptible thing called technology, or sermons on the merits of Zero Economic Growth, or forecasts about the "greening" of America. Those sweet-hearted conceits are luxuries to be indulged only by the most privileged minority in wealthy societies. Whatever popular support such ideas had in the 1970s in the U.S. [not much, it now appears], it evaporated when the hot sun of competition began to beat down, and U.S. workers in large numbers began to lose their jobs.)

Government's broad economic policies have more leverage than its moves on behalf of specific industries or groups of workers, and deserve concentrated attention. When government pursues policies that result in high inflation, high interest rates, and large deficits, or all three, any special-aid projects it may devise have little chance of invigorating the private sector. Those government actions send all the wrong signals and evoke all the wrong reactions.

In an inflating economy, companies become more casual than they ought to be about inefficiency and obsolescence. Employees put top priority on getting their pay and benefits to rise fast, with or without increased productivity, so they will not lose ground. The consequence is that production costs and product prices rise. Companies caught in an inflating economy thus are at a disadvantage versus competitors from countries with economies inflating less rapidly: If they raise prices, they lose sales; if they reduce prices, they lose profits—Catch 22. The financial message during inflation is to go into debt and stay there, because when the debt is repaid in the future, it will be with cheaper dollars. Thus, the worse the inflation, the more likely that a company's production plants, its operating efficiency, and the soundness of its balance sheet will deteriorate together.

In an economy that is not being inflated, the incentives turn the other way. Success belongs to the producers who keep costs tightly controlled, work hard to improve output per man-hour, and do not allow themselves to get overextended with debt. It is easier in this environment to keep plants in repair, and hence competitive, because depreciation allowances provide enough money to cover replacement costs. Returns on investment are real, based on the performance of products and services in the marketplace, and not on the chimera of price rises. The manager who "plans ahead" and makes prudent investments likely to pay out long-term no longer appears to be the too-cautious fool but the wise steward.

Any programs mounted in the name of industrial policy must first accommodate to the needs of national security, and the priorities emerging from that quarter may, on some occasions, override direct considerations of economic efficiency. The economic costs ought to be identified, to be sure, but it might not be sensible to allow them to be decisive. Government has to be on guard against actions that favor particular industries but leave the nation strategically weaker in the bargain. (Need it be added that government also ought to be on guard against political plays of another kind, involving attempts to wrap the flag around self-interests? One can always find an elected official prepared to proclaim that the republic may fall unless the Navy keeps building ships in his district.)

Beyond national security, Federal policy also ought to respect the interdependence of large and small firms, and of high- and low-technology markets: They are tightly interlocked. It must respect as well the realities of international trade; the incentives required for innovation and technological development; and the maintenance requirements of the infrastructure, the buzz word for highways, railroads, communications facilities, educational structures, and other necessities of an industrial economy. (Again, an obvious caution: One Congressman's "pork barrel" is another Congressman's "infrastructure.")

The amount of interlocking in the economy is not self-evident. Low-technology industries are often important customers of high-technology firms. "Triage" the first and the second will go into deep depression. Policies that discriminate for or against companies on the basis of size would be equally unproductive. Most of the new jobs being created come from small firms, and that is a reason to favor them; but most of the existing jobs are in medium and large organizations, and that tilts the scales the other way. Logic says that business size ought not be a determinant of policy.

Many young, entrepreneurial firms are highly innovative—a plus for them; but at the same time many of them depend for part of their success on inventions that have come from the laboratories of giant corporations. Much of the modern communications and electronics industry, for example, and millions of jobs in its thousands of companies, can be traced back to research done in the Bell Laboratories of AT&T. Many a maker of specialty products for the aerospace industry works his high-tech magic with molecules invented and developed in the labs of Du Pont.

While defense-related research and development contribute products to the civilian sector, the technological spinoff the other way is even more impressive, to defense and aerospace applications, and from R&D that was funded privately by corporations with the civilian marketplace first in mind. Weaken either the big-corporation technological base, or the opportunity for smaller firms to go their innovative ways, and everybody loses. There is thus more than a little danger that the industrial policy debate will disintegrate into political rhetoric about small being "better" than big, or certain lines of technical work being more "worthy" than others. This kind of talk might lead to economic policies that overlook the essentiality of economic units of many kinds. The simplest point about the nation's economic fabric is still its most important one: What we have here is not rows of parallel threads, but a tapestry.

Internationally, U.S. policy must adapt to the facts of nonfree competitive life. Different countries play by different rules, and in no case does an open market hold sway, with national governments wholly uninvolved. American-based firms often find that their rivals from other countries, rather than being strictly private businesses, are organizations owned or strongly supported by governments. Boeing goes against Airbus, a firm backed by European governments. U.S. chemical producers making man-made fibers—who must eat whatever losses they may suffer in the market—go against Italian plants which, in hard times, have been run at a loss to preserve the jobs of their employees, with such losses covered by government resources.

Some countries preach free trade for their exports and protectionism for imports, though simple arithmetic shows that the world could not operate if everybody behaved that way. A number of nations subsidize the industries they want to encourage, write or interpret their antitrust laws to favor the home team, and continue to put protective rings around their domestic markets—and then protest the "protectionism" of nations that retaliate.

Private-sector companies must shape their plans accordingly. Capital investments, R&D budgets, and marketing strategies have to fit the facts as they are, not be driven by idealized notions of a world in which trade is truly free and open-market principles apply without fetters. To suggest a specific example, a company might see a way to open up a new technology with a relatively modest research expenditure, and the world might be the better for it, but the company is not likely to follow up (at least not with its own money) if it has to risk millions to put the innovation into production, if another country is prepared to subsidize its own firms so that they can quickly move into the same product line with a lower selling price, and if the rules of trading fail to address those inequalities.

A central fact of the times is that all the leading nations of the free world are trade dependent. Their governments and most of their industries are battling for positions in the world markets. Among the major nations, one-third to two-fifths of the GNP is generated by international business. In the U.S., it is estimated that 70 percent of what we produce is in competition at home or abroad with the output of other nations. Thus, I surely would not propose that the U.S. raise the drawbridge—Fortress America—and block its markets to outsiders. A national policy in our country that failed to encourage two-way trade would produce economic disaster for the U.S. as much as any other nation. All I suggest is that we need governmental policies that respect the realities of trade, unpleasant as some of these may be, and that the private sector and government ought to work together to assure that international commerce is, in fact, equitable if not free.

What all this is saying is that a nation cannot hope to strengthen its competitive position by concentrating on a few industrial sectors and ignoring the general condition of the marketplace, that condition reflecting the past and present efforts of all manner of governmental agencies. It can even be misleading to speak of the subject as "industrial" policy, if that denotes industry as a thing apart, for the problems can be understood only in terms of the economy as a whole, and can be successfully addressed only in that broader framework.

To the extent that a central government can be said to be capable of constructing a successful industrial policy at all—i.e., that it can intervene in ways that might be useful, without making matters worse—the main components of that policy will rest in such places as the Federal budget, where government action makes for red ink or black and determines the extent to which the nation's total resources are diverted from the private sector; in the incentives to innovation and capital formation; in the Federal Reserve System, which can powerfully affect inflation and economic activity through control of the growth of the money supply; and in Federal supplements to state and local educational and training programs, which influence the baseline skills of the labor force. The least desirable steps that might be taken—and some of these could actually set back real progress—would be more bailout bills passed by Congress to save critically wounded companies, or strongly protectionist trade policies.

It would also be a major mistake to run a national policy mostly or entirely based on the technologies that happen to be in the ascendancy at the moment. The technologies that would be ignored might not be truly disposable. While there is lots of opinion on the matter, no one really knows what the right future mix of technologies and industries will be. Within my lifetime the glamour industries have included, at different times, railroads (the coming of the diesel-electric locomotive heralded a new era), nonferrous metals (inexpensive aluminum was a blockbuster development), radio-television, plastics, synthetic fibers, and aerospace, née aviation. None of those today has the celebrity status enjoyed by the newer marvels of electronics, or by molecular biology, but they are no less vital to the nation's continued well-being than was the case when they drew the big crowds at World's Fair expositions.

As great a mistake as any we could make with respect to industrial policy would be to assume that, if we had the right one, it would lead us to quick solutions. The desire to produce a quick turnaround is understandable, but foolish all the same. It ought to be realized that, if it took several decades for world competitive conditions to evolve to their present state, it is likely to take some time to change them again in major ways.

What is needed—and this is where business and government can find common ground for cooperative action—is not a "New Industrial Policy" so much as a new economic attitude, one containing a policy vision broad enough to encompass all of the nation's economic interests. The necessary task is to maintain an economy in which there is a balance among goods-producers and service-producers, and one in which mature, basic industries coexist with young, fast-growing entrants, such that none is made to prosper by denying essential support to the others. There is no argument for particular companies to be preserved, or for the balance among economic sectors to remain fixed, or for every imaginable commodity to be made in the U.S.A., at whatever price, so that it need not be imported, at perhaps a lower price. There is a need, though, for the nation to retain pluralism in its private sector organizations.

To return to the initial point of this chapter, there is much room for better management of government. In pursuit of that objective, it would be helpful to have a mechanism through which the executive branch can obtain a better analysis of economic problems, together with suggestions for action that honor both theory and practicality. The President already gets all the general advice he needs. He and the Congress also receive, from disconnected sources, all sorts of petitions for special help, many of them driven by sectional politics. What is missing, and what the private sector can help provide, is a forum in which knowledgeable individuals can sift through the evidence and the options, ask what the implications might be for various courses of action, and then advise the nation's Chief Executive so that he can make wise choices.

To suggest a few examples, it is not enough in my judgment for the President's economic advisers to tell him that the nation fares best when market forces are left to operate on their own, true as that may be. Also needed are answers to concrete questions. Assume that efficient markets (or the thumb of other national governments resting on the scale of trade) indicate that primary metals can be bought at lowest cost to us if they are made in foreign lands. Is it important for the U.S. to maintain production capacity in basic metals anyway? If so, how much capacity do we need? For all metals, or only some? Should the sewing industries, which have provided entry-level jobs for millions of workers, be allowed to disappear from our shores? If so, what plans can be made for the people who would have held those jobs? Should aircraft and ship production be allowed to decline here on the grounds that we can buy the products elsewhere?

Each of those questions has its own group of stakeholders, but nowhere in government is there a place where the diverse views can be brought together, and the different responses thoughtfully explored. Too often, what passes for reasoned discussion is no more than a smokescreen of rhetoric, hiding groups working diligently to protect nothing but their own interests, as when diplomats talk to one another at a garden party, while the generals draw up the troops into battle lines.

The fact is that there is no single government official or agency with a predominant voice on all issues relating to the economy. Anti-trust officials, mostly lawyers, do their thing without consultation with anyone else. The Departments of Commerce and Labor behave as though they were not the two sides of the same coin. There are dozens of other agencies, each with a piece of the jurisdiction, but nowhere can the people be found who will address the economy as a whole, in terms of establishing the best policy mix. With reference to industrial and economic policy, there is no single agency with jurisdiction in the same sense that the Department of State exercises jurisdiction over foreign policy.

One way to correct this is to establish within the White House a Presidential advisory group including corporate leaders, the heads of key labor unions, and selected cabinet officers. The group should be issue-oriented, have its own small staff to assemble and organize data and proposals, and have opportunities to interact with various agencies of government. The value of the group's contribution ultimately would depend on the quality of the participants and on what the President did with their recommendations. The group itself would offer advice only, and would not have substantive powers—otherwise, the President would rightly be charged with having set up a shadow government not properly accountable to the public.

Such a group would have to limit itself to a few existing or emerging issues, and the agenda would necessarily change with circumstances. High-quality staff work would bring together the facts and analyses, to serve as a basis for dialogue among the industry, labor, and government representatives, pointing toward tradeoffs, concessions, and vision. Ultimately, the process would produce a set of alternatives for consideration by the President.

There would be some issues for which no satisfactory answers could be found. That should be recognized, too. There simply are not good answers for all problems. This approach goes to the fundamental point, though, that we need a better process than we have for dealing with issues relating to our economic performance. If there are not ready answers to many of the issues that need attention, despite all the prescriptions offered by economists, then that is all the better reason to try to improve the way the nation reaches decisions in a case-by-case approach. Perhaps there will come a day when we will pull together all the economic policy functions in one cabinet department, and give the head of that department responsibility for what we might then be willing to label "industrial policy." Placing the Departments of Labor and Commerce under single leadership would certainly be a step in that direction. Until that day comes, though, we need a process that promises to address issues of a kind which now are ignored or touched on only at the fringes.

There is a precedent. In 1974, during the Ford administration, a Labor-Management Committee was created and given official status. The group met with the President on a monthly basis. All members of that group came from the private sector and, while their work drew no widespread publicity at the time, they were a distinguished band. Among those included were the heads of the AFL/CIO, and the unions of steelworkers, auto workers, mine workers, and seafarers. The business group included, among others, the chief executives of General Motors, General Electric, Alcoa, Sears Roebuck, the Bechtel Group, and what is now Citicorp. (The group was later severed from its official White House connection, because of new "sunshine" rules, and since then it has been the private Labor-Management Group mentioned in Chapter Two.)

Useful in its first life, such a White House group could be even more effective now. The need for it is more apparent than it was a decade ago, and the climate is better. It is seen now that the interests of labor and management are largely congruent, and that no industrial policy worthy of the name has a chance for success unless it can rally broad public support, beginning with the people who manage and work in private companies.

The private sector can be effective in such a role only if its leaders bring some objectivity to the table, and present their views with a perspective that deserves general attention. For profit-making businesses and labor unions alike, the easiest task is to lobby for immediate interests, but the steps that will net the most are those that bring about improvements in policy. Those who work in the private sector should not underestimate what they know, or how much help their knowledge might provide. The private sector confronts decision-makers daily with problems that are at one and the same time human and technological, data-based and subjective, and national and international. The people who carry the burden of decisions make their share of mistakes, but at least they have had practice in dealing with all the variables that are crucial to policymaking. They ought to know how to attack problems without complicating them further, and to have a better grasp of what is workable economically than most people who have made careers exclusively in government.

At the same time, leaders in the private sector should not underestimate the difficulties of selling what they know. There is still the feeling that those people who come forward with offers to work with government have a poor grasp of what is politically practical, and are untrustworthy. Sooner or later, when the public requires government to deliver better economic results, government will have to turn to the parts of the private sector where people know how to do that. On an issue of the magnitude of industrial policy, business, labor, and government ought to be able to find common purpose, and cooperate on the process for attaining it.

6

More Justice, Less Law

THE JUDICIARY is the neglected stepchild in the family of government. When the serious business of governance is discussed, it is usually in terms of the legislative and executive branches. Their policies are the ones that affect all of us every day. Their problems are the ones commanding public attention.

The judiciary is meant to be an equal among equals, but in the popular mind it stands apart. It is seen by many as America's national theater. The Colonists used to attend trials as a diversion, and this mind-set is still with us. If something that happens in the judiciary is noteworthy, it is often because it provides comic relief, as with a juicy Hollywood divorce, or high drama, as with a murder trial. The lawyers who make it into the pages of *People* magazine are not the ones who handle blockbuster cases or privotal issues in the law affecting millions of people, but the lawyers caught by the flashbulbs at the end of a celebrity "palimony" suit. The problems of the legislature are day-to-day news, but those of the courts tend to go unnoticed in the media until they provide the stuff of exposés: the TV news special that shows what a mess the criminal-justice system is in, or the revelation that the jury convicted an innocent man, reminding us again that law and justice are not the same thing.

There is no denying that the law can be compelling in its human interest, but the fixation on the judicial system as entertainment is regrettable. It deserves attention for more substantial reasons. Especially in the United States, the judiciary has a role of great importance in social, political, and economic life. Here, more than in almost any other nation, we look to our system of courts to resolve differences among private parties and between the private sector and government. Without a strong, well-ordered judiciary, neither personal liberties nor the organizational structure of American society could survive. The system has served the nation well, but it is not sturdy enough to meet the demands now being placed on it. The judicial circuits are overloaded, and society is asking the system to solve problems it is ill prepared to handle.

Based on experience as a lawyer and a businessman, I believe that the administration of justice will become progressively worse until two conditions are met: the amount of litigation is reduced, meaning that the private sector and government both must turn to other methods of dealing with many conflicts; and the managerial processes of the judicial system are improved. Just as there is room in the other two branches of government to apply principles of management to the public's business, there is room for this in the third branch.

The shortcomings and policy questions are not being ignored within the judiciary itself. They are subjects of lively debate, and have brought forth various schools of thought about reforms and restraints. Derek Bok, Harvard University president and former head of its law school, spoke for many when, in his 1983 annual report to his board, he criticized the American legal system as "grossly inequitable and inefficient," and faulted law schools, his own as much as any, because they train students "more for conflict than for the gentler arts of reconciliation and accommodation . . . [and fail] to acquaint them with the larger problems that have aroused concerns within the society." Well placed as that share of the blame may be, the rest of society has too much at stake to let the law schools shoulder it all. The rest of us are not exempt. A large segment of this problem is a private-sector creation, and useful correctives will have to come from cooperative action. It may be added, not incidentally, that many of the problems of the judiciary, and of the private sector with it, are specifically of business' making.

Private institutions in general and businesses in particular should by all rights be staunch supporters of the judicial system. If business seems less than enthusiastic, perhaps it is because companies have had more days in court than they wished at the invitation of government. The judiciary is not the enemy, though. In the main, the influence of the judicial system on commerce has been overwhelmingly beneficial. Were it not for the court system and its traditions, there would be no competitive-enterprise system in this country. The judicial system has served as the intermediary between the regulators and the regulated, limiting the former as much as it has compelled the latter to perform. It has been the enforcer of antitrust law, and thus the best friend of business in keeping the marketplace open to competition. It has refereed the patent system, providing a strong incentive for the nation's technological advance by securing to inventors a limited-term right to exclusive use of their originality. It has provided the forum for the resolution of disputes between companies, and for clarification of the ground rules for commercial transactions. Most of all, the judicial system has provided private organizations as well as individual citizens with protection against the government itself. There is surely room for improvement here—we are not as free as we ought to be—but it remains true that if the U.S. firms operated under the rules that apply in most other judicial systems with which the world has experimented, the liberties of commerce would be less than they are, not greater.

The problems of the judicial system go back in time. More than half a century ago, Judge Learned Hand said that if he were on the other side of the bench he would "dread a lawsuit beyond almost anything else short of sickness and death." Even earlier, in 1906, the noted judicial scholar Roscoe Pound said in a now-famous address that "there is more than a normal amount of dissatisfaction with the administration of justice in America." Seventy years later, a "Pound Revisited Conference" found the dissatisfaction still there, refocused and in some ways amplified.

To define a problem correctly is to begin to solve it. There are a dozen reasons why the judicial system is in trouble, but mostly they come back to the way the system is managed, and to the expectations society places on it. Without excusing the judiciary from its responsibilities, society has itself to blame for most of the flaws. The courts, after all, have no agenda of their own. They deal only with issues brought before them by others in government or by private parties. If courts are overburdened, it is only partly because of an abundance of criminal cases. The pipes also are plugged with cases brought by lawyers acting on behalf of private individuals, businesses, and government agencies. If courts are less efficient than they should be in dealing with issues, it is largely because of limits imposed by a system the sitting judges did not create and are unable to change except in small ways without outside help. The court system was constructed to meet the needs of post-Revolutionary and early industrial America. It has been expanded but not reformed, and it does not fit the conditions of the closing years of the twentieth century. The principles of justice to which it pledges allegiance are timeless, but the management approach is archaic.

The signs of strain are familiar. Court calendars are jammed. Legal proceedings take too long and cost too much. Lower courts in some cities are so burdened with criminal cases that they have become little more than people-processing centers, moving defendants past the bench, to jail or freedom, with no more than a few minutes to spare for each of the accused. In many civil actions, the only true winners are the lawyers who stretch out the cases through pretrial maneuvering while the meter runs.

Cases can become interminable. Probably the best-known example is the antitrust case against the IBM Company, which carried squadrons of lawyers through thirteen years of continuous work and 66 million pages of documents before a newly appointed assistant attorney general called for a review of the issues, decided that the market was not monopolized and that the Department of Justice probably would not prevail, and dropped the case. In scale and duration, the IBM case is only an exaggerated example of what occurs frequently, in actions pressed either by government against private firms or by company against company.

One factor in the growing unit-size of cases is their technical complexity. The magnifying effects can be seen in today's patent disputes. The first patent case to fill one full volume of court proceedings was the battle over Marconi's and Tesla's inventions in the early days of radio, a case on which the Supreme Court ruled about forty years ago. Contrast that with the records accumulated in a more recent case involving the basic patent rights to polypropylene, a plastic used in appliances, cars, cordage, and other applications. The case began in 1958 and continued through 1982, with three American firms and one from Italy each claiming that its research gave it priority of invention. By the time the dispute went to trial in a Federal District Court in Delaware, the documentation had become so voluminous that engineers had to check the blueprints of the building to make sure that the courtroom floor would hold all the file cabinets. Speak of the weight of evidence. The U.S. patent, first awarded to the Italian firm Montedison, was reassigned as a result of the trial to Phillips Petroleum. That decision was upheld by an appellate court, and the case finally ended when the U.S. Supreme Court declined to hear a further appeal.

The expense of it all cannot be ignored. Not everyone with a legitimate call on the courts' time has the celebrated deep pocket of the large corporation or a Federal agency. While few cases can rival the IBM antitrust action or the polypropylene patent battle, many are prolonged to a point where they require sacrifices beyond the resources of many private individuals and organizations, counted either in time or in dollars. As a practical matter, some people are simply unable to utilize the courts to assert rights that are properly theirs. It is a well-known principle of the law that justice delayed is justice denied. Justice that is too expensive and time-consuming can amount to the same thing.

The rule with jurors is that many are called and few are chosen. As Chief Justice Warren Burger pointed out in his 1981 annual report on the state of the judiciary, less than one-half of jurors required to appear ever serve in a trial, and those who do serve spend up to two-thirds of the time in jury lounges, waiting. There is also the question of the competence of jurors to deal with some of the issues dumped in their laps. One American habit (this is not duplicated elsewhere) is to try a large portion of cases before juries of laymen, even cases involving complicated scientific and medical issues. Thus, we have jurors whose education in biology and physics ended in high school trying to find the meaning and relevance of data fully understandable only to scientists, doctors, and engineers, looking for the fine line between fact and opinion in the testimony of expert witnesses who disagree with one another. The guidance of such cases is often in the hands of a judge whose education in science matches that of the jury. Even in the best of circumstances, the interests of the litigants and the public may be lost in that process.

As for the judges, the best generalization is that they are underpaid and overworked. Even the most diligent among them cannot find time to give many cases the care and thought that is deserved. Early in the 1980s Federal judges were resigning at three times the rate of the 1950s and 1960s. The average age of those leaving was fifty-six, which is to say that the public was losing the services of seasoned judges during ten- or fifteen-year periods in which they would still be in their prime. Most of the resignations relate to pay. Based on the purchasing power of their salaries, judges have enjoyed a steadily declining living standard for several decades. The highest paid are the judges on the Federal bench, and even they now find it difficult to put their children through college. One Federal judge of my acquaintance recently sold his sailboat. It was not a fancy yacht, just a weekend cruising boat for the Chesapeake Bay, but he could not afford to keep it.

Matters are not helped by the fact that a few of the brethren who cling to seats on the bench are incompetent or lazy, or have even become marginally senile. Their jobs are protected by lifetime appointment. In *Beyond the Fringe,* a British revue that made the trip to Broadway some years ago, there was a monologue by a man who wanted to be a judge but "didn't have the Latin for it," and so had to settle for a job as a coal miner. Pointing out the differences in the two lines of work (an absence of falling coal in the lawyers' Guild Hall, for example), he said that when a miner becomes too old or sick or stupid to carry on he has to go, while with the judge there are no such marching orders. That slanders judges as a class, but skewers a few in particular, and woe to the litigant whose misfortune it is to appear in their courtrooms.

The judicial workload has been expanding steadily, with no end in sight. The Supreme Court's docket has tripled in the past thirty years, to more than 4,000 cases per year. The Court is able to accept less than 5 percent of the cases others want it to hear (it is the only court with such control over its agenda), but even then it is clearly impossible for all nine justices to devote close attention to all the cases. They cope by putting strict limits on the time allowed for oral arguments before the Court, by having law clerks do much of the research and drafting of opinions, and by disposing of some cases without explaining their action. This Court has the prerogative, which it uses, of settling an appeal from a lower court with a single word, "denied" or "affirmed." In 1982, the Supreme Court issued 143 opinions (fifty-eight of these in a flurry of activity in the final three weeks of the term), which works out to an average of sixteen opinions for each of the justices.

The lower courts are even more heavily laden. There are ninety-two Federal District Courts staffed by about 500 judges, and about one quarter-million filings are brought before them each year. There is a backlog of nearly 200,000 cases, about three times what it was in 1960. Above the District Courts are the thirteen Circuit Courts of Appeal. There, 144 judges are expected to deal with 25,000 appeals a year, or about 175 cases per man or woman.

Off to one side is a part of the judicial system most people never see or want to see. It deals with bankruptcies, a half-million cases per year. To the other side is the administrative-law structure, another invisible judiciary as far as the public is concerned but a bench that includes more than 1,000 people. Its members are paid as staff members of Federal agencies, but they exercise many powers of judges. They handle an estimated 300,000 cases a year, or more than all the Federal courts combined.

Like the regular courts, this quasi-judicial system can move without deliberate speed. In 1973, the FCC staff moved to lift the license of a Lansing, Michigan, broadcasting company, on grounds that the station operator was not serving the public adequately. As of 1981, the case had progressed through the FCC's review process, and a decision had been made to revoke the license. At last report, a decade after the filing, the case was on appeal to the full Commission. This may not be the end of it, though. FCC rulings may be carried on appeal to the Circuit Courts, and thence to the U.S. Supreme Court. This case may have more years in it.

Beyond all of the above is a much larger judicial sector, the state and local courts. More than 95 percent of all cases that go to trial are handled at this level. Setting aside traffic violations and matters that may be heard by justices of the peace (often nonlawyers), and counting state courts only, we are looking at well over 100 million filings per year. There are also administrative-law judges at the state level, in parallel with the Federal ALJs but two or three times as numerous.

Why is there so much business for the judiciary? Time and tradition are part of the answer. The momentum has been building for two centuries. Alexis de Tocqueville, the French political philosopher who saw America as clearly as any visitor before or since, wrote in the mid-nineteenth century that "scarcely any political question arises in the United States that is not resolved sooner or later into a judicial question." A century before that, in the Colonial period, lawyers were prominent in public affairs. That may help account for some of our historic reliance on judicial institutions to resolve differences that other societies handle in less formal settings. Half of the signers of the Declaration of Independence and about the same fraction of the delegates to the Constitutional Convention were lawyers. Law was the training ground for many early Presidents: Madison, John Adams, Jefferson, Monroe, Jackson.

If the country once seemed to be run by lawyers, it now is overrun by them, in the judgment of many. There are about 600,000 active attorneys in the U.S., or about one lawyer for every 400 citizens. The ratio of lawyers per 1,000 population is twice as high here as in any other leading nation, and three times as high as in most. U.S. law schools graduate more new lawyers per year, by a multiple of more than two, than the total number of lawyers in Japan. Thus appears our litigious streak: It is not that the Japanese, Germans, or others are more law-abiding than Americans (though they may be), but that most of them turn more quickly and easily than we do to private negotiation in preference to litigation. When two Japanese companies have a quarrel that requires resolution, the first inclination of their leaders is to sit down and work out a deal. It is considered bad form to take the matter to court, and that step is rarely taken. The same is true, though to a lesser extent, in Europe. In America, people are likely to sue first and talk later.

It is the way lawyers are trained here. They are schooled as barristers rather than solicitors, to use the British distinction, and do not take naturally to the skills of counseling and mediation. The image held before us is not that of the friend and trusted adviser steering clients away from trouble, but of the hired hand who is an expert at sharpening and dividing issues that already exist, and in dealing with them in an adversarial setting. This is not an entirely fair picture—some of the most effective lawyers in America fit the prescription of counselor and avoid courtrooms entirely—but neither is it an incorrect one. Lawyers in this country have for generations been trained to fight, and it is hardly remarkable that many of them spend much of their time doing so. The opportunities for doing legal battle have expanded continuously, in keeping with the growth of government, its tense relationships with the private sector, and the brawling instincts of many within that sector, versus the government or in quarrels with their own kind.

It stands to reason that with the increase in the size and reach of state and Federal government units there would be more points of potential conflict between government and private citizens or organizations. This alone does not account for the litigation load, though. On a relative scale, government is a smaller factor in the U.S. than in many industrial democracies, and those other countries do not have as great a judicial overburden as we have. What is involved beyond size are the attitudes of people and the changing relationships between individuals and institutions.

With time, the individual has reduced the number of obligations he is willing or able to shoulder on his own, and consigned more responsibilities to his neighbors and to organizations public and private. Reasons for this are close at hand: the greater complexity of life, increased interdependence, an expanding technology that presents people with products they do not know how to fix and with risks they do not know how to measure or counter. Whatever the driving forces, when the individual demands more of government or private corporations in this country, his demand translates rapidly into more work for the judicial system.

It was once believed that the rise in administrative government would ease the pressures on the judicial system. The thought was that agencies would serve almost *in loco parentis,* helping to shelter the citizen from life's risks and harm, clarifying and enforcing the rules for organizations to follow, and thus reducing the calls on the formal judicial system. It has not worked out that way. Government's expansion has been a judicial growth hormone. There have been more review boards and procedures, followed by more compliance hearings, lawsuits, trials, and appeals.

The reason goes back to the operating style of governmental executives and, even more, to the mind-set of legislators. In creating agencies and writing the laws controlling them, legislators have named the problems to be resolved more clearly than they have told their agents how to deal with them. The agencies have been left to find answers on their own, and frequently the judiciary has had to move in to maintain order. We thus may rephrase de Tocqueville: There is scarcely anything that is legislated in America that is not soon litigated.

A current sign of this is the extent to which the courts have gone beyond their traditional role of weighing evidence and puzzling over legislative intent, into the making of law from the bench and the supervision of its enforcement. Today, judges are running prison systems and mental hospitals, issuing edicts to police and fire departments on minority hiring, and redrawing the lines of voting districts. The operations of the Boston school system were for eight years directly supervised by a Federal judge, W. Arthur Garrity, Jr., who assumed that responsibility and issued more than 400 rulings to enforce it, in keeping with a court order that the schools be desegregated. Perhaps such extensions of judicial authority are proper or inevitable, perhaps not. In either event, they blur the separation of powers (why haven't the legislators and administrators done their jobs?) and force the question of judicial competence. If institutions are not well run, it does not follow that judges necessarily have the talent to run them better. The qualities of mind that make for wisdom on the bench may not be those that make for a good school superintendent.

Much judicial action emerges directly from new or relatively new law. I can illustrate with a personal example. One item that crossed my desk every month when I was a corporate executive was a legislative-affairs bulletin, summarizing the state and Federal activities of greatest impact on my company and the chemical industry. In one sample edition, nine topics were covered. Only one of these qualified as "old business" for government. That one had to do with the upcoming monetary and budgetary matters. The other eight emerged from laws that went on the books after I first became an executive, and related for the most part to activities that had previously been subject to fewer if any Federal controls. The topics ranged from new product-liability codes to clean-air and solid-waste-disposal requirements, from patents to payments to foreign-government representatives to secure business, and from antitrust issues to pesticide registration. The covering laws included the Resource Conservation and Recovery Act, the Toxic Substances Control Act, the Federal Insecticide, Fungicide, and Rodenticide Act, and the Foreign Corrupt Practices Act, not one of which existed ten years earlier. This is not a complaint against these laws, but it is worth noting that almost every item in this monthly bulletin was the subject of some sort of judicial proceeding or had been in the recent past. Either government had sued business, or business or special-interest groups had sued government. Whether the difference was serious or minor, it had come to a point where they had to say, "We cannot work this out, Judge. You decide."

As might be expected, many of the lawyers added to the profession in the past twenty to thirty years have gone into corporate employ, with a rapid build-up in the staffs of governmental affairs divisions. At the time I joined Du Pont Company, governmental affairs was a unit of modest size enjoying little corporate status. It operated out of Wilmington, Delaware only, because some people in management continued to resist opening a Washington office. By the time I retired, governmental affairs involved a staff of forty, ten of whom were in Washington, and the company had specialists in various locations tracking state and local issues as well as national concerns. When IBM

was in the throes of its antitrust case, the company's chairman, refer-
ring to his general counsel, Nicholas Katzenbach, said, "Nick has the
only department in IBM with an unlimited budget—and he always
exceeds it." Whatever else the expansion of government has brought,
it has been a Full Employment Act for corporate lawyers, as well as a
boon to the private law firms that many companies retain to handle
litigation or other special work.

Everyone has learned how to use the judiciary, and sometimes
abuse it. Parents have sued school boards for letting their youngsters
graduate from high school as functional illiterates. College students
have sued because they felt professors graded them too harshly. Professors have sued universities because they were denied tenure.
Among the newly skilled in the litigious arts are activists and community groups. They have coupled the law to the tools of television and
press publicity to win their points. Some public-interest groups use the
legal process almost exclusively. As someone has aptly said, the smart
activist long ago stopped lying down in front of bulldozers and started
filing lawsuits.

Like everyone else, they are entitled to their day in court, but what
is of concern is the way the days stretch into weeks and months. More
lawyers have learned the old art of using the courts as the battleground
for a war of attrition. When the strength of the case might not over-
whelm the enemy, these lawyers lob round after round of procedural
mortar fire over the lines in the hope of exhausting and dispiriting the
opposition. What is new is how many have learned that any number
can play this game. Especially when litigants feel strongly about the
outcome, they are often willing to fight far into the night even when
the odds are against them. Whether they win or lose, they entangle the
judicial system in minor matters that advance the law by only the
slimmest of margins, and frequently set the interests of society back a
step or two.

An illustrative case comes from Delaware, where a plan was put
forward in the 1970s to expand and rebuild a network of hospitals that
had been merged into a single Medical Center with one management.
Plan Omega called for the closing of some facilities and the moderniza-
tion of a center-city hospital to provide a limited range of services in the
city of Wilmington, plus construction of a large, full-service facility on
a plot of ground a few miles outside city limits. The suburbs had
expanded in the manner familiar in hundreds of postwar American

urban areas, making an out-of-town location most convenient for a majority of people in the metropolitan area. All of the existing hospitals were in center-city, though. There was none in the suburbs. That provided half of the stage-setting for trouble. The other half came from the fact that the city, again in familiar fashion, was then in economic decline and its population was increasingly becoming older, less wealthy, and more black and Hispanic than the suburban population.

Plan Omega was immediately attacked as discriminatory. City-based groups rallied support from minorities and from the mayor's office, and proposed a counter plan under which the major medical facilities would remain in center-city, with a satellite unit in the suburbs. The hospital board and health planners soon found themselves in court, defending Omega against the argument that the rights of the poor and the elderly, the groups most in need of medical help, would be violated by the "flight" of the hospital to the suburbs. The plaintiffs were not assuaged by the argument that adequate emergency facilities would remain in the city, that transportation among the units would be provided, that the out-of-town location was at the center of gravity of population, and that the proposed "downtown" plan would add about $20 million to Omega's estimated $80 million cost, meanwhile making medical care less convenient for the majority of citizens.

This was a case where there were only losers. After almost a decade had passed, the courts found in favor of Plan Omega and construction was started. The democratic process had been honored and everyone's views had been heard. However, litigation did little to change people's minds. The citizens on each side came out of the dispute about where they had gone in, and meanwhile the world had not stood still. While the case wound its way to its last appeal, inflation did its dirty work. The cost of hospital construction climbed at a far more rapid rate than prices in general. Plan Omega's budgeted $80 million thus became $170 million. The extra $90 million had to come from the community to be served, for the Wilmington Medical Center is a private, nonprofit organization drawing on local sources for its capital facilities.

One has to wonder how often communities pay such a high price in delay and dollars because they thrust on the judicial system problems it was not designed to handle and can resolve only in a laborious fashion. Perhaps the Omega case best symbolizes how little experience most of us have with other mechanisms for solving social problems, and how little trust we place in them.

At times, zealousness alone is enough to keep a dispute before the courts despite repeated discouragement. The Du Pont Company plant at De Lisle, Mississippi, was mentioned earlier in connection with the amount of government regulation of commerce. That same plant was the subject of a round of lawsuits filed by a private organization named Save The Bay (St. Louis Bay, which opens into the Gulf of Mexico). The people in this organization, summer-home owners from the New Orleans area, and mostly retired, did not want the plant in the vicinity. The company took the position that the plant would be neither an aesthetic nor an environmental hazard. It was to be built away from the water's edge, screened by vegetation, and the pollution-control equipment was designed to prevent any harmful quantities of waste from going into the air or the bay. The company had built other plants meeting equally high environmental standards, and had that record to show. The community was generally supportive of Du Pont. The plant meant new jobs and tax revenues for an area in need of both. Local and state authorities agreed with Du Pont's view that a clean environment and the plant in question could coexist at De Lisle.

Save The Bay filed a string of legal actions in an attempt to block Du Pont. They began early in 1975 with a suit in Mississippi Chancery Court against the state Air and Water Pollution Control Commission, to force further public hearings on the waste-disposal permits that authorities had issued to Du Pont. The end of the string did not come until 1983, when a Federal court handed down a decision on an appeal involving the railroad line to the plant. (By then, it may be added, the plant had been built and run for four years, without at any time exceeding the waste-discharge limits.) Other than the court and commission already mentioned, the Save The Bay suits called upon the time and resources of the Mississippi Supreme Court, the U.S. District Court for the Southern District of Mississippi, the U.S. Fifth Circuit Court of Appeals, the U.S. Supreme Court, EPA, the Corps of Engineers, ICC, the U.S. Coast Guard, Harrison County, and, of course, Du Pont.

Save The Bay prevailed on but one point. After the Chancery Court denied the early request pertaining to hearings, Save The Bay appealed and the state Supreme Court reversed. More hearings were ordered. Thereafter, the courts found that the permits had in fact been based on substantial evidence and met the test of law. From then on, Save The Bay lost every round. In this instance, I would not dwell on the costs. Du Pont spent well over a half-million dollars on legal fees, and presumably the bills on the other side were also substantial; but had there been a meritorious issue at stake, this might have been a reasonable price to pay to resolve it. The critical issue here is the amount of judicial machinery and governmental apparatus called into action to consider arguments of little substance, mounted by a small group of citizens lacking the community support to attain their ends by other means. An objective, independent arbitrator could have seen early in the dispute that this was a situation where a company had the intent and capacity to build a plant within the spirit and letter of all the covering laws and regulations, and was under the watchful eye of public authorities who were doing their jobs properly.

To keep the point in balance, it must be added that the tables are sometimes turned and David has just cause to hurl stones at Goliath. The De Lisle example is one of a company that knew what it was doing and was prepared to prove it in court, letting its track record and the evidence speak to the complaint against it. That is not always the corporate mode of behavior. Some business representatives hauled into court leave the clear impression that they think the principal goal of the judiciary is to harass them, and that plaintiffs or judges have no business intruding in corporate affairs.

One judge of my acquaintance is a good witness on this subject, for he has heard a long list of cases involving business in the courts in Delaware, the place of incorporation for many companies. He has seen the worst as well as the best of executives in action, including some who found court proceedings "so far beneath them that they lost their composure.... They came with the premise, 'I know what's right. How dare you challenge me?' as though they were infallible and their own houses were in perfect order." All that need be said about that sort of behavior is that it amounts to contempt of court. (It may prove so by strict legal construction, too, if the business representative has the bad luck to encounter a less forgiving judge than this one.) It also leads to a thought, not lost on this judge or any other, that if courts fail to use their powers of compulsion in the face of such arrogance, some individuals in the private sector will do nothing to correct the problems that brought them to court in the first place. The bigger they are, the harder they can be made to fall. A swollen ego wins no more friends in the executive ranks than anywhere else, and most business leaders are smart enough to know that the buddy system stops at the edge of the law.

Some expansion is needed on the point about the judicial system being used to attain social goals. In one sense, it has always had that function in America. The courts have reflected changes in public views and priorities, even if they have not gone so far as to fulfill the adage that "the Supreme Court follows the election returns." What is under inspection here, though, is something beyond this reactive, deliberative role. This is the notion that the judicial system ought to be an active instrument of change, fomenting it in some instances and blocking it in others, according to ideas of the way the social and economic structures ought to look. To use a homely example, it is one thing to say that mom-and-pop grocery stores have been one of the nicer features of American life, and we should wish them well. This is a social statement with which many of us would agree, especially if we grew up in the days of the corner grocery. It is entirely different, though, to say that mom-and-pop stores ought to be protected by the courts against the inroads of supermarket chains, and that judges have a duty to block mergers and acquisitions that might make it tougher for little stores to compete. There, the judiciary is being asked to put its thumb on the scale of justice to tilt it, toward one kind of private economic unit and against another kind, without a clear legislative mandate and against the probability that the result will be higher costs for consumers, whether they like it or not. There is in this sort of request an impatience with the democratic process and a sense of frustration because the world is changing. "Somebody ought to stop it," is the message.

Maybe somebody should, but "Who?" and "How?" are not idle questions. Arguably, the courts are among the least qualified branches of government to take on the role of social mentor. It is not self-evident that the judiciary ought to determine and enforce social policies when these have been endorsed in no legislative proceeding. No one elected judges to redress the balance among competing institutions and individuals, or to determine the proper composition of the marketplace.

Roscoe Pound spoke years ago about lawyers becoming "social engineers," and he did not mean it as a compliment. In his time or ours, very little could be found in the training or experience of lawyers and judges to suggest that they are better qualified than the rest of the citizenry to decide whether supermarkets are better for society, all in all, than mom-and-pop stores. Nothing in the judicial method equips courts with special wisdom for defining society's broad directions and weighing complex questions against them. To the contrary, as suggested earlier, the courts and the individual lawyers who are their officers are best at pinpointing issues, even splitting hairs, so as to reduce to the narrowest permissible base these areas where decisions must be made. In this sense, it is fair to say that the business of the law is to look at the little picture, not the big one.

The judiciary has nonetheless become a forum for people who clearly are determined to be social engineers, and two areas in which their handiwork can be seen are liability law and antitrust law. While these two are essential areas of the law and are not to be challenged *per se,* at least not by me, their extension beyond classical boundaries is worth more than passing examination.

The history of liability law is largely the story of a steady march from *caveat emptor,* let the buyer beware, to *caveat vendor,* let the seller watch his step. There has been an even wider view that when harm is suffered, someone other than the victim probably is responsible and the injured party deserves to be compensated. Increasingly, this belief has been reflected in legislation augmented by a stream of court decisions.

It is an easy position to defend, at least to a point. The arguments in its favor hinge on the technical complexity of products, services, and modern life in general. In a complex society, each of us is vulnerable to harm due to his or her own ignorance. The more technologically loaded the products and services we buy, the higher our chances of being victimized by fraud or negligence. A nineteenth-century farmer buying a horse could see what he was getting. He did not have to be a veterinarian to look in the horse's mouth and get a rough idea of its age. You cannot roll back the odometer on a horse. I am not able to tell from my own knowledge, though, about the condition of a used car, or whether the new diesel automobile I bought is well designed and properly built. I must depend on the assurances of others that the transmission will not fall out. It is the same in countless other areas of the marketplace. We all look to others for some warranty of performance of the things we buy, and we must largely trust to others for our safety. Thus, when anyone argues that he has been hurt through no fault of his own, there is at least a chance he is right.

That argument does not explain away the mammoth amounts of liability litigation seen today, though. The hazards of being inexpert, and thus not being able fully to protect ourselves by our own wits, are not new. Life became complex long ago, and for centuries people have been obliged to place trust in others. There is a deeper trend at work here, toward the transference of responsibility from the individual to society, whether or not the risks are self-evident and whether the technology is complicated or simple. We have also made it immensely profitable for individuals and organizations to press for as much of a transfer as they can get His Honor to honor. A study of records in Cook County, Illinois, found that in the 1960s and 1970s, the average judgment in product-liability cases was $275,000.

The eighteenth-century citizen was no wiser about his doctor than I am about my automobile (or, for that matter, my doctor). He had no way of knowing whether the doses of sulfur and the bleeding with leeches were helping or hurting. Yet, when it appeared that harm had been done by doctors, there was not the quick recourse to courts of law that we see today. Until comparatively recently, it was rare for a patient or a surviving family to sue a physician. In contrast, malpractice suits are commonplace today and the dollar awards to plaintiffs are so large that physicians typically must pay from $10,000 to more than $50,000 per year for insurance. Experts in the health-care field report that there is also a thriving business in defensive medicine, with doctors calling for a wider array of tests and treatments than they think medically necessary for their patients, simply to defend themselves against the potential charge that they did too little. The exact cost of defensive medicine is unknowable, but estimates put it in the range of $5 to $10 billion a year in the U.S.

Liability litigation has reached a point in our society where it has turned into a form of income-redistribution system. Each patient pays doctors and hospitals slightly higher fees than would otherwise be charged so there is enough money to put into an insurance pool, so that substantial sums can be dispersed to injured parties in the form of court-awarded damages or out-of-court settlements. The same process obtains with other purchases ranging from toys to toasters. The settlements reported in the press may be laid against the maker of a product or the supplier of a service, but there is no getting around the fact that the cost is really paid by the public. Eventually, that cost ends up in the price of products and services.

Also to be remembered is that there are many transactions today in which an individual of ordinary experience is no better or worse qualified than his great-grandparents to evaluate risks and avoid life's ordinary hazards. Yet the different generations have not addressed responsibilities in the same way. We apply far more stringent conditions today than our predecessors did. Consider an example of the kind that frequently appears in court: a toy for infants. Mothers of normal intelligence have always been able to see that dolls with small buttons for eyes may be a choking hazard for babies. The assumption of nineteenth-century society was that mothers should be careful and make sure the buttons were tightly sewn on so that babies could not pull them loose. Today a judge and jury may well hold the doll's maker negligent for putting such a product on the market. A court may also consider the fact that some mothers are mentally retarded or blind, and therefore may not easily be able to exercise normal caution. The "reasonable person" test of law has at least in some measure been replaced by an "unreasonable person" rule.

Caveat vendor has come to mean that seller no longer meets buyer only in the relatively simple context of contract law. ("We trade in good faith. My claims are honest. You know what you are buying. We agree on terms.") There is as well an overlay of fiduciary responsibility, with seller under some obligation to care for the buyer and even anticipate his possible shortcomings. That may apply not only when products are used as intended but also when they are abused, even against repeated warnings. The law has gone beyond the old roller skate on the front walk, followed by the delivery man's suit for a back injury. Today, a car is speeding and a tire explodes; the tire-maker is sued—even though the car was going 100 miles an hour and no one in his right mind supposes that the tires were designed to stand such stress. A skier goes off an icy trail, hits a tree, and sues—despite posted warnings of poor conditions and admonitions to "Ski at your own risk." Children obtain some blasting caps used to detonate explosives, these go off, some youngsters are maimed, and there is a suit against the blasting-cap makers—even though the blasting caps were labeled as hazardous, were sold only to people trained in their safe use, were supposed to be kept under lock and key, and had been stolen. The justification given is that the law should protect not only against intended use but also against anticipated use even if it is irresponsible.

A distinguishing feature of liability actions today is the chainlike search for someone to make good, to cover the damages, to pay the price for wrongs. A basic tenet of law is that when one party is clearly responsible for harming another, the negligent party must pay. It is not always possible to pinpoint blame, though, and the trend in law has been to help claimants by lifting some of the burden of proof from their shoulders, spreading it more widely among potential defendants. If Sears, Roebuck is not found accountable as the seller of the lawn-mower, maybe the manufacturer which supplied Sears will be; if not (or also), the claim may go against the firm that made the engine. It has become routine for liability cases to have a chain of defendants, each with counsel to protect itself against the bill for damages landing in its lap. Naturally, that becomes costly.

Today, there are doctrines of strict liability and of shared liability. The first holds that if someone is hurt by your product, you may be liable even if you were not negligent. The second says that when several people offer the same product, each supplier may be responsible for damages even though the person who has been hurt cannot identify the company that supplied it. Such a case occurred with DES, diethyl-stilbesterole, a fertility drug prescribed in the 1950s. Twenty years or more later, some daughters of DES mothers developed cancer, and the drug was declared to be the cause. There was no way to prove which of the makers of DES had supplied the product the mothers had used, so the court ruled that the plaintiffs could collect from all companies, in proportion to each one's share of the market.

Added to all of this is the opportunity for class-action suits in which individual plaintiffs, perhaps none of whom has been harmed enough to make a suit worthwhile on his own behalf, are joined in a single suit. If the class is large enough, the prize for victory may be huge even though no one plaintiff stands to win much, and the temp-tation to litigate becomes irresistible, if not for the individuals in the class, then for the lawyers. Under a contingency-fee arrangement, plaintiffs' lawyers are paid only if they prevail, but the fee is substan-tial, commonly one-third of whatever they win. Lawyers thus have every incentive to encourage clients to sue, the more the merrier, ei-ther by banding into a single suit or by becoming links in a chain of cases against a single defendant. In one example of mass litigation, two young lawyers in the Midwest sought out hundreds of individuals to represent in suits against the A. H. Robins Co. of Richmond, Vir-ginia, for a product that allegedly had caused infections and miscar-riages. Their law firm won settlements of about $10 million from the company, mostly without having to go to trial, and obtained fees for the firm of more than $3 million.

The scales are tipped against defendants. There are no matching incentives for them. They cannot hope to win, only not to lose too much. The most that potential defendants can hope to collect are some of their own court costs and legal fees, and often not even that. The lopsided nature of the contest is enough to keep the courts choked with suits for damages, some of them pathetically weak and many of them meant to extort settlements from defendants.

A textbook view of antitrust brings forth the image of the Department of Justice breaking up illegal monopolies, moving against price-fixers, preventing cartels, and otherwise doing the necessary work of keeping the marketplace open so that competitors will not be driven to the wall by unfair tactics. The excesses of the past—the trusts of the early Industrial Revolution, their discriminatory pricing and predatory practices—were more than enough to justify the creation by Congress of stern laws to curb such abuses. The most venerable laws anchoring the philosophy of antitrust action in this country are the Sherman Act of 1890 and the Clayton Act of 1914. Supplementing these are other pieces of legislation, including the Federal Trade Commission Act (also 1914), the Robinson-Patman Act of 1936, and the Celler-Kefauver Amendment put on the Clayton Act in 1950.

Correct as the standard view may be, it shows but a fragment of what has taken place under the rubric of antitrust. Over the years, many actions filed by government have been meant not to maintain the playing rules but to determine economic outcomes. These have been efforts to limit the unit size of businesses and tilt the marketplace away from concentration toward small, decentralized structures. Further, most antitrust actions have not emerged from the Antitrust Division in Justice at all, but have been launched either by private organizations against one another or by the Federal Trade Commission. It is these supplemental roles of antitrust, rather than the classical mission of the Justice Department, that account for an overwhelming majority of the cases.

The FTC comes into this picture through its dual jurisdiction: The commission was set up to police the channels of trade through investigation and regulation, but it is also permitted to pursue antitrust actions as a remedy for what it regards as wrongdoing. It has carried out its work so diligently that it has often been accused of going overboard and using the mantle of public interest to shape the marketplace in ways that do not draw public enthusiasm. This reached a point in the

1970s where FTC won the dubious title in Washington as the "national nanny." By all odds, the largest filers of antitrust suits, though, are businesses themselves, not government agencies. When Senator John Sherman put forth the proposal that such private actions should be permitted, he predicted that this avenue would rarely be used. He was wrong. Private filings have grown steadily in number, and now outrun the other kind fifteen to one.

What drives the plaintiffs are the prospects for improving their own market positions at the expense of other companies, and the lure of treble damages. The multiple-damage remedy provides that in some circumstances successful plaintiffs may recover for the actual damages done to them, multiplied by three. The multiple-damage remedy is found in only a few places in common law, chiefly in antitrust but also in some cases involving patents and banking affairs. A piece of antitrust heavy artillery, it has become an American institution. It is not an American invention, though. It originated in English law. The English did away with it a long time ago, however, because they wanted to put a stop to the bounty-hunting. In the U.S., the multiple-damage provision survives, and if it has done some good, it also has given rein to some of the least admirable qualities of the legal profession.

Antitrust actions are intercompany weapons in the competitive wars of high technology. A direct hit can remove a rival's advantage held through patents. The patent system is meant to award inventors a legal limited-term monopoly, but it is against the law for patents to be used to sustain business practices or positions that constitute illegal monopoly. If Company A can convince a court that Company B is engaged in an illegal attempt to monopolize, then the court may compel B to license any patents that are critical to that attempt. Company A, having invested nothing of its own in the process of invention, would then have B's technology available to it. Not surprisingly, when a company chooses to assault another's patent position, it is commonplace to include an antitrust charge in the complaint.

Private antitrust actions can be enormously useful devices, helping to keep the market open, forcing the courts to double-check the validity of patents, and keeping competitors on their toes. Those worthy objectives are often lost in the shuffle, though, in a surfeit of suits that yield no gains in the form of increased competitiveness working to public advantage. In the words of one law professor (now a Federal judge), Richard Posner, "Students of antitrust laws have been appalled by the wild and woolly antitrust suits that the private bar has brought—and won. It is felt that many of these would not have been brought by a public agency and that, in short, the influence of the private action on the development of antitrust doctrine has been on the whole a pernicious one." Business, as has often been observed, is frequently its own worst enemy.

Not that it lacks for outside antagonists. The particulars of some FTC cases are worth noting for what they reveal about the politics of antitrust. In 1972, the FTC staff brought a "shared monopoly" charge against four large breakfast-cereal makers: Kellogg, General Mills, General Foods, and Quaker Oats. Instead of alleging that the four had conspired to fix prices, FTC tried to show tacit collusion. A key feature was the contention that these companies had unleashed a steady stream of new products for the supermarket shelves, meaning to discourage would-be competitors and thus to keep themselves free to charge higher prices. The case dragged on for nine years. Quaker Oats was dropped en route and the remaining three continued the battle. At the conclusion, an administrative-law judge ruled that the companies had not enjoyed "monopoly profits" and had not kept competitors out. In point of fact, one of these competitors, Ralston Purina, had gained impressively in its market share. The judge said the defendants had every right to compete by offering new products, and he found it ridiculous to prosecute companies for offering too much variety to consumers. The defendants estimated the cost of defense at about $24 million, not counting whatever allowance one wishes to make for the time and energy of their managements.

One can only wonder why such a case was pressed at all, except on a "no fault" premise of antitrust law that says the top three or four companies in an industry ought not be allowed to hold more than a stated percentage of the market even when there is no showing that competitors and the public have been harmed. That view enjoyed a certain following in political and judicial circles, and once seemed to have been the guiding philosophy of the FTC chairman. The issue is whether, in effect, successful competition is to be permitted only if it does not become too successful, and whether the law should be stretched to put a cap on corporate size or market share.

Another case with the same earmarks was filed by FTC against eight oil companies: Atlantic Richfield (ARCO), Exxon, Gulf, Mobil,

Shell, Standard Oil of California, Standard of Indiana, and Texaco. The case was brought in the wake of the OPEC oil embargo and the round of price increases that took place in 1973, when "Big Oil" was even more of a whipping boy than usual. FTC charged the eight with collusion in pricing and marketing practices. Eight years later, after extensive pretrial investigation of company records going back more than two decades, FTC dismissed the complaint. The commission did not admit that its charges could not be made to stick, but merely said that the case had gone on for such a long pretrial period that it was no longer in the "public interest" to continue it. Another factor may have been a change in command that had been announced in FTC, with the chairman from the 1970s being replaced by a new man who had a much more conservative view of the limits that ought to prevail in FTC activism. In any event, there was abundant evidence, both when the case was filed and during the investigative stage, of the competitiveness of the oil business. The industry shows few of the signs that would be apparent if it were in the hands of price-fixers—vast profits for conspirators, with their rivals on the ropes. The large producers have been surrounded by dozens of other firms of small and medium size, and, despite the meteoric rise in world petroleum prices, U.S. oil companies have not been exceptionally profitable. Their return on stockholders' equity averaged about the same as that of industry in general during the 1970s. To the extent that there was evidence of market prices being manipulated over the years, the controls in question came from government itself rather than the big oil companies.

One conclusion that comes out of both these cases is how little attention antitrust law gives to self-correcting powers of a competitive economic system. There has been great concern that where a few firms have a large market share, they will use all sorts of tactics to keep competitors away: tie-in sales, boycotts, predatory pricing, acquisitions of key suppliers and customers, and the like. In practice, though, there are few times and places where such tricks can be made to work successfully, because potential rivals are not quiescent. They will not take it lying down. Not only do they have options, but the options also are often more effective than any antitrust action government can mount.

This point has been well made by Frank Easterbrook, a law professor at the University of Chicago: "In most cases monopoly power is self-correcting. If one firm discovers an inelastic demand for some product, so that it can charge a monopoly price, other firms will make the same discovery. There is nothing like self-interest to concentrate one's attention on such things. Other firms will enter the market (or expand their production) and erode the position enjoyed by the first. Persistent monopoly power should be rare indeed; rival firms should outstrip courts in rectifying monopoly."

The final case to be mentioned here involves Du Pont, and once again an element in it was the De Lisle, Mississippi, plant. (It is not coincidence that one industrial unit is cited three times in these pages to make related points about the ways the judicial system and the private sector come together: once in reference to governmental regulatory activity, once because the judiciary was called upon to resolve a plant-siting dispute brought by private parties, and once more in this realm of antitrust.) De Lisle is one of several Du Pont plants making a product called titanium dioxide. Most people have never heard of titanium dioxide, but nearly everyone uses it. It is the white pigment used in paint (in lieu of lead, whose toxic properties are well known), plastics, and numerous other products, including toothpaste. There are six U.S. producers of titanium dioxide. Du Pont has a larger market share than any of the other five, having climbed to the top position in the 1970s.

It may have been that rise to the top that offended FTC. In any event, in 1978 the agency staff, with approval of the FTC commissioners, filed an "attempt to monopolize" charge against Du Pont under Section Five of the Clayton Act. The complaint used language that has become familiar to all who read newspaper accounts of antitrust filings. It asserted that the market was relatively concentrated (true—the top four producers accounted for more than 80 percent of the sales); that there were high barriers to entry (not so—other firms could muster the money to build a plant if they wanted to, and purchase technology elsewhere or develop it on their own); that Du Pont had refused to license competitors to use its manufacturing technology (true—Du Pont had the best process, had paid an awesome price to invent and refine it, and intended to make the profits from it); and that Du Pont had followed a pricing strategy (putting the price low, not high) so as to frustrate new entries and old competitors (untrue—the facts showed that competitive conditions had determined the market prices. There was no evidence that any competitor had been harmed by unfair practices). FTC proposed draconian remedies: Du Pont should be forced to grant licenses royalty-free to its competitors, and should sell off two of its four production plants, one being De Lisle. The divestiture would have covered more than $300 million of Du Pont assets.

This was obviously a test case brought by the FTC staff in an attempt to extend the making of law by a regulatory agency. Whether or not the FTC staff went looking for a case to make its point, one can only infer that the objective was to use antitrust law to make the marketplace conform to someone's idea of what was right, regardless of what competitive conditions and technology had created. There was no legal or factual base of support for the "attempt to monopolize" charge. The events that had occurred were not Section Five violations. In the trial, no competitor came forward to claim harm or to support the FTC complaint in any other way, though the agency had subpoenaed documents from several companies associated with the product. Weak as the case was on its merits, though, it was of consuming interest to industry and the legal profession for a special reason: It raised a fundamental challenge to invention and technological development. Du Pont had built a better mousetrap, the world was beating a path to its door, and FTC wanted to knock Du Pont back so that other mousetrap-makers would have an easier time in the market.

The trail to Du Pont's technology had been long and difficult. For decades, everyone had made pigment from titanium ores by using an extractive process based on sulfuric acid. That works well, but it creates severe pollution-control problems. For every ton of finished product, there are three and one-half tons of spent sulfuric acid to be disposed of. In the 1940s, Du Pont began working on a different process based on chlorine. This reduces the waste-disposal problems, but introduces chemical-engineering headaches of the worst kind. Chlorine is used at high temperatures, and in that condition is among the most corrosive materials known. Ordinary process equipment—pipes, valves, containers—disintegrates in days or weeks. A minor amount of one impurity, vanadium at five parts per million, turns the final product yellow instead of white. Some ore stocks contain large amounts of iron, which is easy to remove via the sulfate process but difficult to remove in the chloride process.

Du Pont had no exclusive on the chloride route. Anyone who wanted to develop the technology was free to do so. The basic reactions had long been in the chemical literature, and there were no composition-of-matter patents protecting the products of the reactions. A few companies elected to try the chloride route and discovered, as did Du Pont, that they had to risk millions of R&D dollars and accept more millions in operating losses during the debugging period of production start-up. In Du Pont's case, an ordinary plant start-up may take three or four months; the first chloride-pigment plant took three years, by the end of which period the operating losses added up to nearly as much as the capital investment in the plant.

Where other companies failed or turned away, Du Pont finally succeeded. It found a way to make high-quality pigment safely, efficiently, and reliably, and its chloride process became the lowest-cost manufacturing process in the industry. That is why Du Pont could make a profit at a low selling price. Du Pont put the chloride process in existing plants and then began drawing plans for an entirely new site, De Lisle. That new plant thus stands as a symbol of a technological triumph that predates its construction by many years. At the time the case was filed, De Lisle was still unfinished. Among its other demands, then, FTC was trying to force the company to give up the most modern production unit in the industry before getting a pound of product out of it.

Du Pont won this one. An administrative-law judge, Miles Brown, ruled against the complainant after hearing the case. An appeal was filed with the commissioners, and the commissioners ruled against their own staff. The final opinion was written by Commissioner David Clanton, who alone in FTC had voted against the original filing. By the time all the evidence was in and reviewed, his reading of the merits of the case had been vindicated and his position had become the unanimous finding of FTC. Commissioner Clanton's written opinion makes two points of pivotal nature about the limits that ought to apply in law: Actions ought to be judged by what the evidence shows has happened, as versus attributed motives; and it is not government's role to dictate a course of action for private firms, or impose theoretical models of the marketplace, but only to rule on whether actions have conformed to laws. As was said about another case by a senior circuit judge, Ben Duniway, "The antitrust laws do not grant the government a roving commission to reform the economy at will."

Had the FTC staff prevailed on this action, the judicial system would have sent two different messages as chilling to society as to private industry: "No fault" antitrust is to be the nation's policy toward dynamic, successful companies, and prudent men should not risk their own money to build better mousetraps. A certain outcome of "no fault" antitrust would be to bias R&D in large companies away from entrepreneurial projects unless government was willing to pay for them. The larger the risks, the greater the anti-innovation bias.

This case had extraordinary importance for Du Pont because for years this company has been the industry leader in research, with technical budgets running into hundreds of millions of dollars per year. Dozens of man-made fibers, plastics, and other modern products of the chemical industry, now made by many different producers, originated in Du Pont laboratories, and almost all of the science and engineering behind them was paid for with company money. The implications are far more general, though. No corporate management could justify putting stockholder dollars and good technical talent behind innovative projects if competitors had only to wait until the mousetraps were built and debugged, at which time the government would intervene to pave a broad new avenue to the doorsteps of the noninnovators and stock their shelves with the same products.

This chapter opened with the observation that the quality of justice would be strained until ways were found to manage the judicial system better and to reduce the amount of litigation going on in it. It should by now be clear that efforts in both directions might be well placed. If there is good news here, it is that some of the best minds in the legal profession have been turned to the need for judicial reform. Law schools, private foundations, state and Federal units of the judiciary, and business organizations have brought forward numerous proposals, some of which have already been given field trials. Enough has been learned from the experiments to suggest that the outlook is far from hopeless. It is thus in order to look at the major ideas about judicial reform and the prospects for at least a few of the companion steps needed to lighten the judiciary's burdens.

To the credit of government, much of the pressure for change and many of the ideas have come from its own ranks. Beginning with the top, there has been action by the Judicial Conference of the U.S., the senior policymaking body of the judiciary. The conference is headed by the Chief Justice of the Supreme Court and includes twenty-seven Federal judges from around the country. Beneath this is the Administrative Office of the United States Courts, created by Congress to do what its name implies: run the system. This, too, has been working to improve the judicial system, as has an in-house organization of the Department of Justice. Created in 1964, this office in Justice was given expanded duties in the 1970s under two attorneys general, Edward Levi and Griffin Bell. It has generated plans for various court reorganizations and for a revised Federal Criminal Code. At the state level, there is now a National Center for State Courts, which Chief Justice Warren Burger has complimented as being one of the truly important developments in judicial administration of the twentieth century. The private sector has been active as well. An Institute for Civil Justice was established within the Rand Corporation in 1979 to do empirical analyses pointed toward more efficient and equitable civil proceedings. The Brookings Institution, Ford Foundation, National Association of Manufacturers, Chamber of Commerce, and Business Roundtable all have sponsored projects on improving the judicial system, as have various law schools. Finally, there have been various special studies conducted by judges, academicians, practicing lawyers, and governmental representatives. Three notable ones were conducted in the 1970s under Professor Paul Freund, Professor Maurice Rosenberg, and Senator Roman Hruska.

At the risk of distorting the work of these groups by summarizing too briefly, their efforts mostly point toward two simple objectives: to reduce the workload of higher courts and speed the disposition of cases by improving court administration, staff work, and the distribution of cases; and to develop new (to our society, at least) pathways for resolving differences, the last to be done by providing incentives to use alternative forums and by changing attitudes of lawyers as much as clients, going back to precepts taught in law schools.

The main thrust in judicial management has been to expand the bench and back it with modern tools, including executive services. The number of judges has been increased. In 1978, 140 new Federal judgeships were authorized by Congress. More primary and appellate courts have been established at both the state and the Federal levels. Eleven of the Federal circuit courts now have paid executives to relieve judges of administrative work, and there are pilot programs to provide similar services in five of the district courts. Judges speak of going "on line" with computer-based systems for record-keeping and case management. With some enthusiasm, they report that their opinions no longer are delayed by the wait for "hot metal" typecasting, but go straight into print from the courts' word-processors. Technology has come to justice.

Several additional changes in court alignments have been proposed. One suggestion made years ago is to create a National Court of Appeals, interjected between the Supreme Court and the circuit courts. The Supreme Court would serve as gatekeeper, like Saint Peter, letting some cases through the turnstile to the high court, and turning others back for decisions by this new lower court. The idea has been recommended by both the Freund Committee and the Hruska Commission, but is at a standoff. Its supporters believe such a new court would free the senior justices to concentrate more on pivotal issues that are "ripe," as lawyers say, for review. Detractors claim it would only add costs and delay without easing the load. A more limited change has been proposed by Chief Justice Warren Burger, to set up a panel of twenty-six judges from the circuit courts to hear and decide all cases that reflect intercircuit conflicts. He sees this as a temporary move, and one that would relieve a substantial amount of the pressure of the Supreme Court's workload.

Another thought is to create new courts to handle regulatory review matters. The cases in question would be those stemming from laws dealing with safety, health, welfare, and pollution control. A variation of this is the call for "science courts" to put decisions in some such cases into the hands of people with technical training, as against lay judges. The reasoning behind such proposals is that the issues involved can best be resolved by specialists who concentrate on particular problem areas in society, as Federal judges do not. The argument has it that the legal issues in such conflicts are often trivial and need not consume the time of Federal courts, while the factual questions are beyond a nonspecialist's comprehension.

Last in the string is a recommendation to abandon diversity jurisdiction. This is the practice under which litigants from different states bring their case to a Federal court for adjudication even though the issue falls under state rather than Federal laws. Diversity jurisdiction is a holdover from an agrarian past, when it was felt that "hometown" judges might look with more favor on their neighbor than on outlanders. Removal of such cases to a Federal court was seen as an equalizer. In today's more mobile and presumably less parochial society, it is surely questionable whether diversity jurisdiction is still needed. By the estimate of the Chief Justice, its elimination would cut by one-fourth the workload of the Federal district courts, and by one-sixth the work of the appellate courts. Those cases have to go somewhere, though, and the question dividing opinion on this proposal, as on the other two, is whether the judicial system overall would better serve the public if the change were made.

My own view is that the most productive route is not for Congress to add layers to the system by creating more courts. Nor is it to create a quasi-court structure with scientists and engineers trying a rule objectively on issues which are technologically loaded, but which usually prove to be entangled with social concerns as well. We should concentrate first on steps to fill in the weak spots in the existing judicial system, to allocate the available resources in better fashion, and to equip courts with more and better staff support.

As a place to begin, the Federal bench should be managed as a unified resource, rather than as a confederation of independent districts and circuits. The talents of judges and the needs of the regional courts should be matched without allowing geography to be a binding constraint. In the present system, the Federal district and circuit courts operate with much autonomy and not much interchange. The presiding judges parcel out case assignments among their own justices in whatever way they think best. The statutes permit Federal judges to be loaned to other districts or circuits, but in practice there are few calls for this. Judges mostly hear cases in their own regions, and do not specialize in particular types of cases.

The thought of doing something about this is not exactly new. William Howard Taft, when he was Chief Justice more than a half-century ago, suggested that when the dockets became unbalanced it would make sense to move judges from one district to another to work off the backlog. He was not able to sell the idea. There were too many problems, notably transportation, communications, and a preference of judges for home and hearth. They were afraid that Taft would turn them into gypsies. The idea has fewer drawbacks now than it did then, though, and perhaps its time has come. It could be used not merely to balance the workload but also to apply the talents of judges to cases where they can do the most good.

The weakness of the present scheme is the premise that judges are interchangeable—that is, equally good at handling all of the kinds of business that come before a court. They are not and there is no way to make them so. Thomas Jefferson may have been the last man trained in the law who could aspire to command all of the useful knowledge around him and not embarrass us by his audacity. No one in Chief Justice Taft's generation could have been so bold, even if equipped with Jefferson's mind. Today, it would be laughable to suggest that a judge who has spent years becoming steeped in the intricacies of tax law could by sheer intellect and application make himself the equal of any of his peers on every other kind of complex case that might come before him, whether it dealt with antitrust, patents, or environmental law. Even assuming that superior intelligence were universal among judges, they still would display differential experience, talent, and interests. Logic would seem to say that judges ought to be assigned selectively, but for the most part the system discourages this. It tends not to draw on its own strengths.

We should not make too little of the point about interests: This can make a difference, hard as judges may try to keep such feelings out of their cases. As an example, there are a few judges who like to handle patent cases and do an exemplary job with them; but most judges will go to almost any length to avoid them. When assigned a patent case, they carry through, but not happily. Forum-shopping is frowned upon (and widely practiced) by lawyers, but a lawyer would be less than human if, given a chance, he did not try to steer his patent case away from a judge known to hate them. Usually, though, he does not have that option. In some districts, the presiding judge assigns the cases, and in many districts the cases are drawn by lot.

What might be substituted for the haphazard system that prevails is an arrangement under which sitting judges are assigned to cases, across district lines where necessary, through a process that gives priority to demonstrated skills. This envisions no major change in structure. The district and circuit courts would stand as they are. Routine cases would still be routinely assigned. However, for more complex cases, the presiding judges would turn to a data bank with records on all sitting judges, akin to the skills banks used in industry, to find the best judge to assign. The presiding judge would be under no compulsion to follow this lead, but the option would be there.

There could of course be complications in such a national approach. Some quarrels among districts are predictable, along with horse-trading of the kind baseball teams do. A presiding judge might be able to borrow a relief pitcher only if he were willing to give up a utility infielder for the duration. Court dockets are no respecters of anybody's lineup, and there would be times when no amount of optimizing by the court's computer would yield a perfect batting order. There could be times when any presiding judge might have to settle for a second- or third-stringer. Unless there were restraints, the most competent judges in the liveliest areas of the law would be asked to spend unconscionable amounts of time on planes and in motels. Yet these are not insurmountable problems. They arise routinely in the private sector with the periodic realignments of management and staff. They can be dealt with to the satisfaction of all if managed with reason and balance.

The question is not whether such an approach is problem-free and perfect in result, only whether it is better than the approach we now use. What it would offer is access in an antitrust case to a judge who has unsnarled such cases before, and in a technological case to a judge who has some skill in untangling science and engineering puzzles. The hope is that complex cases of every variety would be administered more firmly, move more rapidly, and be less likely to wander off on tangents. Litigants who had more confidence in the judges they faced might be more willing to have cases heard without juries, and perhaps to settle their differences en route, either of which would be a big time-saver. Decisions would be more secure against appeal, a time-saver for other courts. One thinks twice before taking an appeal from a decision by a judge who has been upheld in similar cases. Appellate courts are known to give heavy weight to such a judge's analysis of both the evidence and the relevant law, as by all rights they should.

The vision of a national judiciary can also be used to strengthen the Federal bench when new judges are to be appointed. With a central index of information on court loads and staff capabilities, the Attorney General, bar associations, and others advising on appointments to the Federal bench would have a common base for reviewing possible candidates. That guarantees nothing, to be sure. Good advice is not always taken—the President makes the appointments with the advice and consent of the Senate, and the traditions of that house award a courtesy veto power to Senators from the areas where the nominees live. Ordinarily, Senators give the nod to people in their own states, and, however able the candidates may be, they may not be the people best fitted to the courts' current needs. Senators might not be much swayed by "Yes, but" arguments about the need of the judiciary to meet some greater good, but the suggested approach would at least generate some pressure for the selection process to give greater weight to the question of balance on the bench. It ought to improve the chances that new judges would not just clear the first hurdles, winning blessings from Senators and the bar association, but also meet the test of providing talents that fit well against the foreseeable problems of the courts. Again, it is a question of better, not best. Currently, when a district or appellate court is especially in need of another judge good at antitrust work, it is only a nice coincidence if the next judge appointed fills that bill.

It sets people's teeth on edge to say this, but if the door is opened to change in the way the judiciary is managed, the opportunity should be used to establish a performance-review system for judges. Both the judges and the people who come before them would benefit if there were periodic reviews to point out areas for improvement of performance or broadening of skills. Judges are a protective lot, and wary of moves that smack of outside meddling in their affairs. They should be sensitive, for our protection more than theirs. However, what is indicated here is not an outside review but an inside one. Appraisals would be made by senior judges. There would be no threat to the integrity of the judiciary, nor would judges be diminished as individuals. No one's stature is reduced when others help him or her do a better job. If good management calls for monitoring of performance in other walks of life, this should apply no less to the judiciary, where in many jurisdictions the job appointments are for life.

There remains the problem of cases where few if any judges are expert, the ever present example being disputes in science and high technology. Currently, as judges are quick to admit, the questions that arise in such cases can easily put them in impossible positions. As was said by David Bazelon, former Chief Judge of the Court of Appeals in Washington, in connection with a case involving EPA and the Ethyl Corporation, the judge who tries to play amateur scientist may state conclusions that sound plausible but are in fact simplistic, and hence probably wrong in some critical dimension. The judge who tries to brush up on his neglected science background is moving in the right direction, and he can find college extension courses tailored to that need. All must beware of the ninety-day wonder, though, and it would be the height of folly for a judge to suppose that he can learn enough, quickly enough, to rule on a fine point in physics or chemistry. Yet some cases hinge on just such niceties.

One alternative to this quandary was brought forward by the late Judge Harold Leventhal of the Circuit Court for the District of Columbia. He suggested that judges not try to rule on technical detail but concentrate instead on the process by which various positions have been established by the litigants. Are the positions defended by work that is orderly, logical, and complete? Are the key elements clearly identified, and separated from points that are secondary? If necessary, the bench can call for help from the litigants. Judge Henry Friendly, in an opinion on one patent case, went out of his way to thank an appellant for providing the court with a brief titled "Background Chemistry." This is not the sort of brief-writing that is taught in law schools, but the judge presiding in this case admitted he would have been helpless without it.

This still falls short, though. In the best of conscience, a judge could still reach beyond the limits of his competence, award victory to the side which had the most impressive-looking charts and numbers (but maybe the weaker argument), and, at the least, drive the case to an appeal. What is needed is a way of fortifying judges with the services of scientists, engineers, or others with specialized backgrounds, while keeping the control of the courts in the hands of the judges. This can be done if such specialists are employed by the courts and report directly to the judges rather than to any of the litigants. In other words, create a staff that is professional and disinterested. The trouble and expense involved in developing such in-court services could be justified if the skills were available throughout the judicial system— i.e., if the system were managed as a unified resource.

There would be concerns about a warping of the judicial mind. (Who are these counselors whispering in the king's ear? Are they manipulating him? Are they really in charge?) There is a way to prevent both that distortion and the fear of it, and that is to make the technical staff's reports a part of the public record. Certainly, it is poor economy as well as bad jurisprudence to deny the courts the kind of help they need to reach decisions that are as solidly based as possible.

The nation could pay more attention to the quality of its judicial work if it paid its judges more. Salaries in the judiciary are a disgrace. The pay falls so far below any reasonable mark that the consequence, barring change, will surely be the loss to the nation of the services of many of the people best qualified for judicial work. As a result of some recent pay increases, the average salary in the states for general trial judges is $45,000 to $50,000, and for state supreme-court justices, about $55,000. Federal judges receive about $70,000. These are not poverty wages, to be sure, but the pay is only a fraction of what most candidates for judgeships could make in private practice. Further, except in some of the lower courts, judges cannot make extra money by practicing law on the side. Judging is a full-time job, and there are obvious problems of conflict of interest. While judges may look resplendent in their robes, there is not much glory in the work except for the nine on the Supreme Court. All suffer financial punishment for their public service, with few perquisites in return.

This is not to suggest that pay is everything and that we ought to feel sorry for judges because they make less than corporate counsels and partners in big law firms. However, anyone who thinks judges are overpaid can look at the arithmetic and see that from the 1930s to the present, while almost all groups in society have been improving their living standard, judges have been marching steadily to the rear. In the 1930s, salaries of Federal judges were tax-free. If their pay scales had moved upward simply to offset the taxes they now pay and to match inflation, with no real increase in discretionary income (a poorer deal than anyone else in our society has been asked to accept over the past half-century, with the possible exception of schoolteachers), judges today would receive nearly twice what they are paid.

It helps not at all to suggest that judges make as much as other people in the public sector, or to remind ourselves that there are plenty of people who would gladly take a seat on the bench. Some of these are individuals wealthy enough not to have to care about the money. Are we willing to turn over crucial powers in society to people whose chief credential is a large bank account? Others who want the job are young and ambitious and see a judgeship as a steppingstone in their careers. Even if they are competent, they will not stay for long, and one must question putting even the right people into the right bench for the wrong reasons. There are also some wrong people. More than a few of the willing candidates are lazy lawyers who look upon a judgeship as a sinecure. Above all, the job calls for energy and a lively mind.

There is a political instinct, backed by no logic, to keep the pay of Federal judges on a par with those of Congressmen, and the pay of state judges on a level with the governors' cabinet officers or senior aides. These are different lines of work, though, and there is no reason for linkage. It is important to keep the main point foremost. What matters more than anything else is whether the judiciary can attract and keep top-quality people. The system is entirely dependent upon the intelligence, integrity, and judgment of the men and women on the bench. That combination of talents is always in short supply, and whatever works to reduce the pool of candidates meeting these criteria works against the public interest. If there are reasons to change the pay of legislators, as I have argued earlier that there are, this is a separate matter.

What we should look for in the judiciary is candidates with a genuine love for the law, who wish to serve because they genuinely understand the importance of the law in society and want to be part of a useful effort. The present package of pay and benefits unquestionably drives some of these people away from careers on the bench. It takes nothing from the people now serving (most of whom are better than society has any right to deserve, considering the way we treat them) to say that the system ought at the least to neutralize the incentive of pay. We do not want to create a bench padded with people who are there for the money, but neither can we afford a bench weakened by the absence of people who could not afford to take the job.

Justice would move more swiftly and equitably if judges took a firmer hand in managing the flow of cases. There is no justification for most cases dragging on year after year, complicated though they may appear to be. Cases could be handled more expeditiously if a few of the procedural rules were changed, and if courts were equipped with specialized staffs to help with complex cases. The most effective single step would be to put limits on the discovery procedure. As it stands, discovery is a classic case of reform run riot. A relatively recent arrival on the judicial scene (it dates from 1938 changes in the Federal rules of civil procedure), discovery allows a liberal collection and exchange of information before a trial begins. It is a good idea because it helps keep trials short (well, shorter) and avoids guessing games ("What are those fellows going to spring on us next?"). Trial by surprise makes for good television drama, but it does not produce more equitable decisions. In theory, discovery should also save money. It is less expensive to scour records in advance and take depositions from individuals than to take testimony in court from a long list of witnesses, hoping that one or more of them will cast light on the facts of the case.

Discovery does not save money, though, nor does it save time, at least in many instances. It has been turned from its initial purposes into an open-season hunting license used to call forth gigantic amounts of information, most of which, experience shows, has no bearing on the issue in question. Much of what it produces is trivial and redundant. Nicholas Katzenbach reported that in the IBM antitrust case some officers of the company were deposed five, six, or seven times and were repeatedly asked the same questions, including some that would have been expected only from a reporter for a high-school newspaper ("When did you become chairman?").

The element of greed has injected itself into discovery proceedings. Taking depositions is a relatively easy way to make a lot of money. Federal District Judge John Grady, speaking of cases in his court, estimates that one-half of pretrial depositions are conducted to generate legal fees rather than to benefit clients. Lawyers and clients who want to play games with discovery should be penalized by being forced to pay their opponents' expenses whenever the courts determine that the discovery requests were misleading and had no solid justification. There would be fewer fishing expeditions if the fishermen had to pay for the trips.

The worst situation of all is created by cases of bare-bones pleading, where there is no case at all until discovery makes it so. Someone believes that wrong has been done but is not sure how and why. He files suit alleging a violation of law, offering few if any facts to back up the charge. Then he demands all sorts of information from the defendant, saying in effect, "Judge, I can't get my evidence because he's got it hidden in his files." The theory is that if you ransack enough closets you will find a skeleton or two; interview enough people, and somebody's tongue will slip. Thus, the first set of interrogatories is followed by a second set, then a third. Weak cases produce massive discovery.

Limits ought to be placed on this form of warfare. The quality of judicial patience has been strained. Plaintiffs need the help of courts to get their hands on relevant materials, but strict tests should be imposed by judges to be sure the quests are relevant. Bare-bones complaints should be reviewed by judges in preliminary hearings, and if a judge finds nothing more than suspicion standing behind the plaintiff, the complaint should be tossed out. If the beginnings of a solid case exist, then the court should provide the full privilege of discovery; but again there should be a limit. If after a reasonable time discovery has failed to generate significant evidence, it should be cut off. Courts have more important work to do than to carry on interminable cases of indeterminate merit.

"Loser pays" is not a bad rule to impose more generally in civil actions. It is a tradition in this country for each side to a dispute to pay its own lawyers' fees, but there are many costs to consider—document fees, travel expenses, payments to expert witnesses—above and beyond the billable hours of the lawyers. These costs are far from trivial, but only rarely can the party who is successful in court recover more than a portion of them. Especially if you are a defendant, you can win the case in court and still lose it at the bank. To level the scales, the U.S. should adopt the practice followed in many other nations and have losers recompense winners. If both sides knew that the courts had lost patience with fun and games, and that the costs of their excesses would henceforth fall on themselves, they would be less prone to avalanche discovery proceedings, stalling tactics, and similar frivolous actions.

It is not considered polite to talk about this, but there clearly is such a thing as a strike-suit bar, and it is time the legal profession stopped tucking it away like the drunken old auntie in a third-floor bedroom of the family homestead. The "strike-suit bar" consists of lawyers who stimulate litigation to earn fees, usually awarded by the courts. In most cases, the named plaintiff has no substantial interest in the merits of the case. The lawyer is the real party in interest, and his interest is in fees. This branch of the bar adds to the burdens of the judiciary without redressing genuine grievances.

At times, even legitimate cases get out of hand, as with one recent private antitrust suit in the paper industry. U.S. Judge Joseph McGlynn, Jr., was so appalled by the size of the fees sought by the plaintiffs' lawyers—out of a settlement of about $50 million, the lawyers asked for $20.3 million in fees—that he cut their award by about four-fifths. The event that caught the judge's attention and triggered an investigation was a petition by one of the plaintiffs' attorneys protesting the fees asked by others on his own side. Before issuing his own opinion, Judge McGlynn had the benefit of a lengthy report prepared by a law firm not previously involved. This firm had been brought into the case by a group of plaintiffs to audit the size of the fees being asked. "What we found was ugly," a senior partner in that firm was quoted as saying. "Like sharks in a feeding frenzy" was the comment from another lawyer.

There are at least two ways to curtail these shenanigans: Reduce the profits of the lawyers, and give their clients another way to proceed that will be more equitable to them. The lawyers in the strike-suit bar defend their actions by insisting that they really are doing a form of public-service work: They permit people who are not wealthy to assert their rights, and smaller companies to keep themselves from being bullied. This tends to constrain people who might otherwise do intentional harm. Rather than argue with that theory, perhaps we should take the strike-suit bar at its word, but sharply limit the size of fees the lawyers are permitted to collect, especially for class-action and antitrust cases. Judges have considerable discretion in determining fees, and should use their authority to clamp down on what can only be called lawyers' avarice.

The companion suggestion is to apply more broadly the principle that undergirds workman's-compensation cases. An employee injured on the job does not have to prove that it was his employer's negligence that caused the accident. He does not have to go to court and stand the risk that he may come away empty-handed if a jury decides against him. If hurt, he is entitled to collect, but the offsetting fact is that the amount provided by workman's compensation is limited. The objective is to provide him enough to pay his medical bills and return his lost wages. Neither employee nor employer is expected to "come out ahead."

A modified version of this could be applied in such areas of liability law as medical malpractice and exposures to toxic substances. A patient would not have to prove that the scalpel slipped because the doctor was overtired, or that the hospital dispensed the wrong medicine, only that there was injury traceable to this piece of medical attention. Victims of environmental hazards would only have to show that they were harmed and that the cause was these hazards, rather than some other source that yields similar symptoms. They would not be obliged to identify a particular manufacturer to which blame clearly could be assigned. A court or review panel would then have to deal only with the question of amount: "What will it take to make this person financially whole again, so that he will not be burdened with expenses he did not bring on himself?"

We have only scratched the surface in better court management, but when all is said and done the judicial system is incapable of resolving its problems by itself. It is not the courts but others who are responsible for the judicial workload, and for many of the system's shortcomings. Courts are asked not only to do too much but to do things they are poorly set up to do. To use a distinction offered by former Attorney General Edward Levi, we have asked judges to stop being dispute-solvers and become problem-solvers. The courts have not usurped this power so much as they have had it thrust upon them, by Congress, by governmental agencies of every kind and size, by litigants, by social reformers, by us.

Whether ideas for improvement surface within the judiciary or close by, most of them cannot be put to work without the approval of people outside the system. The recommendations of the Chief Justice and his colleagues on the Judicial Conference go to Congress, which can turn them down. Higher pay for judges, specialty staffs for the courts in complex cases, the rewriting of criminal codes and liability laws to achieve greater consistency and equity, the broader use of the workman's-compensation approach—in each of these, the judiciary is at the mercy of state or Federal legislators for money, approval, or both.

The same holds for some other changes that have been proposed in the private sector. For example, many of us concerned with the workings of the patent system believe that a large slice of its problems would disappear if the United States shifted the basis on which it awards patents. Currently, the U.S. will grant a patent only to the individual who can prove he is the true inventor. This is not always easy to establish. In some other countries, the patent goes to the first person to file for it, a far easier point to decide. With rare exceptions, patent reviews show, the first-to-invent and the first-to-file are one and the same person. A change to a first-to-file system therefore would work an injustice on very few. What this change would do, though, is simplify the work of the courts by stripping away all manner of contests over priority, trials that tend to be distinguished by much wrangling over who did what research and when. Courts would then only have to deal with the much easier questions of who won the race to the door of the Patent Office, and whether an invention meets the test of patentability (the idea must be nonobvious, and not the sort of minor modification one would expect to occur to any craftsman in the field). The courts cannot go to a first-to-file system, though. That takes an act of Congress.

Change on a broader base will come only if we are prepared to challenge the adversarial system at its core—that is, only if we are willing to look upon courtroom trials as the last resort and not as the first thing that comes to mind. This is beginning to happen. Trials are being stopped in midstream, and cases are being settled short of trial through settlements. A celebrated case in point is the resolution of the Federal government's case against AT&T, which was in trial in 1981 when a consent decree was worked out by the chairman of the company, Charles Brown, and the Assistant Attorney General. This is the agreement under which AT&T divested itself of the Bell System phone companies, and kept its manufacturing and research facilities, Western Electric and the Bell Laboratories. As an offset, the corporation is now allowed to compete in new areas of technology that had been out of bounds to AT&T because of an earlier antitrust decree. In another much-publicized case, senior executives of IBM and Hitachi worked out an agreement to resolve a case against the Japanese company, centered on a charge that IBM's confidential technology had been stolen. With the settlement in hand, IBM dropped its civil suit.

Alternatives to litigation are becoming commonplace. In terms of costs, time, and outcomes, private parties are deciding that they will be ahead in more cases if they stay out of court entirely and resolve their differences privately through some form of mediation or arbitration. That idea is catching on rapidly. A 1981 survey of the American Bar Association found more than 140 alternative programs in operation around the country, and the number seems to grow steadily.

The American Arbitration Association reports that it typically takes less than five months for an arbitration to move from a filing to an award, or one-quarter of the time it takes to move a case through a Federal district court. Mandatory but nonbinding arbitration has been tried in three judicial districts in Pennsylvania, Connecticut, and California. The parties to a suit are obliged to go before panels of three arbitrators, after which, if not satisfied, they can pursue the case to trial. Experience has shown that about four out of ten cases end in arbitration; of the remaining six cases, many are settled in some other way en route, so that only a few end in a completed trial.

Arbitration is not suited to every dispute, but there are numerous other options. California has been experimenting with what has become known as the Rent-a-Judge program, under which parties to a suit agree to hire a judge at their own expense to hear their case. His findings carry the weight of the decision of a regular trial court, and are subject to the same appeals. The advantage is that the trial can take place promptly. Several states, including Minnesota and New York, have set up mediation centers. Neighborhood Justice Centers were set up in the late 1970s in Los Angeles, Kansas City, and Atlanta.

The laymen who served as mediators managed to resolve about one-half of the cases brought to them, which in effect means several thousand fewer cases going to court each year in those three cities alone. There is a National Institute for Dispute Resolution, which is a clearinghouse of information on alternatives to litigation, and on the success of same. There is a Center for Public Resources, which offers judicial panels including some of the best-known names in the law, to sit as neutral advisers or judges in "minitrials." One law professor, Frank Sander of Harvard, has suggested that the courthouse of the future will have many doors, bearing such labels as Arbitrator, Mediator, Ombudsman, and Malpractice Panel, as well as Courtroom. He and others have begun to train their students accordingly. Most accredited law schools now offer one or more courses to introduce students to the arts of counseling, catalogued in proper educationese as "dispute avoidance skills."

Most encouraging of all, there is a growing inclination in both the private and the public sectors to give these alternative pathways a chance. People are learning to differentiate between disputes that can best be resolved out of court because the disputants see the issues clearly enough by themselves, and those that belong in court because they require control under formal rules of evidence and procedure, or because they involve questions of legal interpretation. There is a mounting casebook that suggests that the results in private proceedings can be fully as equitable as those dispensed by judges and juries, and that often there is no route that works better than having the parties to a dispute simply talk out their problems by themselves, with no one in the judgment seat.

There is no question that expense is driving many people to search for the simple solutions. Whatever the incentive, it works. TRW, Inc., and Telecredit resolved a patent-infringement difference in a two-day hearing conducted in private before a neutral adviser. After each side had made its case, the president of Telecredit and a vice president of TRW worked out a compromise settlement in half an hour. The savings in legal fees are estimated at more than $1 million. TRW has used the same approach in a dispute with the National Aeronautics and Space Administration. Aetna Life and Casualty Company turned to a Washington-based organization named Endispute to review some of its pending cases and see if they could be resolved in some manner other than trials. Many more such examples can be expected in the future.

The pressures for change are being felt inside private corporations as well as outside, and are reflected in new job descriptions to go along with the old title of Corporate Counsel. Top managements have become sick and tired of the protracted nature of litigation, of its burdensome quality and unsatisfactory results, and are looking inside their companies for people to help them address problems in better ways. What today's CEO needs in a large corporation is not just a general counsel of the conventional model, an individual well versed in law and skilled at directing cases. The executive needs that at a minimum. What he wants even more is someone closely familiar with the business who can tell him when he is headed for mistakes, and save him from them. The trend in staffing the post of corporate counsel is to find someone halfway between a business executive and a practicing lawyer, with a real gift for anticipating outside reactions to inside actions, plus the negotiating skills to help company departments see, if not the errors of their ways, at least the risks. Often, the individual who fits those specifications is also the person the company wants running its public and legislative affairs. Thus, it is becoming commonplace to see the title "Chief Counsel and. . . ." In Du Pont, Citicorp, and General Motors, the top legal spot is now filled by such an individual, and more examples are being added each year.

What lies ahead for the judiciary is anybody's guess. Its problems have been marked for years, but have not captured widespread public attention. Nor have they gleaned much political sympathy. Among the slowest-moving bills in the legislative hoppers are those that have to do with judicial affairs. Federal criminal-code reform measures that were being discussed in the early 1970s were still being discussed a decade later, but had not passed into law. Judicial salaries, as noted earlier, have languished for years in the hands of legislatures, not because the judges have been forgotten but because the lawmakers have made deliberate decisions not to have the living standards of judges keep pace with the rest of society. There is nonetheless the ferment of change within the judiciary itself, partly driven by outside criticism but no doubt also a reflection of the performance review judges give themselves. They, too, are dissatisfied and eager for change, and the leading voices for reform and improvement of judicial management practices are steadily building a following within the legal profession. It seems to me that thoughtful support from the private sector can be useful and timely.

It surely would be wrong to suggest that the private sector has finally "got religion" and from this day forth will truly be a friend of the court, *amicus curiae*. It is not just by accident or inertia that most law schools still train fighters and are shifting only a little toward counseling. The schools know their market, and fighters are what the market still hires. Certainly among businesses, and to a lesser extent in other parts of the private sector, there remains a large segment that believes the courts exist to be used in every sense of the word. At least a strong minority—no one knows how large, but it must be substantial, judging from behavior—continues to live by a "take no prisoners" ethic. Mediation and compromise are regarded as signs of weakness. Real men sue; they don't settle. In this view, the adversarial traditions of American law exist for one good reason: to separate winners from losers. Most of those people are not likely to change, but so be it. The world can move forward without them. There is within the private sector a growing interest in a less hostile environment for business and government as they come before the judiciary, and for business versus business. This is only practical, given the conditions that now apply, for today an unremitting drive always to be the winner at law will produce nothing but losers all around. There is in the private sector a growing interest in the administration of justice, based on a recognition that the judiciary's problems sooner or later become business' problems. Self-interested and cost-conscious as this may be in its origins, it is nonetheless a welcome trend. Properly channeled, it can add useful support for programs aimed at better management of the judicial system, and lead to still wider use of alternatives to litigation.

In attempting to help the judiciary manage itself better, business is well-advised to enter the arena with caution. The suggestion that the private sector has potential contributions to make will be interpreted by some as an attempt to skew the judicial system to selfish ends. Images dance in the head: Business offers to help in the name of public service, and then rolls its Trojan horse through the judicial gates; once inside, a cargo of malefactors is disgorged to put the torch to antitrust laws, scoop up more wealth and monopoly powers, and otherwise destroy whatever is left of democratic practice. Not only is that a possible reaction; it is the prediction of some business critics in government, law schools, and elsewhere.

They can relax. Nothing of the sort would or could happen. Neither the judicial nor the legislative branches would let it occur. The idea greatly exaggerates the power of business, not to mention the stupidity of its leaders, for such a course of action on their part would be suicidal. They along with everyone else stand to gain from efforts to improve the judiciary that are conducted out in the open, at arm's length. Thus, business should make it clear that it is willing to let people look inside the horse.

7

Don't Shoot the Messenger

MY FIRST exposure to the press, showing it at its worst and indispensable best, came when I was an eleven-year-old boy and my family became part of what was to become a pivotal First Amendment case decided by the U.S. Supreme Court. One day in my father's dry-cleaning shop on East Franklin Avenue in Minneapolis, from a position out of sight, I listened as a thug threatened my father for refusing to bow to the orders of a price-fixing syndicate with mob connections. My father was a Lithuanian immigrant, self-educated, with a deep belief in a man's right to make his own way in the world. He and his business partner had decided that the time had come for them to do their own dry cleaning on the premises, instead of sending the work to a shop authorized by the Twin Cities Cleaners and Dyers Association. The association's bully had come to explain one last time that this little shop would do no such thing.

The syndicate did not deal in idle threats, and it was not squeamish about tactics. Earlier, someone had broken into our shop and put sulfuric acid in the dry-cleaning fluid. One morning soon after my father was given his final warning, which he ignored, four enforcers appeared. They pistol-whipped my father and sprayed acid around the shop. My father suffered head wounds, and thousands of dollars' worth of customers' clothing was damaged. The police were called, but made no arrests. The Minneapolis dailies briefly reported the story and dropped it, never printing the names of the assailants. A complaint was lodged with the county attorney asking for grand-jury action, but nothing happened.

The friend who came forward was an unlikely one, a man named

194

Jay M. Near, editor of a poisoned-pen newspaper called the *Minne-apolis Saturday Press*. Jay Near was a bigot and scandalmonger, a spiteful man who despised Jews and blacks almost as much as corrupt politicians and police. What attracted him to my father's case was the fact that Near saw this as a chance to take on many of his favorite enemies.

The *Saturday Press* went after everybody: the chief of police, the mayor, the county attorney (Floyd Olson, later three-term governor of Minnesota), the Minneapolis dailies ("disgustingly flabby" . . . "I'd rather be a louse in the cotton shirt of a nigger than be journalistic prostitute"), gamblers and gangsters used as enforcers, and Jews ("I simply state a fact when I say that 90 percent of the crimes committed against society in this city are committed by Jew gangsters. . . . It was a Jew who employed a Jew to intimidate Mr. Shapiro and a Jew who employed JEWS to assault that gentleman when he refused to yield to their threats. . . . It was a Jew who left $200 with another Jew to pay to our chief of police just before the last municipal election . . . ," etc.).

The official response to all of this was to gag the *Saturday Press*. The police chief tried to remove it from the newsstands under a local ordinance against corrupting the morals of children. When that did not work, the county attorney moved against the *Saturday Press* under a 1925 state Public Nuisance Law. Olson asked a court to stop the newspaper from publishing because it was "malicious, scandalous, and defamatory." It was all of that and more, and the county attorney might have added that the paper also got the facts wrong much of the time, though in this case most of what it said was true. The issue, however, was not how nasty or intemperate the *Saturday Press* and similar papers were (many other "sheets" were produced in those days), but whether and under what conditions the Bill of Rights permits prior restraint. Can a publication be silenced because it outrages the sensibilities of a community or a judge? The Minnesota law held that it could. The court shut down the newspaper, and the Minnesota Supreme Court affirmed the lower court's order. As it progressed from there, the case drew attention and supporters including, on Near's side, two more unlikely bedmates: the very liberal American Civil Liberties Union, and Colonel Robert McCormick of the *Chicago Tribune*, a powerful publisher not usually remembered for liberal ideas. McCormick joined the team because he could see the potential effects of gag rules on his own paper, and wanted no part of that. Thus, *Near v. Minnesota,* as a case before the U.S. Supreme Court, was no longer a little local story but an issue commanding national attention.

The Supreme Court threw out the Minnesota statute as unconstitutional. What the Court said, in effect, was that even a "rag" has a right to a voice. If those it attacks can show that they have been harmed by untruths, they can collect after the fact on a claim for libel, but neither they nor a community may shut down the presses because a publication is regarded as generally offensive or even disgusting.

Near v. Minnesota is now a legendary case. Much of the present protection of freedom of the press hinges on it. The presiding Chief Justice, Charles Evans Hughes, later said that *Near* was the high point of his career. Numerous subsequent cases have used *Near* as a precedent, most notably the Pentagon Papers case in which the government tried, without success, to prohibit the *New York Times* and the *Washington Post* from printing a purloined Pentagon study on the U.S. involvement in Vietnam.

To close out the story here, the *Saturday Press* had done its job. Before it was silenced, it had succeeded in arousing public indignation. The dry-cleaning association was charged with illegally attempting to restrain trade through price-fixing, and its attorney was disbarred for criminal activity. The police chief was called before a grand jury and eventually was forced by pressure to resign from his post, though the grand jury did not indict. One of the men involved in the beating of my father spent four years in prison. I had the satisfaction of testifying in court to help put him there. The *Saturday Press* is long gone, but the Shapiro cleaning establishment is in business to this day, and doing dry cleaning on the premises. A few years ago, I shared my recollections about this case with Fred Friendly, the distinguished journalist and former president of CBS News. He has since captured the whole story in fascinating detail in a book, *Minnesota Rag.* It ought to be mandatory reading in journalism schools.

It could profitably be read as well in schools of business and law, and in other places where people who are not going to be journalists think about the role of the Fourth Estate. The lesson of *Near* is that the importance of a free press is demonstrated not just when journalism is behaving at its best, but sometimes when it is seen nearly at its worst. To go one more step, the cause of justice and public service falls to shrill voices such as the *Saturday Press* only if the rest of the community, the media included, has behaved irresponsibly. It behooves us all to see that the media, no less than the government, are as good as we can make them.

This ought to be kept in mind as a challenge to the negative attitudes that persist on both sides of the border between the media and the rest of the private sector. As has been true of business and government, business and the media have confronted each other like soldiers in a civil war, forgetting that they are countrymen. In view of the growing attention of the media to economic and business affairs, and the need for such attention, it is time to take another look at that relationship. Not to go into overblown explanations, but anyone paying attention to the world can see that much of what happens today that is important or at all interesting happens at an intersection of politics and economics. Although trade and commerce do not often make exciting headlines, in this area as much as in public-policy matters there is a civic necessity for a broad-based understanding of relevant trends and events. Such an understanding will exist only if it is generated by mass communications. From the side of business, surely, it makes no sense to continue the hostilities. For business' story, the media are multipliers, and indispensable for dispensing facts and figures that business must get before the public. Plain and simple, business needs the media's help. It is time for cease-fire and truce talk.

The charges and countercharges that divide business and the media are mostly familiar, and thus need no more than brief review. Journalists are believed by many businessmen to be biased (on the liberal side, of course) and inept. They are said to reach for headlines instead of a balanced story. They rush to judgment, fire cannonloads of half-supported charges without concern for the wounded left lying in the ditches, and use the First Amendment and "absence of malice" to excuse their mistakes. Often, they cannot distinguish between reporting and editorializing, or between informing and entertaining as functions. Some journalists are advocates who never allow facts to get in the way of their ideology. Some are openly dishonest: they will run stories they know to be not true. Most of them suffer from a herd instinct. If one says a nuclear reactor at Three Mile Island is about to melt down and cause a holocaust, they all say so. Most are functional illiterates in economics and technology. In those areas and others, they are easy marks for those who want to manipulate them, and most of the manipulating is done by the "antis" of the world, "the nattering nabobs of negativism," as they were called by Spiro Agnew at a happier time in his life, before his own crime led to his being defrocked as Vice President.

In the spirit of equal time, the journalists must be given their chance. Journalists claim that many of the people they try to cover (they single out business executives as especially guilty) are inaccessible, close-mouthed, and narrow-minded (i.e., interested only in issues that directly affect them.) There is a belief that the heads of big companies have enormous power and privilege, and with that goes the proportion of duty that William Shakespeare applied to royalty: As more is given to kings, more is expected of them. Most businessmen, though, fall short of noble conduct. With politicians, they share an instinct for lying to the press when it suits their purposes—and seem not to see this as the same as lying to another human being. The business idea of communications, journalists allege, is to try to put a good face on bad facts, to use language to deceive more than inform, and to try to use the media to gain power by manipulating the marketplace. When matters get out of hand, business leaders hide behind their public-relations spear-carriers ("flacks") so that they can avoid further contact with people they cannot control. According to journalists, business executives often hold a thinly disguised contempt for mere reporters, regarding them as frivolous lightweights who do not work very hard or know very much. Perhaps the most common charge against business leaders is that they are hypocrites: The ones who are loudest in preaching for free enterprise and open competition have next to no interest in a free play of information in society, and no understanding that their opinions, like everyone else's, have to stand testing in the competitive marketplace of ideas. Still living in the era of the titans of industry, thinking themselves infallible, business leaders expect to be heard but not challenged.

All those charges are true for specific cases, and false as generalizations. Not much that is useful will come out of a discussion here in the spirit of "Yes you are," "No I'm not." Call that a draw. It might be helpful, though, to look at the mission of the media and their coverage of private-sector organizations, and then consider what is being done about the problems, or could be. The conclusion I reach, going through that drill, is that the news is getting better. Much foolishness has been committed in the name of freedom of the press, and as much in the name of executive omnipotence. Those are hardly original observations. What is more pertinent is that people on all sides of the issues acknowledge past mistakes and are working to correct them. The harshest critics of the media are not outsiders but people in the media themselves. In the past ten to fifteen years, journalists have done as much to retimber their own house as have the people in any other craft or profession. The same shift in attitude can be seen on the other side: People in business have also been rethinking their posture, and facing up to shortcomings. The stereotypes persist on both sides, but they no longer are deserved.

What is the business of this business called the media? Insofar as news is concerned (setting aside the entertainment function which is often the main business, especially in broadcasting), its essential jobs are to ferret out facts, record events, and provide perspective on institutions and trends. Of all the assorted missions associated with journalism, the most fundamental is simply to show the world as it is, warts and all, and that is what the press seems to do best. Though some wish to assign them greater tasks, most journalists do not see it as their job to reform the world or any of its institutions, with the possible exception of their own. Neither do most of them see it as their duty, as journalism professor and former TV newsman Elie Abel puts it, "to clap hands."

The press still errs. There are occasions when some of its members behave despicably. Mostly, though, as reporters and editors go about their daily chores, they are acting not as filmland villains or heroes but only as people holding up a mirror to society. What applies to the press applies as well to other public media—magazines, television, and radio. They, too, have shortcomings, but they, too, can claim that when their people are engaged in serious journalism, the picture they paint is a reasonable facsimile of the real world. (Excluded here is practically all of TV drama and comedy, which continue to present a picture of business as the natural home, as one magazine article summarized it, of "crooks, conmen, and clowns." The fiction writers' description of business—and, for that matter, of journalism—rarely bears much relationship to reality as that word is used anywhere east of Sunset Strip.) When the news media fall from grace, perhaps the best assumption to make, safe until proven wrong, is that what is missing in the equation is not morality or high purpose, but information or possibly experience. In any case, the failings of the media are no excuse for failings elsewhere, or for opposition or obstruction. People who do not like the message have no call to shoot the messenger.

The media look upon private organizations as not much different from public ones, and that view is understandable. Business' turf is not completely private property, in the same sense that a man's home is his castle. For all large institutions, the fact of life is that outsiders have come inside the castle walls, not to visit, like Goldilocks, but to stay. For a private corporation, the two tenants who will not be evicted are the government, which long ago took up residence in one wing of the castle, and the media. My point is that this second tenant has as much right there as the first. Its presence ought not just be tolerated but welcomed because, without the help of the media, private organizations cannot reach their own legitimate goals, and neither can society.

The media influence the people whom the private sector needs and wants to reach. Not only is that influence felt directly through the coverage given to news and views; it is also felt indirectly through the impact of the media on governmental policy and law. Thus, there is a pair of good reasons for the private sector to think seriously about its relationships with the media. Whether a private organization is concerned with its own communication objectives, trying to get people to hear what it wants to say, or is worrying instead about what the government is going to do next, it is best to keep the mind and the intercom-telephone lines open to all wings of the castle.

There is a continuing debate as to how much power the media really have in the counsels of government. Some contend that the media do little more than serve as intermediaries between government and citizen. Claims beyond that, we are urged to believe, are only static from journalists trying to convince us they are more important than they really are. Others say it is foolish to suppose that, and believe the media are truly movers and shakers, powerful forces that help determine the agenda of politics and alter the outcomes. The bond between media and government is so strong, according to this view, that, in the words of one of the deans of the Washington press corps, Richard Strout of the *Christian Science Monitor,* "It can be argued that we are part of the government."

The middle ground says that journalists do put some torque on policy but do so more as followers than as leaders of events. Only rarely do the media ride on the front edge of the wave, initiating political action, championing reform. The media usually come into the middle of the debate, stirring themselves to widespread coverage of issues only after other groups in society have been involved for a year or two, and often much longer. Moreover, if media coverage then displays some preconceptions about big corporations, these usually turn out to be no different from the preconceptions the public has long held about corporate institutions. What comes to the surface is what has been lying below.

Consider as examples the issues mentioned in earlier chapters, and currently being heavily covered by the media: environmental protection, product safety, occupational health, international competitiveness, and the job outlook in the U.S. Each of these was an object of concern, research, and pleas for action reaching into some of the offices of government long before it became a "media issue," meaning a subject commanding general attention from newspapers, radio, and television. The media did not create these, but what they did was to pick up the signals and turn up the volume.

Still, the media have influence of a sort, and, given their scale and presence in the policy arena, it could hardly be otherwise. The Washington press corps is the example to use, because Washington has become the center of gravity of the news business in this country, replacing New York City. Thumbnail numbers make the point: 3,000 different news organizations; more than 4,000 journalists holding credentials for the House and Senate press galleries. The publication *National Journal,* which does its homework with great thoroughness, estimates the total number of "legitimate journalists and news writers" in Washington at 10,000. No corps that large and active, with access to the levers and buttons of government, could be devoid of influence.

In a perfect world, reporters and editors would cover economics, technology, business affairs, and all such matters as thoroughly and skillfully as they now cover the White House and, let us say, the St. Louis Cardinals. It has not happened yet, but the pieces are beginning to fall into place. Business and economic news, once reported sparsely, are now front-page fare. Radio and television news departments take it seriously. Interest rates, industrial output for the past month, the latest on the nation's competitive status versus other countries—each of these is granted at least a few seconds of TV prime time, with a couple of computer-generated charts or graphs thrown in. When a major economics story can easily be related to everyday life—changing employment patterns, for instance—it may even win the highest honor that a commercial network news director can bestow: a full two and one-half minutes of air time. Some wars receive less.

The quality of reporting has gone up. Looking back a decade and more, editors of the nation's leading dailies, with few exceptions, characterize the economics coverage of their own publications in one word: "lousy." Today, many if not most of those same newspapers deserve a performance rating of "good" and are trying for "excellent." Contrast that to Jay Near's day in journalism. Then, few newspapers even pretended to be interested in business and economics, and those that did put these at the bottom of the journalistic pecking order. The business beat was the one for the reporter who had done everything else wrong and was fit only to cover the ribbon-cutting at the new bank building. City editors became enthused about a business story only when the bank failed and the chief teller was caught with his hand in the cookie jar. Then as now, a juicy story was a juicy story. The collapse of the standing order, the hint of scandal, the toppling of idols had always had a chemical attraction for reporters. Some things never change.

Those too young to remember those good old days are encouraged to see a revival of *The Front Page,* Ben Hecht and Charles MacArthur's wacky 1928 comedy about newspapering in the days when reporters wore press cards in the brims of their fedoras. See also H. L. Mencken, the celebrated Baltimore journalist, a man of the same times. In *Prejudices: Sixth Series,* Mencken spoke thus of journalists:

> The majority of them, in almost every American city, are still ignoramuses, and proud of it.... There are managing editors in the United States, and scores of them ... who have never read the Constitution ... there are city editors who do not know what a symphony is, or a streptococcus, or the Statute of Frauds; there are reporters by the thousand who could not pass the entrance examination for Harvard or Tuskegee, or even Yale.
>
> It is this vast and militant ignorance, this widespread and fathomless prejudice against intelligence, that makes American journalism so pathetically feeble and vulgar, and so generally disreputable.... [I]n general journalism suffers from a lack of alert and competent professional criticism; its slaves, afflicted by a natural inferiority complex, discountenance free speaking as a sort of treason; I have myself been damned as a public enemy for calling attention, ever and anon, to the intolerable incompetence and quackery of all save a small minority of the Washington correspondents.

Perhaps Mencken exaggerated, a little.

Media culpa: There are still lots of problems. Some journalists use the pen to advance pet causes, worthy or otherwise. On occasion, some of those journalists, like Near, commit an act of justice, as it were by accident. For the most part, though, the failings of the media today emerge less from bias than from a lack of competence. Most crimes are of ignorance, not spite. In important subject areas such as technology and economic affairs, many journalists do not understand their subject well enough to report on it responsibly. I say that in sympathy, as a simple statement of fact, knowing that lots of other people also have trouble making sense of science and the convolutions of economics. Many of us, including victims of shoddy reporting, probably would not make better journalists than the people who now have those assignments.

I grant the media the benefit of the doubt, err on the side of caution, and hold to an open-door policy of press relations. My philosophy on this is so simple it hardly deserves the honor of such a fancy word: A private organization of any size and substance is best served when it gets full and fair coverage from journalists. The chances of getting that are best when the organization helps journalists get their job done. Ergo, return their calls. Answer the questions. Honor deadlines. Especially in TV and radio, but sometimes in the press as well, journalists live by minutes and seconds. Set up as few filters as possible. Never lie. When you have a problem and the press becomes aware of it, do not try to paper over the facts. Admit them. That alone will go a long way toward keeping them in context. The best way to turn a one-day story into a continuing investigation is to cover up or make light of a situation that appears serious and ought not to be taken lightly. The last thing to do is pick a fight with the media. Common sense says that you do not engage in a war that is pointless to begin with, especially if you cannot win and you can find several good reasons not to fight at all.

Being accessible to the press requires an investment of time, but it pays off and rarely backfires. As for the dangers of giving away too much information, they are overrated. My homespun rule on disclosure is, "If in doubt, put it out." The burden for justifying "No comment" to a legitimate question should fall on the people who have the answers, not on the people asking the questions. There can be embarrassments: A little risk is not the same as no risk. I have met some people in the media who have seemed happiest when they could give me each day my daily lumps; but among the hundreds of journalists whose paths crossed mine in Du Pont or the Business Roundtable, I can remember only a handful whose motives I had reason to question. Most of them impressed me as people sincerely trying to do a creditable job on their stories, and to be objective in the face of what in many cases had to be judgment calls. They obviously wanted to win the respect of their peers, and just as obviously this meant more to them than anything else.

Only rarely have I been misquoted to such an extent that a news story seriously distorted what I said. The number of times I have been set up—misled by a journalist who can only have been trying to spring a trap—is very small. At a guess, those two kinds of problems together represent less than 10 percent of my contacts with journalists; and anyone who is batting over .900 in a public park has no cause to complain.

Television and radio create some special problems, however. With their enormous reach and potential impact, they are vital to the communications of any corporation of substantial size, but they compress stories into such short time-frames that all the flavor can be crushed out of them, and understanding lost. I would not hesitate to go on camera for a live interview, because the chance is mine to choose priorities and make whatever points I want, knowing that there may be but a few seconds available. Viewers can judge the message for themselves, and if my points are badly made, there is no one to blame but myself. The same does not apply for recorded coverage destined for editing before it goes on the air. That is a very different matter. All control is then in somebody else's hands. An hour in front of the cameras can be chopped to thirty seconds or less of broadcast time. The points I thought least important may be emphasized; those I most wanted to register may be ignored altogether. I have no sense of the context in which my comments will appear, no idea what the directors of the show will put in front of my words or behind them. This does not argue against agreeing to such interviews in all cases, only that there ought to be some precise understanding ahead of time because these events do carry hazards.

Being "out front" for an organization requires training and experience. It astonishes me that people who would never think of getting behind the wheel of a car without knowing how to drive it will agree to go on a television program without ever having been in a studio, or enter into a press conference without prior exposure to the interview techniques used by radio and TV journalists. It can only be done well with practice, both to become accustomed to the lights and microphones, and to learn to put forward the main points in a quick, short fashion so that, if all else is lost, at least those points have a chance of being conveyed intact to viewers or readers. Politicians learn to do this early in their careers, when their mistakes are not likely to be serious. By the time they become recognized news sources, most of them are pretty good at it. Businessmen have to get on the learning curve in the same way, before they become senior executives playing in high-stakes games.

Further, they should never underestimate the value of making a long-term investment in good relations with journalists. In more than one crisis or potentially hostile situation, I have seen at first hand the value of an executive being known by reporters as someone with a reputation for credibility. On one occasion, a member of Jack Anderson's staff telephoned me for a reaction to a story they were planning to run. The story as he relayed it to me was completely untrue, and I said so. The reporter replied to this effect: "You and your company have a good reputation, so we'll go back and recheck this, but if it turns out that the story is correct, we'll give it both barrels." The story never appeared, and all concerned were spared a harsh public accusation which probably would have outdistanced any later denials or retractions.

More recently, a *New York Times* reporter came to see me in connection with a story she was preparing on a number of current and former business executives. It was a particularly cordial interview, and when it was over she said, "I want to tell you something. Years ago when I was a young reporter on a Philadelphia paper, I called your office on a story. In those days, a call from an unknown would not have brought a return call from many senior executives, unless maybe it was from the *New York Times,* but you called me back promptly and were very helpful on my story. Now I'm with the *Times,* but I have never forgotten that courtesy you showed me."

The classic example of being open with the media is John deButts. When he became chairman of AT&T, he gave reporters a private number on which they could call him directly. When a story appeared about AT&T that he thought was garbled or slanted, his practice was to telephone the reporter immediately and offer to meet with him to go over the problem line by line. Only after that would he carry a complaint to an editor, or make any public statement.

The best demonstration of corporate "damage control" I have ever seen was by Johnson & Johnson, the corporation whose subsidiary, McNeil Consumer Products Company, makes the Tylenol painkiller. When it was discovered that someone had put cyanide in Super Tylenol capsules, Johnson & Johnson adopted a full-disclosure policy, with around-the-clock information services for the media and with senior executives available to answer questions. The company stuck to the evidence that it had in hand and avoided speculation. When reporters asked whether any cyanide was used in the plant and if the product might have been contaminated before reaching the stores, Johnson & Johnson at first said, "No." The company immediately reversed that when management learned that cyanide was used in a building adjacent to the manufacturing plant, in tests to assure the purity of raw materials. Though there seemed little chance that this could have been the cause (and later checks proved it was not), the company was forthcoming with the information that the answer was "Yes." The company was asked whether poisoned products were only in one part of the country or might turn up anywhere. The answer was "Don't know." The early evidence was that the problem was confined to the Chicago area, and later findings bore that out; but Johnson & Johnson took no liberties with the truth and no chance with the public health. It was the company that made the decision to remove Super Tylenol from markets all over the country. The CEO, James Burke, conferred with the FBI and FDA, and at first there was some opposition there to a total recall. The thought was that this might encourage other deranged people to try a copycat move, to show that they had the power to bring a giant organization to its knees. J&J pushed the decision through, and recalled Tylenol worth $100 million at retail.

Throughout, the company treated this as the crisis that it was. Seven people died of poisoning. In terms of the business impact, too, it was a catastrophe. This was a major product for Johnson & Johnson, with a larger share of the market than all three leading rivals, Bayer, Bufferin, and Anacin. Tylenol and Super Tylenol accounted for about $350 million in sales and about one-fifth of the profits of J&J. Corporate management knew that when Super Tylenol came off the shelf it might be forever, and that regular Tylenol might also be hurt beyond repair through public confusion about the similar labels, or through loss of faith in the producer. Yet because of the way the organization stepped up to its responsibility and turned to the media to help it communicate—to the public's benefit, not its own—Johnson & Johnson emerged from the episode with widespread public support. Its reputation, instead of being destroyed, was if anything strengthened. Some marketing experts were convinced the product would never recover. "A mortal blow," one of them declared. "Less than fifty-fifty," said another; but the product did survive. Legislation requiring tamper-resistant packages for such products was passed, and Tylenol soon regained much though not all of its market position. The way the problem was handled was so impressive that CBS' *60 Minutes* devoted a segment of one of its shows to it. Not to be overlooked is one final point: The media covering the story also distinguished themselves. Journalists responded immediately to the company's candor and openness. It was a blockbuster story and the press played it that way, but the major news arteries told it straight, selected their words carefully to avoid sensationalism, and gave the public a basis for responding sensibly.

An open attitude pays off equally well when an institution is facing genuine abuse. The example I know best comes not from the established media but from a strike force set up under Ralph Nader's Center for the Study of Responsive Law. The group was charged with writing a book-length investigative report on the Du Pont Company and its influence in the state of Delaware. The title of the work that emerged suggests the theme they set out to document: *The Company State.*

The supposition at Du Pont, based on other Nader projects done on organizations public and private, was that the report would be very negative and that the Nader group would do all it could to turn it into a media event. Du Pont decided to handle the project accordingly. The eight "reporters," all young and mostly law students, were permitted to interview dozens of company executives and employees, and were provided written answers to long lists of questions. I coordinated the project for the company (I was then in the Legal Department), and at my insistence all interviews with Du Pont managers were tape-recorded. We wanted a full record of anything we might be quoted as saying. That is certainly not a standard practice with press interviews, but a Nader group investigating Du Pont is not a standard media house-call either.

The published report was about what we expected. It argued for about 800 pages that the Du Pont Company and family controlled in subtle if not direct ways the economic, political, and social destinies of a small state, usurping the role of government and imposing the values of an elite minority. There were errors by the dozen in the book, which also included a new form of arithmetic by which it could be demonstrated that Du Pont was not paying its fair share of taxes. We looked for saving graces, but in vain. Few nice things were said about the organization in this document on life in medieval Delaware. Even gifts to charitable activities did not win favorable mention; these were set aside by the investigators as schemes to manipulate social-service agencies to keep the natives happy and compliant.

The reason to mention this episode is not that the report gained great media attention, but that it gained comparatively little, at least for Nader's team. Du Pont certainly did not emerge as victor—there is no way to win in an inquisition—but the company received more favorable publicity out of it than the authors. As soon as the report was issued, we in Du Pont went through it in fine detail, prepared an error sheet with rebuttal facts, and made that available. Company executives met with the press and went on television. We conceded that the report made a few reasonable recommendations (e.g., Du Pont ought to help the community get more public housing), and noted that we were in agreement because we were already doing what was suggested. We offered to let interested parties listen to the tape recordings of interviews and decide for themselves how accurately and fairly Du Pont and its people were quoted and portrayed. One place that offer was made was on the national Phil Donahue TV show, where I was a guest. Donahue brought up the subject and we talked about it at length on the air.

There is no evidence that the report did any great damage to the Du Pont organization or its people. Public-opinion polls in Delaware and nearby showed that it changed few people's minds about the company. To my knowledge, no one apart from the Nader team has ever listened to the tapes, or wanted to. Perhaps that says something about the credibility of the report. (The Nader team vigorously opposed our taping of the interviews, then later came to us and asked for a set of tapes.) Though Nader wrote the foreword to the book, he said little about it publicly then or later. Post-mortem, the only regret one might have is that Du Pont did not publish a counterbook of its own, to

stand on the library shelves alongside *The Company State.* There is
the possibility that future readers will take the Nader report as gospel,
but if the corporation has been doing the rest of its job in communicating what it is and does, it need not be much concerned about that
happening frequently.

Some of my business friends who do not wear celluloid collars are
still hellbent on doing battle with people in the media, and it occurs to
me that they are working on the premise that working journalists are
like the self-styled reporters of the Nader study team. The theory was
circulating in the 1970s, and gained some following in business and
elsewhere, that something called "the new class" was taking over the
pivot points of opinion- and decision-making in this country. Edu-
cated in the liberal arts at universities on the East and West Coasts,
well left of center politically, new classmen were to be found in key
slots in government, think tanks, and the media. Journalists who fit
this mold would be natural allies of social activists, unionists, environmentalists, the liberal wing of the Democratic Party, and other
groups determined to bring a particular version of reform to the nation. They would be anti-Republican and out of step with the more
conservative, Middle Western values one usually associates with people of commerce and industry. What makes the "new class" line of
thought noteworthy here is the claim that its members were calling the
shots in the news outlets with the most political and social muscle,
namely the *New York Times, Washington Post,* and *Wall Street Journal; Time* and *Newsweek;* the Associated Press wire service and one or
two others; and the news departments of CBS, NBC, and ABC. These
are the media elite, the group to which lesser lights in journalism must
defer, the inside ring, the group that can steer national policy and
shape national opinion to the extent that anyone in journalism can.

The "new class" thesis has been pushed much too far, in my judgment. It does not explain the situation so much as it explains it away:
Blame it all on the Ivy League on the East Coast (with special demerits
for the Yale Law School), on Stanford and Berkeley on the West
Coast, and on similar dens of iniquitous liberalism in between. Not
only do they produce Nader study teams but their minions are all over
the castle, subverting the place. Whatever one makes of that thesis in
government or among Nader's raiders, it will not wash in the media. At
least some of the supposed soulmates of new classmen, people it theo-
retically favors and who ought to be happy about that, report that they

feel just the opposite. Many leaders of organized labor, to take one example, believe that they and the union movement have been given anything but a fair shake by the media.

Moreover, journalists as a group do not show the biases they are supposed to display. A great deal is known about the makeup of the journalism fraternity—family background, schooling, and the like. The Washington reporters in particular have been studied in microscopic detail by Stephen Hess, a senior fellow at the Brookings Institution. Based on data from several hundred journalists, Hess concluded that, while journalists are not just average folks and there are some leanings, there is no stampede to the left. The ones who work for the elite organizations do tend to come from the highly selective colleges and universities. They have more years of education than the footsoldiers of journalism, often including graduate degrees. As a group, however, even the elite corps hardly fits a "new class" stereotype. Journalists are not one-sided or cohesive in their views. In Washington, a majority of reporters will agree that there is a political tilt in their clan toward the liberal side, but the vote on that is 51:49, hardly a landslide. Asked where they locate themselves in the political spectrum, most Washington reporters claim to be middle-of-the-road or conservative, 58:42 over self-described liberals. Mostly, Hess found that journalists are not given to ideological crusades and few of them have strongly political reasons to be in the field. Their own assessment is that there are fewer examples now of deeply prejudiced journalism than existed a generation ago, either on the side of "raging liberals" or "mossback conservatives."

What this says to me—and what my own experience confirms—is that it probably is not the journalists as a class who are out of step with public attitudes and governmental thinking in this country, so much as it is the people who fasten onto "new class" or other theories to explain their unhappiness with what the media say and do. As far as I can see, and with allowance for some obvious exceptions, the political and social profile of the species *Journalist americus* more or less parallels that of the college-graduate population of the nation, as evidenced by opinion polls on national issues over the past quarter-century. Nonetheless, people continue to devote enormous amounts of energy to agonizing over the faults of the media, energy that in my view might better be spent in revising their own style of operations, that being probably more responsible than any other factor for whatever poor press they are getting.

People in business are correct in sensing a sting in the media's criticism of business performance. An Opinion Research Corporation survey in 1982 confirms the notion that most journalists do not think that the leaders of big companies are doing a first-rate job of running their companies effectively and ethically, and contributing as business should to the economy and to the society. A high percentage of journalists said it is very important for business leaders to maintain competitiveness, keep facilities up to date, build for the long pull, and operate in socially responsible ways, but on all those counts a majority of the same journalists said that most big corporations have not done well. In only one area did nearly all journalists assign high importance to a business responsibility, in this case the maintenance of a healthy work environment (that received a 95 percent score), and also agree in the majority (the score on that was 52 percent) that most corporations are doing "a first-rate job."

It is well not to be oversensitive to this kind of scorekeeping, however. Assuming that the journalistic criticism is half right—and no business executive of my acquaintance would deny that many companies have been badly managed—the media are not picking on the corporate sector in particular. They take a similar unglossed view of government, educational institutions, labor unions, and numerous other structures of the modern world, and are often equally as sharp-tongued in editorializing about them. Louis Banks, former managing editor of *Fortune* magazine and more recently a professor at the Sloan School at MIT, tells the story of attending a meeting convened by Time Inc. to bring together 200 national leaders, and hearing the loudest protests about the media coming from young, energetic, attractive people in political life—people one would have supposed would be media pets. They, too, felt abused and misused by the sorts of media failings that irk business executives.

The only way business can convince the media or the public that it is doing its work well is through demonstrated performance—the facts have to be there—and by making those facts broadly apparent. Executives must be more forthcoming with the media if they want their company and industry problems to be understood. Silence on the part of the leadership avails little. It was said in the days of Pericles that "In Athens we think silent men are useless," and much the same applies today in the public forums in which business is judged.

There is also the question of attitude. One old hand in the Gannett newspaper organization has commented, "There's still a lot of paranoia in the business community." I would like to believe that he, too, is exaggerating along with Mencken, but it is hard to be sure. The editor of *Business Week* magazine tells of walking to a press conference with the head of one of the big auto companies, and asking him, "What are you going to tell us today?" The executive's answer: "As little as possible." The good news is that the executive in question is long gone from the scene; the bad news is that this editor still tells the story, saying there are still people like that around. A reporter for the *Los Angeles Times* recalls a telephone call he made to an oil-company president to obtain more information about a change in gasoline prices, announced in a news release. "Just run it the way I sent it in, sonny," the reporter was told.

One well-known national columnist privately expresses a view that I fear many journalists share: that business executives still have not climbed down off their high horses. If business leaves that impression, it makes a great mistake, a mistake that most people in public office, even those who indeed do have high horses to ride, have learned to stop making.

"Once you pay somebody a salary of $500,000 a year and give him a private airplane," says the columnist, "he gets the idea he is ruling by divine right and his decisions are automatically going to be correct." He adds that some business leaders seem to have the notion that they should control the agenda of public discussion about issues that affect them, forgetting that many other people are affected, too, and have an equal right to say what is talked about.

What falls out of this is the futility of trying to control the news through selective release. Once threads of information begin to come forward, journalists regard a story as fair game whether the timing is convenient for somebody else or not. That is not the way some "newsmakers" see it, though. One CEO of an electrical manufacturing firm was infuriated because a story broke about an acquisition he was negotiating. Some threads of the story had already become publicly known, and enterprising journalists pulled them together, but the CEO was not ready to announce the package. Not being able to shoot the messenger, he did the next best thing and ripped into his staff for "letting the press run this." Such stories can be told a hundred times over, the customary whipping boy being the "PR people" ("You're supposed to protect me from this sort of thing"). Their skins thicken with time, but damage is done. A few episodes like that and, as a business writer for the *Miami News* has said, journalists find that the whole staff of an organization turns "incredibly timid and cautious." Useful communication with the media then ends.

Language is the litmus test of journalists. The words people use tell them whether someone is speaking to communicate or to avoid saying anything worthwhile. Much is made of the genius of government bureaucrats at befogging our mother tongue, but the business world has an equally rich vocabulary of doubletalk which it uses when it wants to get attention without saying much to deserve it. Sample: "We expect to see substantial improvements in selected product lines in the foreseeable future," or "Conditions permitting, we will look at options to avoid undue layoffs at the plant." Such statements tell the outside world next to nothing, as is their intent. They are meant to leave impressions ("progressive company," "socially responsible," etc.), and to build an image not based on facts.

It cannot be done, and only the very naïve would suppose that any journalist worth his salt would fall for this line. By logic that escapes me, though, some executives who would blast any subordinate who tried to blow such smoke at them in a company meeting will try to sell such language to the outside world. They honestly appear baffled when the evening news does not rush their pronouncements onto the picture tube or, worse yet, runs good news about one of the competitors instead. Pick a day at random, tour any daily newspaper's editorial office, and you will find wastebaskets filled with private-sector puffery, business boilerplate, and other unenlightening nonnews releases. Where else would one expect a competent editor to put it?

It is not the job of a lay journalist to unravel the interior data of organizations about which they can know only a little, especially when the organization makes it extra difficult by seeming to talk out of both sides of its mouth at once. The classic example is business' way of stating its profits, which to the unsophisticated often looks like an effort to make the profits look large for the benefit of the stockholders and small for the Internal Revenue Service. At the least, to put it charitably, the numbers warrant some explaining, but instead of steering journalists through them in such a way that the figures make sense, some corporations simply let confusion reign, and then charge that the news reports were "distorted" or "simplistic." Probably they were, but whose fault is that?

It has also not escaped the notice of journalists that there are always some cases where business executives hold back material facts, or deliberately misrepresent them. As but one example, when the news began to break about improper foreign payments by U.S. corporations, there was at first only a trickle of information, and numerous denials of the "yes, but that's all" variety. Then the Securities and Exchange Commission said, in effect, "Tell us and be forgiven," after which hundreds of instances came to view, including some new ones from a few of those "yes, but" companies.

There is as well a distressing narrowness to go with the dishonesty. A columnist from the *Washington Post* puts it this way: "You [businessmen] don't take the press seriously, or the issues. You're not responsive. You don't try to get to the bottom of problems. So many of you sound as though you are reading from a script." That writer illustrates his point with a story that goes about like this: At a time when governments all over the world were filled with concern about the financial stability of nations, with newspapers filled with news of recession everywhere and speculation about the problems of Third World countries over their heads in debt, he and some other journalists happened to have a chance to interview a leading bank executive—"supposedly one of your broadest-gauge people." What the writers wanted to know was whether the banker thought the developing nations might default and, if so, what the consequences would be. All this man wanted to talk about, though, was the impact of all these earth-shaking events on his own bank, which was holding some of the Third World debt. After making sure the journalists understood that his own bank could weather the storm, he lost interest in the subject. In the mind of at least that reporter, here was a CEO to whom the problems of all the rest of the world were as nothing.

Emmett Tyrell, Jr., editor of *American Spectator* magazine, has supplied an even more biting account of the density of some executives who come into contact with the media. Tyrell has recounted a story told by writer Tom Wolfe about a dinner-table conversation Wolfe had with "a titan of industry." Wolfe said that their exchange followed a standard format. Sample question from Wolfe: "Do you think a Polish Pope will change relations between the Vatican and Moscow?" Sample reply: "I met the Pope. Charlie Small, the head of the Light Weight Corporation, got us an audience with him; and it wasn't one of those large ones, only 260 CEOs. You know Charlie Small? He's a Knight of Columbus. You ought to get to know Charlie

Small." It sounds like lines from a play, or something out of Sinclair Lewis' *Babbitt*. Tyrell added this point of his own: "Political intelligence is almost as rare in the business community as in the American Political Science Association." For the sake of all the condemned, I hope he, too, exaggerates, a little; but at least the Philistines can take comfort in the fact that they have learned professors for company.

This takes us to what I believe are the limits of the media and the shortcomings that can legitimately be criticized. The limit is that the public cannot expect a fully balanced picture from the media. Journalists are quicker to seize upon bad news than good, and are constantly torn between the duty to be fair and the temptation to make reports as colorful as they ought to be, or a touch more. Katharine Graham, chairman of the *Washington Post* corporation and former publisher of that newspaper, is one of many in the field who point out that ordinary events are not newsworthy: "The occasional business failure or the isolated crime makes headlines; [but] there are no stories when products are delivered on time, when soup is safe, when candy bars don't shrink." An unknown journalist has given us a model lead for the news story that would describe the world as it really is: "Three thousand students attended Jones High School yesterday, milled in the halls, worked or slept through class, and went out for sports. Meanwhile one student shot the principal."

Journalism is a competitive world. Reporters have to scratch for space. They are usually in a hurry, and always in favor of a story that will rate page-one attention and a byline. This does not make for gentle essays on what is generally right with the world, or for reports from the field that "Nothing worth reporting is going on here." Theodore White, a journalist who has become nationally known for his books on Presidential election campaigns, has been quoted as follows: "You don't make your reputation as a reporter, and I did not make my reputation as a reporter, by praising anybody. You make your reputation as a reporter by gouging a chunk of raw and bleeding flesh from this system. . . . But maybe we've gone too far and maybe there should be someone to call us to account for this. . . ."

The limit, then, is that journalism frequently gives us a dim image, as from a half-silvered mirror; and, as with any half-truth, there is a constant risk that what we hear is a half-lie. That result may be unintended, but the public is still obliged to look elsewhere for the facts needed to achieve a balanced perspective. Even if White's closing comment is taken to heart in the media and there is greater self-restraint, it is not practical to expect the media to tell us all about the students who are not shooting the principal.

The shortcomings take the form of sins of commission, selectively committed. The renowned journalist James Reston has made the point that in covering national and international affairs, many of the reporters know more than some of the officials they cover. No doubt that is true. Many reporters have built up extensive background, while some of the people they work with are political appointees and new to the job. It is not surprising that journalists, especially the ones working for the most respected news outlets, may be far more knowledgeable than some of the people they interview, with Reston himself as a first example. Reston's point does not fit for all areas, though, and over the years it seems to have applied all too rarely to such fields as economics and technology. There, the media's reach has exceeded their grasp, and the resulting coverage has been so lacking in perspective as to constitute a disservice to the public.

Years ago, journalism could be faulted because it fawned too much on technology and technologists, and much of this can be attributed to naïveté mixed with awe. In those days of innocence, the public was treated to a parade of "Gee whiz" stories about the miracles of science, engineering, and medicine. Wonders came at least one a month, with each new issue of *Reader's Digest,* and we were all led to believe there could soon be a world without want, a world without disease. Everyone overpromised—the practitioners of science, the producers of products, and reporters who did not know enough science to realize (or enough skepticism to suspect) that the failure rate for "miracles" is at least 90 percent.

In those days, science writers were like the little girl in the nursery rhyme: When they were good they were very, very good, but when they were bad they were horrid. Most reporters admitted to being technological illiterates. To some editors, a science writer was anyone who could spell p-e-n-i-c-i-l-l-i-n, and many failed to get a passing grade on that. I do not exaggerate. Some years ago, when Du Pont was enjoying unusual success in creating a string of new products based on synthetic polymers, a newspaper reporter decided to do a round-up on progress in this field, and asked for an interview with the director of our Central Research Department, Dr. Theodore Cairns, a distinguished scientist in his own right. Our man was well into a spiel on the intriguing things that could be done with polymers—new plastics, new fibers, composite structures, and the like—when the reporter said, "Excuse me, Dr. Cairns, but could you spell 'polymer' for me?" I have two witnesses.

Now, the problem has swung to the other pole. Starry-eyed belief in the goodness of technology has been replaced by the fear that it will soon do us in. Overexpectation has given way to an excess of fear, with the media giving us new reminders every day of the problems and perils of technology. What we have now are not only some well-placed warnings, but with them a barrage of distortions that has left the public more confused than informed.

Some of the most serious problems exist in reference to toxic substances and public health. As before, the quality of media coverage ranges from night to day. The best-qualified science and medical writers, many of whom have college degrees in science, have covered that unfolding story with considerable skill, winning the respect of health professionals, industry people, and others who realize how complex the problems are, and how difficult it is to report on them in simple language without falling into the error of oversimplification. A large part of the reporting and editing, though, has not come even close to that standard. To use the media's own label, there has been much "pack journalism." Technological illiteracy is still with us.

Key words and tag lines serve as shorthand reminders of the topics in question: DDT; Three Mile Island; pesticide-contaminated cranberries; chlorinated hydrocarbons such as chlordane and heptachlor, later banned from use; health hazards (probably cancer?) reported from saccharin, cyclamates, nitrites, and caffeine; nuclear wastes, described as a ticking time bomb; Love Canal, and a study that showed chromosome damage in people living nearby; reports that Tris, a chemical flame-retardant used in children's sleepwear had been found in lab tests to be a mutagen; PCBs; "deadly" dioxin. "A Deadly Gamble: Chemical wastes stalk the unborn" was a typical headline.

For years, it has been recognized that cancer can be caused by some materials made and used in industry, and the consensus among cancer specialists has been that such occupational sources might account for 1 to 5 percent of all cases. Then came a sudden announcement from the Health and Human Services Department, delivered at a press conference by the Secretary himself, Joseph Califano, that the number was not in the 1 to 5 range but more probably was as high as

38 percent. From another quarter came an announcement that exposure to low-level radiation, long regarded as the cause of a small number of cancer cases, was a much more significant health hazard than had been suspected. New studies proved that, we were told. A report surfaced that there was an excess of leukemia cases, above the number to be expected in the general population, among workers at the Portsmouth Naval Shipyard who worked with nuclear submarine reactors. In a 1982 series of articles an Atlanta newspaper reported twenty-five cases of a rare, potentially fatal blood disorder, polycythemia vera, in and around the Savannah River nuclear-materials plant in South Carolina, and linked them (journalistically, not scientifically) to exposure to radiation. The newspaper also reported abnormally high infant and fetal death rates in the area. The stories, which were widely distributed by wire services at the time, were retracted *in toto* by the newspaper a year later, a rare move.

These and similar shocks made for headlines and continuing coverage in public media, and in many instances led to swift, aggressive governmental action. Products were banned. Government bought the homes of the Love Canal residents and relocated the people. It did the same later with the town of Times Beach, Missouri, when dioxin was found there. Surely a great deal of publicity was to be expected from such disaster projections, and in some cases the response of authorities was undoubtedly appropriate and desirable. What was frequently missing, though, in the government's actions and even more in the media coverage, was reason or balance. The way these incidents were handled caused near-terror, unnecessarily, much of it unjustified not merely by hindsight but by the information available at the time. It is not quite a case of shouting "Fire" in a crowded movie theater, but almost.

Reflecting on this class of health and safety problems as a group, Dr. William Lowrance, head of Rockefeller University's Science and Public Policy Program, said this in a paper published by the American Association for the Advancement of Science:

> This rash of accidents, disruptions, and disputes has left the public and its leaders fearful that the world is awfully risky. . . . [T]here is a feeling that as with medical catalepsy, in which the simultaneous firing of too many nerves draws the body into spasms, the body politic has been drawn into a kind of regulatory catalepsy by too many health scares, too many customer warnings, too many environmental lawsuits, too many bans, too

many reversals. A related complaint is that we are afflicted with excessive government intervention, often of a naïve, or trifling, or nay-saying sort. Among professional analysts as well as the public there is a conviction that many risk-reduction efforts are disproportionate with the relative social burden of the hazards.

He is right, and the public media bear some of the responsibility for inducing "catalepsy."

One by one, the health and safety problems are being sorted out, or already have been. They are worth reviewing for the lessons in them. The contaminated cranberries, pulled off the market just before the Thanksgiving selling season, were later found to be safe for human consumption. The great cranberry scare was a false alarm. Asbestos is not a false alarm. More and more evidence has shown it to be a serious, long-range health hazard. It is known that large numbers of workers have been exposed, and that harmful effects may appear years later. DDT is now seen as a pesticide that should be used with great care and selectivity, and perhaps only as a "last resort" chemical. Along with some other pesticides no longer licensed for use in the U.S., it is a molecule that does not readily break down in nature. DDT harms more species than it should, birds among them, and for most applications there are substitute chemicals that decompose rapidly and thus do not have long-term toxic effects. Despite the fact that DDT was in widespread use for years, though (it was even sprayed on people with Flit cans at one time), scientists say they can find no evidence that DDT has ever caused human cancer.

Cyclamate, the artificial sweetener, was banned by FDA on the basis of suggestive but far from convincing research findings. At this writing, it is still off the market, though an application for reinstatement is under review. We still have caffeine in our coffee and tea, and have been told to stop worrying unless we consume huge quantities, and then the concern is only a "maybe."

The nitrite scare has gone away—another false alarm. It turned out that the microscope slides from an initial feeding test with rats did not show a prevalence of malignant tumors, as was first reported by the scientist in charge of the study. A later review of those slides plus a replication of the tests revealed that animals fed nitrite developed no significantly larger number of tumors than a control group. The FDA Commissioner who announced that nitrite would be banned on the basis of that first study, withdrew his statement on the basis of the later data. The Tris story deals with tests done with a bacterial species, through a screening procedure called the Ames Test, named for its originator, Dr. Bruce Ames. Whether the positive results with bacteria signify a danger to humans, and if so, how much, are not certain. Some other flame-retardants that were considered as substitutes for Tris apparently can cause sterility and may cause cancer. Again, the implications to man are not yet clear. The jury is still out.

The 38-percent figure on occupational cancer was but one episode in a long series of misstatements and misunderstandings about environment as a cause of that disease. The first blunder centered on "environment." Cancer specialists use the word to cover all of the factors that surround people in daily life and affect their health: what they eat, whether they smoke, how much stress they suffer, where they live, where they work, and all the rest. This was mistranslated in some media, though, to signify "environmental" problems in the sense of industrial pollution and, even more narrowly, to denote exposure of workers to fumes or to materials with which they work. When people in industrial regions heard that cancer experts were saying most cancer is caused by environmental factors, they understandably became upset. The 1-to-5-percent figure was supposed to put this in context, but that message did not always get through. The government's statement that the occupational quotient was at least seven times higher than that also caused an understandable stir. At the 38-percent level, we are talking about hundreds of thousands of cancer cases per year. There was, though, no solid statistical basis for that figure, nor any broad support among people doing cancer research. The report made a good news story, but it polarized positions, diverted attention to the wrong areas, put the Secretary out on a limb, and did no good for the cause of public education.

The awareness of potential dangers to humans from chemical dumpsites has been building ever since the Love Canal incident began in 1978, and this has been one of the most heavily covered stories in journalism history. Health officials believe such waste sites deserve priority attention and have urged immediate clean-up of the ones that are most likely to be most hazardous. There is little argument against that. Yet scientists have repeatedly made it clear that this is an area of vast unknowns, yielding only slowly to research. A 1981 symposium of fifty-five scientists came to these summary conclusions: "Not only do we not know how severe the human health effects are from disposed chemicals, we are still far from being able to agree on how best to go about assessing those risks." And "Although analogies can be drawn among waste sites, chemical, geological, or medical generalizations not based on detailed, site-specific analyses should always be considered unreliable."

That is about as plain a statement as scientists make, and it leaves us with only one certainty: Public commentary about such problems as Love Canal ought to be framed in the most careful language, with all of the caveats. Wild-eyed charges that dreadful things are happening to people, or equally rash claims that there is nothing to worry about, are more than a little irresponsible and are not readily forgiven as poetic license.

As for the story about chromosome damage to people who lived in the vicinity of Love Canal, there was no truth to it. It was accepted on more or less blind faith at the time—it was largely the basis on which the Love Canal properties were bought and the residents moved out— but after that study became public it was reviewed by other scientists and discredited. One reviewer commented that the study was so badly designed that it never should have been done in the first place. Other studies have since been conducted. They show no incidence of chromosome damage that could be attributed to Love Canal. The rate among the exposed population is not higher than for people living nowhere near Love Canal. Some officials who based their own statements and decisions on the study later apologized, as did some television journalists who had given the story the full treatment. Whether such retractions ever catch up with such allegations, though, is another matter.

The media's handling of radiation hazards leaves at least as much to be desired and, again, is to be faulted not by second guessing but on the basis of what was known at the time. It has long been public knowledge that radiation is everywhere around us. The earth itself is mildly radioactive and some of the granite in it, more so. The planet is bombarded daily by radiation from space. Most of us receive some added exposure from medical and dental X-rays. No one says a little radiation is good for you, but the concern goes with the dose. The smaller the amount of exposure, the lower the chance that an individual will suffer genetic damage or cancer from radiation. At very low levels, the likelihood becomes one cancer case or less in a population of millions. None of this is arcane science. It is what anyone can learn from a high-school science course or by reading a layman's primer.

Against that background, consider the media reports that emerged when new concerns were expressed by one scientist about the hazard of low-level radiation. Scientists had reached a consensus in 1972 on the question of how much should be considered dangerous, after evaluations by committees from scientific organizations from all advanced countries. The question a few years later was whether the risks had been underestimated, so scientists took another look. One scientist familiar with the data said yes, low-level radiation might be significantly more dangerous than had been thought earlier. That was a tentative conclusion. The overwhelming majority of others reviewing the same data said no. The "yes" report (it is remembered as the Mancuso Report, for Dr. Thomas Mancuso) was picked up by the media; the "no" reaction largely escaped journalistic notice. What surfaced hardly anywhere in the popular press was another conclusion reached by many reviewers: the 1972 assessment of risk was probably too high.

The Portsmouth shipyard workers were a case of a tentative "yes" being overturned or withdrawn soon after an initial claim hit the headlines. The story of excess leukemia cases received the publicity; less was heard about the scientific reviews that said that conclusion was wrong, or about the author's withdrawal of that initial claim.

The rare blood disease polycythemia vera has not appeared more frequently in the vicinity of the nuclear-materials plant than elsewhere. Twenty-five cases would be more than expected for a population group of the size in question, but that is not the number of cases confirmed by a review conducted by the Federal Centers for Disease Control. CDC reported that more than half of the alleged cases were of a different, nonfatal disease called secondary polycythemia, which can come from various causes including cigarette smoking. True polycythemia vera was confirmed in five cases, a number that the CDC said would not be unexpected for this population. As for the claim that babies were dying at "consistently higher" rates than average, a study of statistics for three counties in that area actually showed lower than average death rates in the reported age group. An editor of the *Atlanta Journal and Constitution,* the newspaper whose reporters had put together the news story about the twenty-five cases, later was quoted as saying the publication should not have run with the story as it did. After follow-up research by different reporters, the paper ran a front-page story retracting the original series. Several bits of evidence, readily available, might have served as warning flags on the story. One was that the link between radiation and this disorder has not been established. Another is that radiation levels had been monitored in and around the Savannah River facility continuously since the plant was built nearly thirty years earlier, and gave no evidence that any employee or plant neighbor had been exposed to enough radiation to cause any health problem. An objective judgment would have been that the claim of twenty-five cases was on shaky ground from the start.

Three Mile Island is a tale too well known to need recounting here. It is remembered as the most serious nuclear-power-plant accident in the U.S. It ought to be remembered, as well, as a journalistic fiasco. No one at TMI or in the government agency concerned with reactor safety seemed to be in control of the situation, or the release of information. Reporters got their stories where they could find them, and much of the time, got them wrong. Initially, the reports of a loss of cooling water and a meltdown in one of the two reactors at the site touched off media fears that a true disaster loomed, a Doomsday scenario. Later, when that quieted down, there was a groundswell of fear that the radiation released would do long-term harm to people in the surrounding Pennsylvania counties: birth defects, miscarriages, thyroid defects, and cancer. There were reports of cows dying mysteriously on a farm nearby.

However, the reactor never was a "bomb" ready to go off, and the amount of radiation released was not large enough to represent a hazard to the public. No one, man or beast, received an overdose. It turned out that the cows had died of natural causes. The report that babies born the next year showed thyroid defects was based on a statement from one source. That produced a *Boston Globe* headline: "13 Thyroid Defects: Probe Set at N-Plant." However, even at that time health officials were saying that there was no basis for public alarm because there was no medical evidence that radiation at the level of the TMI release had ever caused hyperthyroidism. A scientist who was a member of the study group created by the President to investigate the TMI disaster, the so-called Kemeny Commission (named for its head, John Kemeny, a distinguished mathematician and college president), said that he could assure everyone "unequivocally" that there was no connection between the thyroid defects and TMI. Such caveats appeared far down in the news story, though.

Several journalists who have reviewed the coverage of TMI, as carried by both print and electronic media, have said that the truth about nuclear power and its problems or promise cannot be learned by reading the newspapers and watching television. I would amend that: The truth on TMI would not have emerged from a casual sampling, but would have been found only by people lucky enough to have encountered the accounts of trained, careful science writers who had done their homework on nuclear-power issues before the reactor at TMI lost its coolant, and therefore were able to write about it without losing their cool.

The stock defense for uncritical reporting is that journalists are only reporting what others say and do: "We don't judge," they argue. But of course they do. They make judgments all the time: the editorial decision to run a story instead of holding it back for further checking; the decision to print an accusation if it comes from one source, but not to do so if a similar charge is heard from another source; the writer's judgment that the denials belong in paragraph nine and do not get billing in the lead; the news director's decision to assign staff to the development of a solid background piece (an expensive and time-consuming proposition) instead of going with a spot news account—all these are judgment calls based on somebody's sense not just of what is catchy but also of what the responsibilities of the media should be. The coverage of technology is the most serious kind of business for journalists as well as government officials, industry leaders, and everyone else who has to make decisions about complex and frequently hazardous activities. There is a special obligation to get as many facts as possible before deciding that it is time to sound an alarm, precisely because so many laymen do not have the technical background to make judgments on their own.

What is known about this dumpsite? Do nuclear reactors explode if they overheat? Have there been other reports of this disease in this area? What do other scientists say? What's the reputation of the man bringing me this report? (In the polycythemia case, one of the key sources was a doctor whose license had been lifted.) Do I know the source to be careful and thorough, or is he perhaps one of those people who twist data to suit another master—an employer, an activist group, or anyone else who might want the conclusions to come out his way? Am I being allowed to see the back-up data, or only undefended conclusions? How much exposure to radiation is regarded as a health hazard to humans and how much are we talking about here? What is known about the correlation between tests on laboratory animals and possible effects on humans? Are we dealing with serious, irreversible health hazards, and thus should lean over backward to be careful, or is this a smaller-scale problem? These are the kinds of questions any professional would ask before drawing conclusions. They are analogous to the questions good reporters routinely ask when they are covering politics, international relations, or other fields in which they are comfortable. No vast educational background is needed to deal with them, only a reasonable familiarity with the field which an intelligent layman can acquire. One must conclude, though, that this sort of healthy skepticism has been all too rare in the media's attention to the problems of health and safety, just as it was scarce in the days when science and technology came in for fulsome praise in the media.

In a quite different vein, consider the media's treatment of the "energy crisis" of the 1970s. What did the public media make of the shortage of natural gas that drove some suppliers to ration their commercial customers, and the scarcity of gasoline that had cars lined up for blocks at gas stations? That question has been explored by the Media Institute, a watchdog group sponsored by private companies, including broadcasters. After analyzing nearly 1,500 television reports, the institute concluded that the coverage was anything but enlightening. Those who depended on the TV accounts, this study decided, would have been in a complete muddle. My recollection is that the print media did better but still fell short of minimum standards for careful, thorough reporting. Generally factual accounts citing places where shortages existed shared space in newspapers with the wildest kinds of stories regarding the origins of the problems: Reporters dutifully noted charges that oil firms were holding back supplies. There were vague reports about tankers filled with oil, lying off the Atlantic Coast, keeping needed oil off the market.

Does this denote a media bias against the oil companies so deep-rooted that it overcame all sense of objectivity? That was one charge leveled at the media at the time, but there is perhaps a simpler and more believable explanation. The public was given an incoherent account because the economic reasons for shortages were rarely brought forward, and perhaps that was because many journalists had no idea of what those reasons might be. Further, as the study of TV coverage showed, reporters drew heavily on government sources, which predictably led to few stories suggesting that government's own policies, rather than skullduggery or stupidity on the part of the private sector, might have something to do with the problem. More contact with petroleum economists and resource experts in industry and universities might have cast a brighter light on the nation's energy-supply problems and prospects.

Memory might have warned more editors and writers that the rumors about the ships were suspiciously like the old accusations that Big Oil had created a motor oil that never needed changing, but had killed the product to protect its business; or the one about Du Pont buying up the patent on the way to make nylon stockings that would never run, so that women would forever have to buy new nylons. Those who went looking for evidence to support the contention that the crisis was a creature of the oil companies did not fall for the harebrained stories that ran in some publications. Some curious people chartered airplanes and flew out to sea to look for the anchored tankers. They found ships carrying grain and coal (which could have been mistaken for tankers), some empty tankers, and some full ones headed for port or waiting for dock space so they could unload—normal ship movements. The U.S. Coast Guard reported that during the period when shortages were said to be particularly severe, an above-average number of tankers arrived at U.S. ports. The crisis stories ran day after day, but the central information that the public needed most of all—that the nation had a distribution problem but was in no danger of "running out" of gas and oil—had a hard time finding its way past the panic stories.

A problem in the coverage of the energy crisis, as with the health and safety stories, was that few journalists had enough advance experience in the field to bring good judgment to fast-breaking news. Stephen Hess' study showed that among Washington writers covering energy affairs, few had majored in economics or science in college. Hess quoted one, a political-science major, as saying she was just "sort of shoved into the energy slot." Another reporter, formerly a foreign correspondent, said he was put on the energy beat because interest was heating up on Capitol Hill and he had to become the "expert," but admitted that "this scares me because I don't really understand the technicalities of the subject at all." When asked what subject they wish they had studied more in school, many reporters today will answer, "Economics." When asked what is wrong with their coverage of issues, many will say that too many members of the craft flit from subject to subject, touching the surface but having no time to dig in.

It is not difficult for journalists with a bit of imagination to find sources who will help them with perspective. On energy issues, for example, there are consultants, university-based study centers, and industry associations, any of which could have steered reporters toward an understanding of the causes of the shortages. With Three Mile Island, journalists would have found at Du Pont headquarters, not far from the scene of the accident, a number of individuals with decades of experience (dating from the dawn of the nuclear era in World War II) in reactor operations and safety. As far as I know, no reporter ever called those people to ask whether a meltdown was likely and if so, what the hazards would be.

The redeeming feature in all of this is that people in the media are aware of the weaknesses and excesses, find the situation unsatisfactory, and are doing something about it. They are trying to clean the stable and improve the breed, and are having some success at it. They can use help and cooperation from other institutions in society, but already have all the critics they need, including many within their own ranks. Dan Cordtz, the economics editor for ABC News, says, "I can be a lot more critical of TV than the critics," and he follows up with specifics. In public forums and meetings of editors and publishers, people in the media hear themselves labeled as "insular," "arrogant," "doom-criers," and "sensationalists," and take that to heart. Surveys have shown that the credibility and stature of journalists have slumped in recent years—not to the same levels as those of people in some other walks of life, perhaps (politicians, big-business leaders), but on curves with similar slopes. Louis Banks probed these animosities in an article in the *Atlantic* which bore the blunt title: "Memo to the Press: They Hate You Out There."

It is not outside critics alone, but people in the media as well, who deplore the use of the First Amendment as a shield against wrongful behavior. One example is a 1982 film, *Absence of Malice,* starring Sally Field as an aggressive reporter who writes stories that prove to be both false and damaging, and who pauses to review her ethics only after one person is dead and another's reputation is shattered. The script was written by a former newspaper editor. A nonfiction comment has been made by Fred Friendly, who has said that journalists' arguments against tighter self-regulation of their work reminds him of the arguments businessmen made before the Sherman Antitrust Act was passed. "I care a lot about the First Amendment," Friendly explained, "but . . . because [journalists] are not constitutionally Accountable (with a big 'A') to government doesn't mean that they are not accountable (with a small 'a') to [readers]. . . . There's a difference between being legally accountable and being morally accountable."

If Mencken was held to be a traitor to his class, Fred Friendly and others who hold similar views are more like prophets being honored in their own time. There are numerous and widespread programs to make reporting and editing more responsible and journalists more knowledgeable. Special emphasis is being given to the two weak areas mentioned here, economics and technology. With Ford Foundation sponsorship, Friendly arranged a series of seminars for business and the media in cities around the country, beginning in 1977. The seminars were led by law-school professors, who used the Socratic method and hypothetical cases to probe the conduct and motives of people on both sides. The American Newspaper Publishers Association, American Society of Newspaper Editors, Associated Press, and National Association of Broadcasters have conducted training programs, briefings, or conferences to upgrade journalists' skills.

Journalism schools have added special programs to provide stronger background in science and economics, and there are less formal projects in science under the sponsorship of the National Association of Science Writers and the Council for the Advancement of Science Writing. Scholarships and internships have been created. At New York University, a new graduate-school program has been launched to train journalists who already have undergraduate degrees in science. At the American University in Washington, there is now a National Center for Business and Economic Communication, providing instruction and conducting studies under the guidance of a veteran journalist, Louis Kohlmeier. Rockefeller University's Science and Public Policy Program is headed by a scientist who is helping bring together journalists, government policymakers, business representatives, and others with the objective of improving understanding of such problems as toxic-substance control.

House critics have acquired formal status. One mentioned earlier is the Media Institute. That has outside support. Another, created in 1973 by journalists themselves with foundation financing, is the National News Council. It serves as a forum for complaints about unfair or inaccurate reporting, and it publishes critiques.

Journalists have become self-critical in public. Once, there was only an occasional, lonely voice, the best known of which was probably A. J. Liebling's. He used to chide his fellows in a series titled "The Wayward Press." Today, in-house criticism is more common and, Mencken would be happy to hear, no longer considered treasonous. Editors and publishers meeting in convention agonize over past failings. Newspapers have ombudsmen to field and review complaints, and a column set aside for corrections, retractions, and clarifications. When the *New York Times* and the *Washington Post* both discovered, in separate incidents, that they had run stories fabricated by reporters, one a series that won a Pulitzer Prize, it was their own editors who broke silence and corrected the mistakes. A Chicago television station, WBBM, did a one-hour show examining reporting techniques. Public television ran a series on print and electronic journalism, exploring libel cases among other topics. ABC's *Viewpoint* show has served as a forum for criticism of TV news practices. CBS has done one program looking at the journalistic practices of its own lead show, *60 Minutes,* and another one-hour program on the question of individual rights of privacy of people in the news, versus the rights of the press to run its stories. The latter was another use of the case method, with a Harvard law professor prowling the aisle, firing questions at such celebrity "students" as Lauren Bacall and Dan Rather.

For all of this introspection, it remains that there is still a credibility gap between the media and many of the private-sector organizations they cover, as with the media and government. Journalists still do not think much of the way some business leaders do their job, and vice versa. However, the bright side of this is that it is apparent to all concerned that the media and business are dependent upon one another and must continue working toward change and accommodation. The trend toward increased coverage of economic and business affairs can be expected to continue. There will be more staff, more column inches and broadcast time, and, with luck, more efforts to dig behind the headlines. It is reasonable to expect a slow but sure improvement in quality, with less of what Dan Cordtz has labeled "Here they come; there they go" journalism, and more of the careful, thoughtful, and informed reporting that distinguishes the craft at its best.

That increases the attractions of an open-minded attitude toward the media on the part of all the news sources, be they public or pri-

vate. There is no need for anyone to take injustice and sloppy reporting lying down, but neither should the private sector be hypersensi-
tive. It is far better to take in stride whatever negative stories there are
as long as they are relatively harmless, and to invest energy in building
stronger relationships with the people in the media who are reviewing
their own performance and raising their own standards. We have,
after all, come a long way from the days when newsmen took payment
under the table to run stories favorable to business in the New York
newspapers; when "PR" in business meant flying turkeys off rooftops
with roller skates strapped to their feet, to stimulate pre-Thanksgiving
turkey sales; and when such critical public commentary as was needed
to keep people and institutions on the straight and narrow was delivered, in all too many communities, in the pages of such journals as the
"Minnesota rag."

8

The Climate Inside

On a sunday morning some years ago, when I was a newly minted chief executive officer, I was in a Washington, D.C., hotel room doing some light reading to kill time while waiting for a meeting to begin, and came across an article criticizing corporate management and boards of directors. I have forgotten the name of the author and the publication, but it struck me at the time that this was one more bit of evidence that discussion about life in the corporate interior was increasing, with little comment from the people with firsthand knowledge. It was almost as though an inverse relationship existed: the more intense the criticism, the smaller the chance that it was coming from anyone who was or had been a director or executive in a corporation. Most of the information offered the public was secondhand and much of it was simply wrong on the facts. There were abundant theories and numerous proposals for reform, but little by way of practical understanding of the functions of boards and managers, and only a passing recognition of the changes that were taking place on the boards and in the management practices of large corporations.

I resolved then and there to do what one man could to redress the balance, and to offer, for what it was worth, a voice of experience. In the intervening years, I have taken as many opportunities as possible to speak to the issues myself, and to encourage other businessmen to do the same. Other executives have shared my concern, bringing the Business Roundtable into the discussions, making strong presentations to the public and Congress, and conveying corporate points of view to the public media about corporate policies, accountability, and internal operations. At one point, I found myself sharing a platform at

Carnegie-Mellon University with the man who then headed the Securities and Exchange Commission, Harold Williams, in what was supposed to be a debate about what ought to be done to govern companies better. We may have disappointed our audience because we agreed on almost all of the main points. We are both gradualists.

In retrospect, I can see that the voices from the corporate interior were offered none too soon. The criticism of the American corporation has become a growth industry. All aspects of governance and management have been examined in incredible detail, from the composition of boards and the question of what should be done, if anything, to change the selection process, to the working environment on the shop floor and the question of what can be done, if anything, to make employee-employer relationships more amiable and productive.

One stimulus for this vast and still-growing commentary was a series of revelations in the 1970s of overt wrongdoing in the executive suites—bribes to foreign government functionaries, illegal or questionable political payments, and the like—damning in number and seriousness. Another was a wave of feeling that most companies make bad use of human resources, and that American industry must adopt new ways of working lest it lose out to foreign rivals whose managers understand the human animal better. How new those proposed changes really are is one of the points for attention here. My own feeling is that we are going back to some old-fashioned approaches that should have been more widely adopted in their time, and still deserve to be followed.

All in all, the discussion has been healthy and useful. It has led private corporations to rethink the basic responsibilities of leadership, strengthen their boards, do some necessary housecleaning, reexamine their work environment, and share more information with the public. The corporations are the better for that. With respect to the major issues that float to the upper reaches of the corporation, though, the commentary continues to be shot through with misinformation. It is clear that many outsiders have no idea of how much time and energy corporate directors and managers devote to the very questions that most concern critics, and I can only conclude that the persistence of myths is at least partly the corporations' fault. Not enough people running corporations have taken the public enough into their confidence, explaining what they are trying to do and defining the standards which guide them. Because there has been failure of that sort, though, and conceding that there was misbehavior in high places, it still does not follow that society should accept as well founded many of the "facts" purporting to reveal what generally goes on in board-rooms and executive suites, or many of the reform proposals that have been advanced.

With this in mind, I plan to come at this subject from the top down, looking first at the issue of governance and then at questions regarding management. Having chaired one major corporate board and served on others in the fields of banking, insurance, aircraft man-ufacture, health care, and computers, along with a couple of universi-ties and philanthropic foundations, I have reached several conclu-sions. By stating them, perhaps I can explain the presence of this inward-looking chapter in a book that is otherwise external in view. The conclusions are these: What goes on inside large companies is as important to their public acceptability as what goes on outside. The way a large corporation fits into the political and social matrix is heavily dependent on the climate established by the board, not by its statements alone but, more importantly, by its actions. The corporate environment is to some extent shaped by everyone in an organiza-tion—and it is customary to bow in the "we're all in this together" direction—but the creation of a healthy internal climate begins with the board of directors. It is the board that decides a company's charac-ter, to use a quaint term in which some of us still believe, and if the directors are deficient in their lead, the subordinates cannot be expected to fill the gap. Indeed, the subordinates chosen by the board may be the problem.

The point was made earlier with reference to government that when units are not operating effectively, the place to send the consul-tants is not into the operating agencies but to the higher reaches of the executive and legislative branches, for that is where the problems are probably rooted. So it is with the corporate interior: If there is some-thing wrong with the behavior of a private organization, the reasons are likely to be found in the policies and attitudes set forth by the board. Opposite that, and more positively, when an organization is respected and trusted in the outside world, it is likely that trust and respect will be found in wide measure among the people inside, at all levels, as a consequence of policies and attitudes emanating from the top. To a much greater extent than many outsiders suppose, people within organizations sense what the boards and the senior management think is important, and thus what the real corporate priorities are. Moreover, to my way of thinking, there is no way to differentiate between a corporation's inside and outside faces. I find it a contradiction in terms to say that a particular company has a good understanding of the public-policy process and does well at government relations, but does not understand corporate governance issues and does a poor job in its employee relations. A company can hardly do well at one of those tasks if it does badly at the other.

If the standard test for corporate management has to do with economic performance—how well the company makes and sells goods and services—the test questions for corporate governance go beyond that. At stake are the institution's legitimacy and accountability, its probity as much as its product. Some people have firmly concluded that the boards of large corporations flunk their performance reviews on all counts. In this view, corporate governance is a smooth phrase for a cynical process by which power is seized by a handful of corporate princes. Big corporations are seen as rogue elephants loose in the land, elephants which pay no attention to where they put their feet. Corporate directors are seen not as people who provide necessary windows to the outside world, but as window dressing, or sleepy sentries. Stockholders are perceived to exercise no real authority. The election of directors and the appointment of top executives are seen as charades, simple exercises in self-perpetuation. The outside forces supposedly keeping business in check (regulation, antitrust law, market competition, collective bargaining, state chartering laws, and other agencies of constraint) are regarded as singly and severally inadequate. It is claimed that business has crippled, coopted, or corrupted them one and all.

From that vision and its lesser variations have come a variety of proposed correctives, some modest, some draconian. Congress has been urged by some of its members to break up the biggest companies, regulate all of them more tightly, and bring them more under the Federal wing by requiring national corporate charters in place of the charters now issued by the separate states. One objective of that would be to turn private corporations into what Professor George Lodge of Harvard once called (and recommended) "nationally chartered community-oriented collectives."

It has been suggested that corporations be required to have boards made up mostly or entirely of outsiders, i.e., individuals not employed by the companies; that constituencies be given board seats (perhaps by quota—so many women, so many blacks, so many community representatives, etc.); that labor-union representatives be given board status, following the lead of West Germany with its codetermination policies, or in the manner in which the Chrysler Corporation, when in the throes of refinancing with government-backed loans and concessions from employees, placed on its board the head of the United Auto Workers, Douglas Fraser. It has been proposed that boards be equipped with their own staffs, strike forces of auditors free to roam the organization, beholden only to nonmanagement directors. One package plan would put nearly all of the above ideas in force at once, and impose them on the 700 or so largest corporations in the country. That one came from Ralph Nader's Corporate Accountability Research Group.

A more temperate view is surely in order. The thrust of this chapter is that the foundations of the present system are sound, the methods of governance are defensible in terms of both ethics and democratic principle, and the proposed curatives are more dangerous than any disease from which the private sector suffers. Some changes are needed to remedy past mistakes and reflect new conditions, but such changes should come in an orderly way and are being made. Pat formulas for "restructuring" should be viewed with great skepticism, on the grounds that what fits one corporation may not be suited to another. The drastic reform suggestions ought to be opposed *in toto,* for they would yield the worst of all possible outcomes, a double-negative trade-off: The most valuable qualities of the enterprise system would be sacrificed to gain the least attractive features of the governmental system. In effect, we would swap the track record of General Electric for that of the U.S. Postal System.

If one agrees with the claim that the engine of economic progress in the United States has been enterprise set up by private individuals for private purposes, then it should follow that major change is in order only if the present system has failed woefully. There is nothing in our national history or in a comparison with other societies to suggest that this is even remotely the case. The last, worst way to tune the economic engine is to call in a band of inept mechanics and issue them sledgehammers.

What is most wrong with the prescriptions for major change is their premises. The "facts" about elephants are incorrect. There is no runaway corporate power in the marketplace or political community. Both commercial competition and governmental regulation are persistent, effective, and almost ubiquitous, as by now is entirely clear to the leaders of the large as well as small corporations, if not to business' critics. Some of the proposals for reform are surely prescriptions for chaos. Consider "constituency directors," for example. One well-justified principle of corporate governance is that all directors be committed to the overall well-being of the organization, and be pledged individually and collectively to seek the best balance among competing interests. The objective is the long-range good of all concerned. To say that some directors should henceforth be seated because they represent specific constituents is to guarantee that boards would soon lose whatever sense of common purpose they now have (if anything, they need more of it, not less). Directors would be permitted, even urged, to deal with the separate purposes of groups whose flags they fly. This would drive corporations in exactly the wrong direction, away from a focus on long-range, board-based objectives, toward short-term deals, vote-trading on policies, and log-rolling in the corridors outside the boardroom. We would be encouraging the very qualities that many people, including some who favor this idea, find most reprehensible in the political process.

The Noah's Ark proposal is probably not to be taken seriously—its political support has never been great—but it is worth looking at the consequences as an object lesson in what boards are not supposed to be. The internal maneuvers within interest-group boards would be Byzantine, and it is difficult to see how individual directors could avoid the obvious challenges of their accountability. Stockholder suits would pop up like crabgrass in July, on the grounds that the directors were looking out for the interests of everybody except the one group that owns the store, the stockholders.

Constituency pleading is not all bad, to be sure. It is one way of avoiding board and management meetings smothered with politesse, and there is something to be said for the tension it creates. However, as has been suggested by a former president of Time Inc., James Shepley, tension that is not drawn from a common corporate commitment can lead to paralysis. It is likely to do that if boards are packed with directors unsympathetic to business problems and realities. On the road to governance by the lowest common denominator, the first casualty would be the institution's appetite to take risks (another quality corpo-

rations could use in greater, not lesser, measure). As Shepley has commented, "the chief executive would be out of his mind who would take
a risk-laden proposition to a group of directors, who whatever their
other merits, do not really understand the fine points of the business at
hand, and whose official purpose is to create 'tension.' . . . "

Always, the question of competence must be pressed forward. Suppose IBM did reconstruct its board to assure seats to representatives
of community groups, employees, women, blacks, Chicanos, and others. As a director of IBM, my first move would be to resign my seat
and sell my stock. I cannot imagine such a board having the slightest
idea of how to make the decisions that routinely confront this firm's
board, decisions that steer an organization in one of the most international, technological, competitive, and fast-changing of all industries.
How could such a board pass judgment on management strategies that
lock in the company for five to ten years? What background would it
have to monitor research and capital-spending budgets totaling billions of dollars per year? The meetings of such a board might well
meet all standards of democratic process, but how many potential
investors would elect to commit their savings to IBM in this circumstance? How many pension-fund managers would sleep well knowing
that the assets for which they are responsible, assets whose earnings
provide monthly checks for retired people, were in the hands of such
overseers? How many other stockholders would join me and "vote
with their feet," pulling out of IBM and putting their money elsewhere? Is someone now to deny us that option?

The point is that being a director of a large corporation is a full
order of magnitude different from serving on a local school board or
community agency. Caring about what is right and just, and even
having uncommon abilities in certain directions, are not necessarily
adequate qualifications for governing corporations of substantial size.
Further, the people who founded or invested in such businesses did
not do so because they wanted to set up miniature, governmentlike
structures in the name of "corporate democracy." They became involved with the intention of making money, which in most people's
opinion is not an antisocial mission, and the first prerequisite for
directors or managers in such organizations is to be able to contribute
skills that enhance the organization's prospects.

A better summary than I can offer on the balance of diversity and
talent has been written by Jacqueline Grennan Wexler, formerly presi-

dent of Hunter College and a woman who has served both as a university trustee and as a corporate director. She sees similarities in those roles and argues a need for breadth in both kinds of institutions, but she also sees clearly the difference between variety and disorganization:

> A corporate board of directors and a university board of trustees should bring the richest possible range of insights and expertise to their deliberations in order to understand all the options available to their institutions to achieve their missions. It is to their *invested* interest that they select their members from a rich range of background and experience.
>
> Trustees and directors will be representatives of many groups and many fields. They cannot, like legislators, be directly accountable to those groups. The call for special-interest directors is naïve. More than any other group, trustees and directors must view corporations and colleges with those institutions' total responsibility and good in perspective. It is in the public interest that our institutions be governed by men and women committed to their integrity, not by those who would manipulate or prostitute them for others' ends.

One of the few places where I part company with a onetime idea of Commissioner Williams of SEC is on his proposal for corporations to have all-outsider boards, with only the chief executive officer representing the insiders, and with the CEO not the board chairman. Such a board, far from holding the hired executives in check, would be the easiest of all boards for a clever CEO to manipulate. He would be the only individual at the board meetings with an intimate knowledge of the company's activities. The fact that he was not the board chairman would be but a minor impediment. If the CEO had any political skills at all, he could assure that the outsiders learned just enough to appreciate the wisdom of his ideas, and not enough to challenge them. Even if directors were equipped with private staff assistants, the board members would never be a match for the one person in the room who spends sixty hours a week on the business and has the whole corporate organization at his beck and call.

Equally, it must be noted that windows pass light in both directions. If we are prepared to argue, as I am, that outside directors help corporate insiders maintain perspective, then it also should be true that inside directors can be vital sources of knowledge for outsiders. Richard West, a former dean of Dartmouth's business-administration school, is among those who have pointed out that it is important for outsiders to be able to exchange ideas and questions with a number of people in management, as peers among peers. This is necessary as part of the process of outsiders building their banks of relevant information about matters coming before the board. Professor West, like Mrs. Wexler, brings firsthand experience to his opinions, having served on several corporate boards.

Federal chartering is a phony issue, plain and simple. It nonetheless has serious overtones, and says a lot about the divergent world views to be found in our society. The essential question here is one of power, not the postal address from which comes a piece of paper bearing a fancy seal. Now the charter may read Harrisburg, Pennsylvania, or Albany, New York, or, more likely than any other example, Dover, Delaware. The proposal is to make it say Washington, D.C., and the reason for doing so, as most of its proponents readily concede, is to remove more authority from private corporate hands. Once in Federal custody, corporate charters could become all-encompassing documents speaking to such matters as market share and product selling prices, and pressing on a national scale a variety of convictions about desirable social policy. Somebody would have to run this Federal function, so we could anticipate a czarlike agency, a Super SEC. The states would be bumped aside as controlling agencies, and many of the existing Federal regulatory bodies as well.

While it is difficult to move the Federal government to action, it is far more frustrating to try to persuade fifty separate state governments to common action, especially when some of the fifty garner substantial amounts of money from the present corporate-chartering process. Hence the appeal of centralization. Once power was coalesced in Washington, it would be feasible to use advocacy politics, for which that city is famous, to reach goals that advocates have been unable to obtain at the ballot box. A Federal chartering agency might be persuaded, for example, to force corporations to sell drugs under generic labels instead of trademarks; or to prevent them from building nuclear power plants; or to prohibit them from shutting down inefficient manufacturing units if that meant laying off workers. In essence, what the champions of Federal chartering have always wanted is not more paperwork to occupy Washington bureaucrats, but more power to reach their own political goals. They want to be able to pull a corporate lever to deliver social "goods," as they define these, whenever they see those "goods" being threatened by economic efficiency. How good some of those results would be is of course questionable.

The debate on all this began long ago. Federal chartering of corporations, far from being a modern issue, was first proposed in James Madison's day, before there were any big corporations or an SEC and the rest of the regulatory structure to keep an eye on them. The issue recurs in every generation, and can be expected to continue doing so. Now as in the past, it boils down to the question of what the public has in mind when it thinks of freedom and rights in the economic area. Do people have a right to form voluntary associations on their own, contained only by the requirement that they not trample on the freedom of others? Or have the rights of association been so abused that the nation, for the protection of the majority, must now revert to a much older philosophy, medieval in its quality, that individuals have only such privileges as a central government, in its generosity and wisdom, chooses to bestow on them? I think the question answers itself. It would be a fundamental break with America's past to turn private corporations into "nationally chartered community-oriented collectives," and no justification for such a break has been produced.

The poverty of state chartering codes is everywhere declared, but never demonstrated. The state of Delaware is routinely trotted forward as the worst of the fifty possible examples—the leader in the race to the bottom, as one law-school professor, the late William Cary of Columbia, put it. Delaware earned this miserable title because the state makes it simple and inexpensive to form a corporation (one local resident used to advertise that he could do it for you for less than $100, without any lawyers), and the costs thereafter are low for non-resident firms. We are asked to infer from this that the state is lax in monitoring the companies to which it grants legal existence, and that other people suffer as a result—stockholders, employees, and "little guy" taxpayers who have to make up the difference because "big guys" are not paying their fair share.

It is an old and tired argument, readily refuted. The chief reason that Delaware is a popular place to be incorporated, certainly for companies of large size, is not that it offers bargain-basement prices—the difference in costs between that state and many others would be a tiny factor in most companies' annual reports. The primary reason is that Delaware has a legal code that is modern and fair, and that is kept up to date by constant review. Corporations find that the legal logic they encounter in Delaware is clear and relatively predictable. Delaware judges who deal with corporate matters have earned national reputations for being extraordinarily knowledgeable, and as a result corporations have developed confidence in the stability and wisdom of the Delaware courts. All of this makes it attractive for many companies to call this their legal home base, and at least 40 percent of the companies listed on the New York Stock Exchange, plus many smaller firms, have elected to do just that.

Though Delaware's presumably scandalous affair of state has existed for decades, nothing convincing has yet been put in the record to show that stockholders or the public have been ill served. If any one company were in a position to abuse the state chartering system and run roughshod over the public interest, it ought to be the Du Pont Company in Delaware. Du Pont is a major taxpayer there and the state's largest employer. At various times in the company's history, members of the du Pont family or company employees, or both, have held positions of authority in state government, including the chairs of governor, judge, and majority leader in the Senate. For a period of many years, the principal newspapers in the state, the morning and afternoon dailies in Wilmington, were owned by a holding company established by du Pont family members, though the papers have since been sold to the Gannett chain.

For all of this, the Du Pont Company is treated no differently in Delaware courts than other corporate organizations, and the company's power to affect legislative outcomes is sharply limited. One bit of proof of that is a state Coastal Zone Act that prohibits industrial development along a long waterfront strip. The Du Pont Company objected when the bill was under consideration in 1971, not because it wanted to oppose conservation policies but on the grounds that this particular legislation was poorly drafted and inflexible. The company has since pleaded more than once for amendment, but to no avail. For all Du Pont's legendary powers in Delaware, this law was passed and still stands as first written.

The parallel holds for the judicial branch: The corporation is given its day in court, but government retains control. If Du Pont directors were to breach their fiduciary duties, they could expect stockholder suits to be pressed with no less success in Delaware than in any other state. What Delaware does not do to or for corporations, however, is to use charters as instruments for telling companies who ought to be on their boards or what the qualifications for directors must be. Nor does the state seek to use charters as weapons for regulating companies in new ways. This, in the eyes of critics, seems to be the true failure of the state chartering system.

Speaking to this subject, Andrew Hacker has presented a picture of the world as it might be with Federally chartered enterprises:

> The vision emerges of chastened corporations, going about their business in accord with the morality of a democratic populace and the rationality of professional administrators. In this depiction, corporations become acquiescent creatures, ready to place social considerations ahead of their own. Thus virtually every value—total disclosure, product safety, hiring equity, free expression, community consultation, ecological purity—takes priority over profits, expanding the enterprise, or persuading people to buy things. I leave it to others to speculate on how well businesses may fare under such a regimen of restrictions. What intrigues me is the advent of a non-economy. In its place we have an ethical schoolroom. Not much may get produced. But what does is exceedingly virtuous. . . .
>
> Corporate chartering will not bring us socialism, or even some close approximation. But it will give us another agency, replete with its forms and regulations, hearings and inspections, guidelines and checklists. Once again the mountain will labor and come forth with a nest of mice. They won't make corporate behavior more moral or rational; or for that matter less profitable. But mice do get in the way and on the whole are not pleasant to have around.

What is it that corporate boards are supposed to do, and can they do it better? The answer to the second part of that question is "Yes." The first part is more complicated; it has a five-part answer. My approach to this is to divide the functions of corporate governance and management the way the U.S. Constitution divides Federal and state power. The Constitution lays out the powers of the Federal branch and stipulates that everything not covered there is the business of the states and of the people thereof. Following suit, a corporate board should lay claim to five basic jobs and delegate all the rest to the corporate executives, or let the duties remain apart from the corporate mission entirely. Attention to these five tasks more or less defines the qualifications to be expected of directors and, by extension, those required of the managers the board pays to run the store.

The board should keep to itself, delegating to no one:

• The decisions on the broad policies and general directions the enterprise is to take.

- The selection of the company's officers, and the provision of a line of succession for people to fill key spots.
- The determination of performance standards, ethical as well as commercial, against which top managers and all subordinates will be judged, and a statement of these standards to the managers in unambiguous terms.
- The monitoring of top management's performance with reference both to the business directions the board has chosen, and to conformity with internal and legal requirements.
- The communication of the board's goals and standards to those who have an important stake in the organization (outsiders and insiders both), and of the steps the board takes to keep the organization responsive to its responsibilities.

What this denotes is a board of active stewards rather than passive trustees. It implies that it is the directors' job even more than the management's to see that corporate resources are put to creative use, against defined objectives, and are not simply warehoused like sacks of coins put in a countinghouse for safekeeping. It also puts a premium on the qualities of integrity, interest, and diligence on the part of each director. There is simply no substitute for these, or for the perspective, experience, and independence of mind required to handle complex problems. In this day and age, there should be no seat in the boardroom of any large corporation for people who have nothing to offer beyond nice intentions, or for those willing only to show up once a month to pour holy water over decisions someone else has already made.

Ordinarily, it is the management of a company that is expected to attend to such matters as product introductions, capital expansions, and the decisions to abandon or downgrade some lines of work while putting more corporate energy into others. This in no way reduces the need for directors with extensive business background, however. With few exceptions, corporate boards must involve themselves in strategic decisions—loosely, those that affect the direction in which the company is heading—and in all large capital commitments. What this comes down to, in effect, is that the board is to be apprised of, and usually votes on, decisions known in advance to be big enough to make an important difference in the company's position and character. When Citicorp decided some years ago to change from a strategy of running a banking operation in a narrow sense, to become a full-range financial-service organization in all parts of the world, the proposals came from the management, but the commitment came from the board. When IBM bet its future on the new world of electronics, giving up punch cards and manual sorters, and when the company later made the leap to personal computers to supplement the larger, main-frame units where it had made its reputation, it was again a matter of the management proposing and the board disposing. When the opportunity to buy Conoco first presented itself to Du Pont, the discussions were between the CEOs of those two firms (and a few other suitors who came on the scene before or after), but the CEOs made few moves in the negotiations and no irreversible decisions without the benefit of their boards' judgment and support.

Given the scale of the acquisition, this is easily understood. The Conoco-Du Pont merger was a multibillion-dollar transaction; but on much smaller ventures the boards are also called upon for advice and nonobjection to management's plans. In Du Pont, as is true for many large companies, major programs do not move forward unless they have the approval of the key committees of the board. For example, if a project involves a large investment, it must have the blessing of the board's Finance Committee, only three of whose ten members are people currently active in corporate management. A Du Pont department may on its own authority redesign the control panel in one of its plants, but if it wants to build a new plant costing tens of millions of dollars, it has to go over the hurdles in the board.

Thus, the absurdity of the picture of a modern corporate board meeting where a circle of dozing directors, individuals long past their prime if they ever had one, not having seen the agenda beforehand, are startled out of their reveries by the sudden question from the chair: "Gentlemen [it is always men in this scenario, old boys with old-school ties], is it okay with you if John here spends $150 million to rebuild the Richmond Works?" In a more correct picture, the ladies and gentlemen of today's board, who mostly will be individuals with extensive business background, will have spent hours preparing themselves for the meeting. They will know well in advance what it is that Richmond makes, how much it might make (i.e., in dollars) if overhauled, what is likely to happen to the plant if the request is turned down, what else the company might do with $150 million, and whether the Finance Committee is able to come up with this kind of money without leveraging the company too heavily. In the best-run boards, directors are provided with advance reading materials on all substantive issues coming before each committee or full-board meeting, with carefully prepared briefing materials augmented by summary sheets. One survey found that in 1982, directors of multibillion dollar companies spent an average of 155 hours—the equivalent of almost four work-weeks—on the business of each board on which they served.

All of this is to say that corporate boards cannot be letterhead operations or dumping grounds for people who have run out of gas, but must be organizations with a balance of individuals who have intimate knowledge of different aspects of business, a capacity for homework, and a sense of responsibility for the long-term health of the enterprise, a sense that extends beyond commercial dealings to encompass a company's long-term reputation with its various publics.

The supply of high-quality candidates for boards is not large, and paragons with all of the desirable virtues are rarely to be found. It is this that makes the case for drawing upon outsiders as well as insiders, and upon women as well as men. Quotas or exclusionary rules should have nothing to do with it. It is simply a matter of casting the net as widely as possible to give the organization its best chance of attracting outstanding candidates. Why limit the search by ruling out groups that account for more than one-half of the population? In many large corporations today, nonmanagement directors make up two-thirds to three-quarters of the boards. Women and members of minority groups are no longer rarities on boards, though they are not yet present in large numbers. There will be more as they gain experience in senior posts in private-sector organizations. The trend to broaden the boards was a long time getting started, but now is firmly established.

Students of corporate affairs have numerous suggestions for ways to improve the oversight function and keep boards accountable. Available for the asking are detailed organization charts covering audit, compensation, financial control, and other areas. There is danger in a tightly programmed approach, though. Boards are as different as your own children, and my experience is that no one system will produce the best results for all. A board could select any of several packages, but should be careful not to put its trust in a piece of paper while losing sight of the objective, which is to be clear about who is responsible for what.

Like many other organizations today, corporations are so complex that they must be governed and managed through committees. It is not practical for every board member or senior executive to stay close enough to all issues to serve as a knowing counselor and monitor. The way the committees are designed is less important than the commitment to staff them with the strongest directors and managers available, and to give them well-defined duties. When this is done, it is a signal to the outside world and to employees that a close watch is being kept on performance. I do not denigrate structure, but if corporations have competent, committed people on their boards, structure and process can easily be made to fall into place. If individuals with the needed qualities are missing or the board is fuzzy about objectives, corporations are in trouble, no matter whose organization chart they follow.

There has been considerable improvement in corporate boards in the past ten to fifteen years. Pressed by public criticism and changes in the law, and stung by glaring errors that have occurred in some large, once well-managed organizations, directors of those and other companies have done a good bit of soul-searching. The result has been an effort, generally successful, to draw stronger people into boards, tighten up responsibilities internally, and build a greater degree of sensitivity to the world surrounding the corporation. All companies listed on the New York Stock Exchange, for instance, are now required to have audit committees chaired by an outside director, and no one currently active in management can sit on those committees.

Most companies also handle executive compensation in an arm's-length manner. Though this is not a requirement, it makes sense, for one of the most destructive mistakes a board can make, destructive to morale inside and confidence outside, is to leave the impression that top management lives in a feathered nest and will stay warm and dry regardless of stormy weather. There have been cases where large companies have been devastated by adversity, even to the point of collapse, while the management took excellent care of itself through some sort of self-managed protective network. Meanwhile, employees have been tossed out and stockholders left to pick over the corporate carcass for whatever scraps remained. To avoid such instances, you need not only an alert board (how did the patient get so sick before the doctors knew it?) but one with a hard-boiled, independent compensation committee.

There is a further prerequisite here, though, and that is good judgment as to what constitutes performance. If a company is rolling on momentum, a do-little management may turn in pleasant-looking numbers for several years while in fact the company's future prospects and internal organization are falling apart. A company battered by hard times may continue for a time to show losses, even though a brilliant management team is taking all the right steps to rebuild and will in future years be recognized as the corporate savior. It takes some wisdom in a compensation committee to know what most deserves to be compensated.

There is still much room for improvement in corporate governance, and the areas that most invite attention are corporate disclosure and communications. They are of course related. For a long time, the unstated principle of private corporations was to let out whatever information was required by law, and keep back everything else. The test question, well known to anyone who has spent time in the corporate interior, was "Have we ever released that before?" If not, it took dynamite to blast the information loose. Today, the appropriate disclosure principle would be the reverse. With employees and the public as with the media, the burden has swung the other way, and the proper test question now is "Why not reveal this information? What have we got to lose?"

It is not just that the SEC and FTC disclosure rules are more stringent now, though of course those have to be obeyed. The corporation's deeper problem is that it must continuously demonstrate that its affairs are in the hands of people who are competent, accountable, and cognizant of the effects that the organization has on society. Establishing that requires more than the release of the quarterly numbers. It calls as well for plain statements about corporate objectives and programs, and about the code of conduct that is being followed.

If there is one common failing of corporate boards, it is that they play their cards too close to the vest. They hold back more facts about the business than is necessary to protect trade secrets, and, worse, they decline to explain to the outside world (and sometimes their own people) how performance is to be measured and what the code of conduct is meant to be. We can scarcely blame a company president for "short-termitis," with the organization putting all its attention on the next quarter's earnings and the devil take the future, if no one has told the president that the board expects and demands a longer-range vision, and that the president's pay and bonus depend on it. Nor can we expect employees to adhere to a code of conduct if the board has not set one forth explicitly, and if employees' jobs put them in gray areas where what they learned at mother's knee does not resolve the ethical questions.

Directors should not make assumptions about what the people below them understand or do not understand. There should be a code in writing and it should be made public. It appears to be impossible to produce one piece of paper that will fit all organizations. Many attempts have been made to do that, but all they have generated are homilies couched in useless language—i.e., language so general it permits no tests for compliance and thus speaks to rules that cannot be enforced. There is nothing to stop each company, though, from preparing its own list of dos and don'ts, citing specifics on the behavior that is ruled out of bounds and noting the penalties for stepping out of line.

As good a model to follow as any is the Sherman Act, which makes the distinction between *per se* offenses in antitrust, and other actions which a judge may rule to be right or wrong in the light of circumstances. Some kinds of corporate conduct amount to *per se* offenses and cannot be condoned because of pleas of extenuating circumstances. An example would be the bribery of government officials. Whether done in the U.S. or abroad, this subverts the process of government. It amounts to an effort by a private corporation to arrogate unto itself powers that, in democratic nations, do not rightly belong in the private sector. Another example would be the sale in one country of a product that knowledgeable authorities in other countries had tested and found to be inherently unsafe in any application. Such a sale would not be justified merely because the nation importing the product was unaware of the hazard.

An example in the gray area is the question of political contributions. Although corporate gifts are prohibited in U.S. Federal elections, that ban does not apply to elections in some states, and it does not exist at all in some other nations. Thus, each U.S. company has to decide for itself whether it will follow the Federal ban in every jurisdiction, or whether it will do as the Romans do. The decision could go either way, for our Federal mores in this instance are not necessarily morally superior to those found in other nations or states, some of which find no meaningful distinction between individual and collective participation in political funding.

The essential is for each company, once it has made its choice, to declare it, so that its own people and others know where they and the company stand. In Du Pont, we carried that a step further and set up a rule covering the personal political contributions of senior executives, as well as a written guideline on gifts of company funds. Members of management were told that they could make personal contributions or not, as they chose, but that the company would maintain a log of requests made to them, and of their response. The log was offered for public scrutiny. Newspapers ran stories about it, but mostly it has gathered dust. In the five years after it was created, only six people outside the company asked to see it—five reporters and a graduate student.

The fact that the register was there was enough of a reassurance that the board and management were aware of public sensitivities about corporate influence in politics, and had nothing to hide.

It is important, too, for the board to operate with an internal climate that encourages frank discussion and permits dissent. There should be no ganging up on directors who oppose a project, no icy glances at the people who persist in probing an issue when everybody else wants to go to lunch. In this respect, directors of corporations (and for that matter the managers reporting to the board) could well take a leaf from the experience of the scientists, and make the clear distinction between challenges to the ideas of others, and attacks on the person: debate *ad notium,* not *ad hominem.*

While efforts have been made to strengthen and empower boards, even more attention has been given to rethinking the responsibilities of corporate managements and improving their performance. Here, too, the quality of the people at the top and the climate they create within the organization are the crucial elements. A primary focus of a CEO is what can loosely be called internal environmental affairs, by which I mean the rules, relationships, conventions, and opportunities that are shaped in one way or another by the front office, and either encourage or discourage talented people from contributing to the organization.

One important day-to-day task for the CEO is communication— digesting information and shaping ideas, yes, but, even more centrally, the business of listening and explaining. Decisions and policies have no effect nor any real existence unless they are recognized and understood by those who must put them into effect. As with a board of directors, an operating business organization acquires a sense of purpose not just because one or two leaders have something in the back of their minds, but because that vision is shared and sold. It sounds banal to say that a CEO is first and foremost in the human-relations and communication businesses—what else could the job be?—but the point is too important to leave to inference. No other item on the chief executive's duty list has more leverage on the organization's prospects.

The misconceptions about the talent search both inside and outside corporate organizations are simply unbelievable. It is still thought that pay and promotion go to those who meet all sorts of unstated but agreed-upon social criteria relating to church, country clubs, and spouse. The truth is that corporations simply cannot afford to play such "how to succeed" games, even if their leaders were foolish enough to do so. The thirst for talent is so great that extraneous factors cannot be allowed to drive the selection process. It is easy to find companionable golfing partners, but at the office an executive with any pride of performance (or survival instinct) will do all he can to surround himself with people who have ability, who know how to work, and whose judgment can be trusted in a crisis. Whether they are men or women, black or white, joiners or loners, or individuals saddled with nagging spouses is and ought to be irrelevant. What has any of that to do with getting the job done?

One of the first lessons a manager learns while climbing the corporate ladder is how little he can accomplish by relying on his own brains alone. The higher an individual goes in management, the more obvious it becomes that an executive is only as good as the group around him. On the way upward, that group expands steadily to include more line managers plus a variety of staff people, including (if he is lucky) some true gems, a few key individuals who are nameless and faceless to the outside world, but who supply data, ideas, proposals, and criticism that contribute enormously to the smooth working of the organization.

How dependent a senior manager is on others is proven by the amount of time executives spend planning and reviewing job assignments, and by their constant searching of the ranks for "unknowns" with extraordinary ability and drive, either to move them upward or to give them special assignments that do not seem to fit in neat slots on the organization chart. In large organizations, there are always plenty of chores like that. In the best-run companies, management is equally persistent in asking whether there are negative factors, perhaps stemming from management's own behavior, that undercut incentives, block ideas, and mask talent.

There is a persistent mythology, too, that management can be reduced to a science guided by knowable, infallible laws. Management systems abound, and some of them contain remarkably ingenious schemes for analyzing information and making decisions objectively; but at its heart the management process remains a subjective craft. It hinges on vision and on the ability of the people at the top to capture support and build institutional loyalty. The qualities derive from a kind of judgment that has yet to be reduced to rules and numbers.

No one ever claimed this is a neat system. It is open to wrong decisions and failures of leadership. Less than deserving people can get promoted, and in every organization, some do. Even the best managers sometimes seem to be right only about 51 percent of the time. These self-evident shortcomings can send us down blind alleys. For a time, some corporate theorists and their management disciples, dissatisfied by the messiness of it all, gave themselves to a crusade to find the holy grail of precision. They concluded that financial management, which is the most rigorous segment of the art, should be treated as the hub of the management wheel, a center of decision more equal than any of the other parts. Plants, product lines, and clusters of services were rolled into "portfolios," to be monitored, expanded or contracted according to month-to-month performance, and bought and sold the way one would treat a handful of municipal bonds. Diversification and growth became ends in themselves, to be pursued whenever they made the earnings statement look better, without much reference to the logic of the resulting corporate structure, the technological fit, the management's understanding of the markets it was entering, or the organization's ability to keep the customers happy. The limits of that sort of conglomerate building rapidly made themselves known, and its principal operating tool, management strictly by-the-numbers, remained only briefly in vogue.

What the experience of recent years has taught us is that some precepts the portfolio managers urged us to dismiss as old-fashioned and nonscientific not only apply to modern problems but may well be the only solution to them, and are surely more effective than the proposed substitutes. Managers in the private sector are now being urged to attend once again to the homely virtues of producing quality products and providing reliable service. Business schools are implored to add production-management courses to the curriculum, and to leaven the number-crunching with the people-connected side of enterprise. Corporations are asked to (re)discover that their primary asset is people, and that people respond logically to incentives. We are now informed that the work ethic is not dead, that people do not like to goldbrick, that most employees will do a quality job if given tasks with identifiable value and rewards for superior performance, that the workplace is awash in potential talent, that workers are usually smarter than some of their supervisors think and can spot management insincerity and waffling a mile away, that most people are not bitterly unhappy about what they do for a living, despite the talk about alienation, and that big organizations as well as smaller ones can harness energies and talents if they go about it properly, with a genuine respect for people. In sum, the proposition is that when management shows people it honestly believes they are important to the organization, they will be important to the organization. When managers look upon employees as "hands," then the company can expect a response in kind: One place to work is as good (bad) as another. Get all you can. Give as little as possible. If the company is not making a long-term commitment to you, why should you show any loyalty to it?

We are advised that it is time for a different mood in labor-management relations. Instead of consuming ourselves with disputes about the way to divide the pie, the time has come for workers and managers to work together to create more real wealth to the benefit of all. Cooperation is in. The adversarial wars which prevailed for decades and spilled over into national politics, with Democrats seen as the party of organized labor and the Republicans as the part of business, are out. As a former official of the United Auto Workers has said, most of our labor relations has been about yesterday. The corporations that now hold the key to the future are those that enlist employees at all levels in the search for solutions to problems and the generation of "better ideas."

What is astonishing is not that these views are widely proclaimed, though surely they are, but that to some people this is new and novel doctrine. Where have those people been? The reformist attitudes I report were ingrained in the thinking of many managers and students of corporate affairs in generations before mine, and the essential wisdom behind this "new" approach does not require further testing. It has been confirmed time and again by the experience of companies that adopted it to their gain, or rejected it to their sorrow.

What drives these ideas forward today, and makes them seem somehow fresh and different, are the pressures of competition from abroad and the agonies of change within the domestic economy. Once-solid industries, long regarded as anchor points for national prosperity, presumed to be so invulnerable that the Antitrust Division considered breaking them up, have either lost market share, as with the Big Three auto producers, or have gone into even deeper decline, as with the leading steel manufacturers. Regional shifts have left some areas struggling while others have boomed. Industrial centers of the North acquired the unhappy title of Rustbelt, and were made to look pathetic versus the boom towns in the Sunbelt of the Southeast and Southwest. Technological shifts have overturned much of the established order. We are warned that the old-line textile-manufacturing communities, those that have not already collapsed, will become economic deserts unless they find other work to do. High technology is everywhere admired; low technology, pitied. Prosperity, thy name is Silicon Valley. That, at least, is the drumbeat.

It is obligatory in such discussions to point to Japan, and that frequently leads to invidious comparisons. While the U.S. was losing relative position economically, the Japanese were gaining in spectacular fashion. They raised their per-capita Gross National Product to equal that of any nation in the world. While U.S. labor and management remained at odds, as did management and government, the Japanese found ways to bring all three forces together into national harmony, with admirable success. All of this is brought forward by some as support for an argument that America must emulate Japanese ways of managing, not just to humanize its organizations but simply to survive.

No doubt we have lessons to learn from others, but we ought not be dazzled by the success of competitors, nor should we be dismayed by what we see around us. There are no mysteries or miracles out there. Most of what has worked well for the private sector in other countries, Japan included, is familiar to the U.S. and is being applied in many places here. A shakeout process is and has been going on in U.S. industry, but that process of decline and renewal is traditional. It accelerates in hard times and slows down when the going is good. The results do not always fall evenly and the process is far from orderly, but for the most part such change comes gradually. The nation can cope with it if resources are reassigned in sensible fashion and steps are taken to provide interim help when large numbers of workers are trapped in obsolete jobs.

It is well to approach those realignments with a sense of history, and a recognition that Silicon Valley is not Shangri-La. In a work force as large as this one—more than 100 million people—the balance among different occupations does not shift rapidly. Industries capitalizing on the newest technologies display impressive percentage growth rates, but they provide relatively few jobs in the aggregate, and not all of those jobs are skilled or secure. Some of the production jobs call for routines that may well be made obsolete by the next round of technological development. On the other side, many companies in traditional industries still have considerable opportunity for growth, much of it resting on their own ability to continue to innovate. What disguises this is that the process is selective: Some companies in mature industries are reshaping their product lines and process technology so that they will remain competitive, and some are not.

To suppose that the road to full employment and bountiful economic progress is to convert companies of ex-steelworkers into computer-repair teams is to ask for trouble. The jobs are not there. There are more production workers in the primary-metals industries than in all of the computer companies. The five largest categories of work associated with computers represent a little more than one-half of one percent of the total work force, or about 600,000 jobs. Assuming that their ranks will expand at a rate several times the national average, a decade from now they will still represent only a small part of the whole, perhaps 2 percent. In the American job market, there are twice as many auto mechanics as computer workers, five times as many janitors, ten times as many health-care workers, nearly twenty times as many people classified as operatives, doing such familiar work as welding and dry cleaning, and thirty times as many clerks, bookkeepers, and bank tellers. Even in a depressed condition, the metals and metal-working industries provide on the order of two million jobs. In the decade of the Eighties, the percentages of the work force represented by sales workers, clerks, craft workers, machine operators, and laborers are expected to remain almost stable, and most new job openings will continue to be found in the long-established career lines.

The worst thing managers can do is overgeneralize from the present, underestimating the ingenuity of people and the resilience of industries. U.S. businesses are still among the most productive and efficient in the world, and in some sectors remain the undisputed leaders. Even in industries and regions battered by hard times, there are encouraging exceptions to ward off dismal conclusions. For example, there are specialty steel firms in the U.S. whose employees outproduce Japanese steelworkers, man-hour for man-hour. There are textile manufacturers doing significant amounts of research and development, and undertaking major capital-improvement programs to convert to new products or processes. Some producers of commodity chemicals, including old standbys such as sulfuric acid which have been manufactured for centuries, continue to make money because they have gone to the trouble to make themselves the world's low-cost producers, through new investment and better process technology.

In New England since World War II, economic growth has been slower on average than in the Southwest, but some New England states in recent years have had above-average growth rates even in manufacturing, an economic activity that is supposed to be dead in that part of the country. The Bath Iron Works in Maine builds frigates for the Navy, and has gained national publicity because it delivers them ahead of schedule and under budget. Meanwhile, on the sunny Gulf Coast, where tradition holds that labor conditions are more favorable than in New England, another Navy contract yard has become notorious for delays and cost overruns. One apparent difference is that at the Bath Iron Works the goals of labor-management relations that are today so strongly touted—trust among the people, a strong commitment to the job and the product, loyalty to the organization, and so forth—were embraced long ago and have been firmly kept in place for several generations. All of this suggests that there is a cluster of subjective factors that permit individual companies, industry sectors, and even geographical regions to buck trends that could well put them under.

If it is true that U.S. businesses would do well to adopt some Japanese management practices, it is equally true that many of those practices bear the label "Made in America." Where the Japanese have beaten us, it is usually at our own game. Much of Japan's success is due to its adoption of strategies and ideas about management that were first developed here. The Japanese backed their entry into world markets with a high rate of savings and capital investment, an open-

ness to new technology whether home-grown or imported, a commitment to employees that has been returned in loyalty and hard work,
and a willingness to adapt products and services to the signals coming
back from the marketplace. It takes nothing from the Japanese to note
that all these would be components of successful economic development for any free-world nation in the modern era, or that these have
been the secrets of success for many of the American companies that
have done well over the years. The Japanese have played for the long
pull and gone back to the drawing board when they have made mistakes. Those two tactics have been immensely helpful to the Japanese
economy, but neither is alien to us. Japanese auto-makers, for example, lost money for years in the American market. The cars first intro-
duced here were heavy, underpowered, plain, and unsalable. Instead
of quitting, the Japanese sought the advice of their American dealers,
and redesigned the product to make it lighter, agile, and attractive.
The rest is history.

I do not want to sprinkle rain on the parade. American firms can
do better in managing all of their assets, the most important being
their people. If the competitive challenge from Japan and other rivals
forces us to relearn some lessons we have partly forgotten, so much
the better for us. All I want to suggest is that management needs perspective and a sense of the basics. Further, I believe that increasing
numbers of managers are displaying that sense. There are bulging files
of case material on plants, offices, and stores that have taken a new
lease on life by putting more emphasis on the human side of enterprise, forgoing "daddy knows best" management.

Companies are trying to shape policies to fit their people, rather
than the converse. As an example, it is no longer assumed that there
ought to be but one employee-benefit program, fitted to the needs of a
prototypical, skilled blue-collar worker, a man who is the sole support
of his wife and two children. Acknowledging that such workers today
represent less than one-fifth of the work force, and that employees
may have a wide spectrum of needs, companies are offering options
and alternatives. Quaker Oats, American Can, TRW, Mellon Bank,
and Du Pont are on a long list of companies that let employees choose
from more than one health-insurance plan, or set aside more or less
money in tax-deferred savings plans, or buy more or less life insurance
at group rates. Some firms are experimenting with cafeteria-style benefits—put whatever you want on your tray as long as you do not exceed

a maximum price at the cash register. Those or other firms are looking at flexible working hours and arrangements under which two people split up one full-time job.

Under such labels as employee involvement, quality circles, and quality of worklife, companies are making extra efforts to draw on minds and not just "hands." Mostly they do it with a series of little steps rather than through blockbuster changes; but, as it says in the song, little things mean a lot. Consider some samples from the clipping files:

General Motors, in stereotype a woolly mammoth of a company frozen in old bureaucratic ways, may well have the most extensive such programs of any corporation. It has dozens of projects at different locations pointed toward management-and-labor cooperation. Probably the best known is one of the early ones, at the Tarrytown assembly plant on the Hudson River north of New York City. In the early 1970s the Tarrytown plant was in line for the title of the worst plant in the company, and possibly in the industry. Production efficiency and quality were low. Absenteeism was high. Strikes were frequent. Union and management hardly spoke to each other except to review grievance proceedings. At times, there were 2,000 of those on file, pending action. Recognizing that GM management might well fold the operation, the plant's union and management leaders broke with the past, opened up lines of communication with each other, and launched a home-grown program to get employees involved in a common effort to turn the plant around. Several years later, Tarrytown had the best quality record in the corporation, absenteeism had dropped, strikes had disappeared, and formal grievances had become rare, not because everyone had stopped complaining but because people had found ways to resolve their differences on the shop floor. They had begun to trust one another.

Chrysler had a similar experience with a plant in Detroit making auto trim. Once described as "hopelessly noncompetitive," it was put back on its feet by the combined efforts of workers and supervisors through changes in work rules, production goals, and management approaches. The plant's output went up by 25 percent. In Westinghouse, more than 10,000 employees, both blue-collar and white-collar, are taking part in small groups commissioned to improve operations. The company has found that, as a result, waste has gone down and product quality and productivity have gone up.

At the Carborundum Company in upstate New York, a blueprint for plant redesign was produced with a $7 million price tag. The company turned the plan over to its operating and maintenance employees and asked for any improvements they could offer. They came back with an alternative plant at half the cost. At the Mead Corporation's paper mill in Chillicothe, Ohio, the oldest plant in the company, it used to take twenty-one man-hours of work to produce each ton of paper. Now it takes thirteen man-hours. The difference is credited to a combination of new machinery, tighter quality control, and better management. Decisions were pushed down the line, work rules streamlined, and employees encouraged to come forward with ideas.

The Ingersoll-Rand Company was having problems in its pump-manufacturing process. There were too many delays and breakdowns. The company was losing market share. Employee task groups were set up to establish new, measurable goals, and to improve communication and reward systems. "Family days" were inaugurated to build a sense of participation. Newsletters were initiated to keep people informed. As a result, complaints about products were cut in half, and on-time deliveries increased by 23 percent.

At the Rushton Coal Mine in Philipsburg, Pennsylvania, in a pattern that has been followed in many other companies, members of the mining crews were trained in all jobs so they could rotate assignments, and the group was made largely autonomous, with the members being held responsible for both output and safety. Both improved. One miner was reported as saying, "Suddenly we mattered to somebody. Somebody trusted us." He went on to add that when a machine broke, the crew rarely bothered to call for special maintenance help. They fixed it themselves. His explanation was that they had come to look upon the tools as their own, like their cars at home. They were no longer working in a mine, but in *their* mine.

A Northrop plant near Los Angeles, where parts were made for Boeing's 747s, challenged its work force to tackle a variety of quality and operations problems, with an invitation to look at anything from shop-floor lighting to work-scheduling and tool-improvement. The company now credits their efforts, along with some other changes, for a 50-percent cost saving on the 747 units.

At Du Pont's Richmond, Virginia, textile-fibers plant, a building needed reroofing in midsummer. The crew was told to work out the project on its own. Instead of working in the worst heat of the day, the men elected to begin at 5:00 A.M. and quit at 1:30 P.M. They increased the amount accomplished each day by more than one-third, and cut a week off the estimated schedule for the project. At the company's Kinston, North Carolina, plant, also a manmade-fibers unit, the mid-1970s was a time of rising labor costs and morale problems. Plant management concluded that too many decisions were being forced to high levels, and that the people closest to the problems, the operators, mechanics, and foremen, were not involved enough in efforts to keep the plant competitive. Management determined to reverse the trends, reduce the ratio of chiefs to Indians, let people manage more of their own work, and encourage them to look for ways to do the work better. Among the results: In a packaging operation, waste was cut 50 percent; in the production area, a pipeline that was going to be installed at a cost of $120,000 was supplanted by a $5,000 substitute that worked as well—someone found an unused line that could be adapted; and in the powerhouse, there were improvements in both costs and generating efficiency. Asked by a visitor what he thought was the most important feature of the new approach, one powerhouse operator looked at the superintendent of that part of the plant and said, "I finally got this guy to listen to me."

As one of the largest users of power in the nation, Du Pont was hard hit by the rapid rise in fuel costs in the 1970s. Its response was a company-wide conservation program which set goals and left it to the employees to come up with ways to meet them. The first 10 percent was easy: Find and fix the leaks in the steam traps; run the boilers as efficiently as possible. After that, it became a test of ingenuity, with more extensive changes required in procedures and equipment. Within a few years, the company was saving more than 20 percent on the fuel needed to produce the same amount of product. In terms of the then-current prices for oil and natural gas, this meant savings to the corporation of several hundred million dollars per year. Other companies in chemicals and other industries report similar percentage savings derived from similar programs.

Not all the examples come from large manufacturing companies. Delta Airlines has had a tradition of caring about its employees, including an open-door policy that makes top executives available to talk about company problems with anyone in the organization. Lay-offs are a last resort. Delta has built such loyalty that at one point, when the scheduled air carriers were in a recession and most were losing money, Delta employees passed the hat and raised the money to buy the company a new plane to add to its fleet. They explained that they wanted to say "Thanks."

The Guardian Life Insurance Company used to handle policyholder services with a clerical staff that was subdivided and fragmented. Several people were involved in each case, with no one having clear responsibility for any customer. Files got lost. Answers to questions were slow in coming. The company then put its people through a new training program and reshuffled the service group around "account analysts," each of whom now takes care of all matters for a group of policyholders in a particular geographic area. There are no hovering supervisors. Each analyst is expected to think of "my people, my responsibility." Guardian reports that output has gone up by one-third since the change was made.

No one has carried this style of management further than W. L. Gore & Associates, a young company quickly growing large, headquartered near Newark, Delaware. Bill Gore, the founder, puts so much trust in employees that he has all but dispensed with any management structure at all. A former Du Pont employee, he was much impressed in the late 1940s and 1950s by a task-force approach to which he had been exposed in technical work. In a task force, little attention is paid to the location of people on the organization chart; much to the contribution their particular skills can make to the problem on the table. When a project is completed, the task force usually is disbanded and the members go on to other assignments, some of them joining new task forces to tackle new problems.

When Gore left Du Pont to strike out on his own, he decided that the right organization for him was not a pyramid but a lattice, where any employee could work one-on-one with any other, and people could figure out for themselves where in the organization they could fit best. Gore's organization has no managers or subordinates, only associates. No one has a title unless he or she invents it. (When one associate on a business trip was asked why she did not have a title as others in business do, she had calling cards printed: "Sarah Clifton, Supreme Commander.") There is, though, a discipline in the organization, based on a recognition by employees of what different people can do, as demonstrated by experience. There is also a history of success. In twenty-five years, Bill Gore built a business with twenty plants, 2,000 associates, and $125 million in sales, with products used in vascular grafts (half a million people are walking around with Gore-tex artificial blood vessels), wire and cable coatings, and breathable but waterproof sportswear.

What works for Gore might not work for the Du Pont Engineering Department, housed in a building next door to Gore's headquarters office. It cannot even be said that what works in one place in a company may be a good answer for other plants or offices in the same corporation. General Motors, for instance, found that the approach that saved Tarrytown could not, at least at the time it was tried, be transplanted to another GM assembly plant in upstate New York. By hindsight, both management and union leaders agreed that at this second location the leadership was too set in old ways to give a different approach a fair try. (Interestingly, national UAW leaders said that the local labor leadership had been mostly responsible for that failure, while a corporate vice president tended to put as much or more of the blame on the plant management. Neither pointed the finger at the other, which says something about the changing attitudes of management and labor in America.)

A review of these examples shows that some variables expected to be important prove not to be so. This sampling does not suggest, for example, that a healthy internal environment can be created only in small organizations and not in big ones. Nor does the case record show success and failure dividing along lines of old versus new industries, blue-collar versus white-collar workers, unionized firms versus nonunionized, manufacturing firms versus service organizations, or high-technology activities versus low-technology. The common threads are not spun from those variables.

What the examples do share are these qualities: Successful programs to make a better work environment have been tailored to particular locations and people. They represent change presented in a form that does not threaten people but promises rewards. They build on the assumption that management people have no monopoly on imagination or common sense. They bring the people who are affected into the planning process; and they send a signal that management recognizes that it may be underchallenging people and has enough respect for them to be willing to try some experiments. Successful programs compliment people. As that Pennsylvania miner said, "Somebody trusted us."

In the familiar image of management, communication is authority at work: It is the captain yelling down the speaking tube, "Fix the engine!" Some corporate captains do yell, but that has little to do with the basic job of management communicating. The essential is not a "command" voice, nor is it the spirit of good cheer in the monthly letter to employees in the front of a house magazine, meant to build morale in the plant and urge the sales force to "go get 'em." It is instead the ability to put yourself in the other fellow's shoes, identify what is on his mind, provide him with whatever information there is to help him understand what is going on, and help him do his job better. As in management's handling of external affairs, it is partly a matter of recognizing how other people may see a problem, partly a sensitivity to the pressures on them, and partly a matter of respecting them enough to share the truth as you see it.

Perhaps more than anything else, the way the management communicates tells people in an organization where the priorities really lie. At one plant I visited as a CEO, there is a woman in the shipping area who handles a giant robot of a machine that picks products of the right size and color out of inventory, packs them neatly in boxes, tapes these shut, and sends the packages on a conveyor to a dock. This woman is nearing middle age. She lost her husband and is working to raise two children. She is determined that they will go to college. Not only does she know how to run this special tool; she seems to understand every part of it and had a hand in programming its computerized innards. Her technical explanations of this are largely lost on me, but that is not important. What matters is not that a chief executive passing through her work area on an infrequent visit did not happen to go to engineering school, but that he and the other managers of the company realize what this job means to her, how hard she is willing to try, and the kind of treatment she and others like her deserve.

"The climate inside" is just a label. It gains a reality when I test it against my own behavior as a manager: As a chief executive, did I meet that woman halfway? Did my subordinates? If the company ever wanted to make a change in the equipment in her work area, if there had to be shutdown or work stretchout during a business recession or because competitors had scooped up some of this plant's customers, would she be the first person told? She should be. No one has a greater stake in the news. If she has to rely on the rumor mill to learn what is happening in the plant, then, call it what you will, her supervisors are not good at communication and one has to question whether corporate management is good at managing. The worst communication practice of all is to say nothing when changes that affect people are taking place. That kind of silence travels fast through corporate corridors, and carries a secondary message: "We don't care about you, not even enough to tell you about something that hits you where you live."

In a speech that got me in trouble with some of my cohorts in management, I once told a group of plant publication editors that they should have First Amendment rights to print news about their company without having two or three levels of managers above them blue-penciling copy because issues are "too sensitive," "the timing is wrong," or there is no need for information because "the natives are not restless." If the information is material and affects employees in some way, why not supply it to them? While I am not aware that plant managers rushed to follow my call, I still think it is a good idea. The point I was trying to make was that employees in most corporations today are mature and intelligent people who will keep information in a proper context if they are given enough of it. They deserve the warts-and-all truth, and management should be very careful about deciding what "they" do not need to know.

Not to be overlooked is the fact that a statement to the outside world, coming from the top, can have a large impact inside, and that may be precisely the reason for an executive to speak out. Early in my work as a CEO, I wanted to make it clear to the organization that I was firmly committed to an open-door policy with respect to minorities and women, and that the company would move these people upward in the organization as fast as their talents would allow. Rather than depending only on a policy memorandum moving through formal corporate channels, I also announced my feelings to the press. Once people saw a clear commitment in the public print, it was clear there was no turning back, and equal opportunity was a nonissue.

I have gone light on Du Pont examples in this book, using them mostly where it is evident that the same points could be made with other companies. I have not wanted to imply that one company has such virtues that its managers deserve special praise. Nor have I wanted to encourage the reader to dismiss my generalizations on the grounds that they are drawn from a sample of one. There is, however, one area where the example of Du Pont is so extraordinary that it begs to be put in this record. The area is employee safety and health protection, and I cite it as the best case I have ever seen of communication being used as the central tool of management. The example comes forward with no hint of self-praise, for the policies behind it were installed long before I had anything to do with managing the company, or was even born.

Consider a few facts for reference. The chemical industry is a much-safer-than-average place to work, despite its potential hazards. Chemical workers have to deal with materials that are flammable, corrosive, toxic, or radioactive. Manufacturing processes frequently involve large quantities of materials being reacted at high temperatures or pressures. A chemical plant also has all of the usual hazards one would find in many industrial settings, ranging from yard locomotives hauling raw materials, to machine tools that can cut or crush, to high-voltage electrical circuits. Yet, over the years, the segment of U.S. industry with the best safety record has been chemical manufacturing. For every incident that causes an employee to lose a day of work in the chemical industry, there are four such incidents on an all-industry average, and in some lines of work the experience is much worse than that. There are twenty-six such lost-time incidents in the trucking business, for instance, and twelve in the meat-products industry. It is hard to believe it is twenty-six times as dangerous to drive a truck as to work for a chemical company, but those are the numbers. (The figures and the ones that follow include occupationally-caused illnesses as well as injuries, and are weighted by numbers of employees and the total hours they work; they thus compare like "exposures.")

Du Pont's accident rate is but one-seventeenth of the chemical industry average. To put that on a national basis, the lost-time rate for all industry is sixty-eight times as high as the rate for Du Pont. Stating this in absolute values, in a typical industrial plant with 1,000 employees, in one year there will be nine job-connected injuries or illnesses serious enough to keep an employee from working. In a Du Pont plant of comparable size, there will be one such incident in a total of seven years and seven months. The numbers do not fall evenly, of course. A serious accident can demolish a plant's safety record and make it look much worse than the national average. Opposite that, there are certain Du Pont plants, laboratories, and offices where for periods of twenty to twenty-five years no employee has lost a day of work as a result of an on-the-job accident or occupational illness. Across the company and even in its "riskiest" lines of work, Du Pont employees are safer on the job than at home. They have less illness and live as long as or longer than average.

The Du Pont record has been compiled in the simplest and most direct way, by setting a policy at the top and carrying it to every corner of the corporation, with support from a communication program that can only be called obsessive in attention to detail, and persistent to a degree that leaves visitors shaking their heads. The board of directors long ago established safety as a *sine qua non* policy: No product would be made, no process utilized, unless it could be done safely. No employee would ever be asked to perform a task unless there was a way to do it without being hurt.

This point of view dates from the nineteenth century, when the owners and managers of the company were one and the same, and du Ponts. Proving that they meant what they said, the early generations running the company built homes adjacent to what was then the only plant, a facility making explosives. The du Ponts worked in the powder yard themselves, alongside the men. There were some accidents—powder-making at the time was a nervous technology, and some employees lost their lives, including a du Pont—but the point was made: No employee should stand a risk that the managers and their families were unwilling to stand themselves.

The priority of safety has reached every corner of the company. There is no way that any employee can honestly say that he "didn't know" about safety first, or that nobody explained that it is part of his job responsibility, or that safety violations are dismissable offenses. Clerical work groups have regular safety meetings, just as production crews do. Staff meetings routinely begin with safety as the first item on the agenda, then move on to production rates, cost control, and other such matters. Safety engineers must "sign off" on a new plant design before the first shovelful of dirt is turned. The Executive and Finance Committees will not even review the project for authorization until that requirement is satisfied. People walking up and down stairs are told to use the handrail. There always is one. As noted in the earlier chapter where OSHA was discussed, "four on the floor" is not a reference to cars with stick shifts; in Du Pont, it refers to the four feet of the chair.

Along with the nagging reminders, employees are given plenty of professional help in staying well and unhurt. Industrial hygienists check plants and laboratories to make sure that reactor vessels are not emitting toxic fumes. A Medical Division conducts epidemiological studies and performs physical exams: Each employee has one periodically. Protective gear is provided wherever needed, ranging from hard hats and goggles to enclosed suits with outside air supply. A laboratory of toxicology and industrial medicine is doing research to determine potential health effects of proposed products and materials used in manufacturing processes. Founded a half-century ago to track down the cause of malignant tumors appearing in workers making dyes, the laboratory is now one of the largest and best-known facilities of its kind in the world. It has a staff of more than 250.

While everyone in the organization is constantly reminded that health and safety precautions are part of the job, the burden falls first on the shoulders of management. If the corporate record were to tumble, the board would have the chief executive officer on the carpet, not the head of the Safety and Fire Protection Division. By the same token, when there is an accident at a plant and corporate headquarters is on the phone, the person they want to talk to is the plant manager, not the safety supervisor.

One of Du Pont's executives, Richard Heckert, tells the story on himself of an early assignment as a plant manager, when he was given a dressing down by his bosses because the plant's injury rate was inching upward. It was made clear to him that unless that trend were capped and reversed, his career as a manager would be short and unpleasant. If one or more subordinates were lax, that was Heckert's problem to solve. The lesson for him was that safety is the first test of a plant manager's competence, and if he failed that test, there would not be any others. He learned the lesson well. The safety record got better and so did Dick Heckert's career. He is now a vice chairman of the corporation.

No exceptions are tolerated. In the 1960s, the company began to expand its businesses in the Common Market and, in addition to building some new plants, bought several facilities from European firms. The safety records of those plants, whether average or better for their own area, were well below Du Pont standards. As a newcomer, Du Pont was advised not to rock the boat, but to adapt to the culture, to avoid being the "ugly American." We were warned, for example, that we might have major labor problems in Germany if management started telling workers they had to wear safety shoes whether they liked it or not. By and large, Du Pont followed the when-in-Rome advice, but safety was a notable exception. A major information program was launched to promote safety and explain the management's point of view about it. The European employees responded—they thought it was a good idea, too—and the rate of accidents and injuries began to shrink. Today, the safety record for Du Pont's international operations is almost as good as for the domestic company.

The most telling anecdote about safety and health, though, comes from a more distant past, and illustrates the crucial role of top management in establishing a climate within an organization. In 1935, the president of the company, Lammot du Pont, was asked to make some remarks at the opening of the company's toxicology laboratory. This was not the best of times for American business, and hardly the moment one would have chosen to spend money on a facility that might not have seemed clearly needed. Such in-house research was a new idea in industry. Only one other chemical company was building any such facility—few industrial firms, for that matter, had in-house research laboratories of any kind at that time—and Du Pont was under no outside pressure to make a major gesture to show good intent. Its safety record then as now was far better than average. The principal objective of the laboratory was largely preventative medicine, and to some that appeared to be a needless expense for a corporation in the Depression.

Lammot du Pont saw it differently. At the ceremonies, he said this: "We will run up against difficulties. For instance, the operating department will want to know 'why the laboratory doesn't produce something.' The sales department will want to know 'why the laboratory works up data that might make our customers believe our products are unsafe.' But we are embarked on our campaign with determination and it is only a question of time before the world recognizes that a very constructive thing has been done." More than anything else management can do, it is statements such as that one that declare the territory in which a company chooses to operate, set its standards, and show where the well-being of people stands in the corporate hierarchy of values.

No course given in school provides a manager with the sense of priorities or the vision that Lammot du Pont showed on that occasion, and no formal schooling can promise to turn out corporate directors with the judgment and sensitivity required to support such a manager. There is much that can be done by way of training, though.

People with apparent potential for managerial slots can be systematically moved around the corporate interior to gain experience in production, marketing, and finance. In the same way, they can be put in jobs that will expose them to governmental and community affairs on the outside, and to the people problems on the inside. The point I emphasize, however, is that the learning process is not one to be reduced to formula. No one can cram for the exams that test the qualities of leadership and governance. Probably it is possible to memorize a few rules that make for good communication or the appearance of same. No doubt prospective or present leaders could learn to improve their management styles and personalities, because some of them have a way of making it difficult for their followers to be either cooperative or creative. However, the tricks of the trade and the "charm schools" will net little unless the people entrusted with authority understand the role of the organization in society, and the responsibilities that managers have to the people joined in the effort.

In Ralph Waldo Emerson's time, it was accurate for him to say that an institution was the lengthened shadow of a man. That is less true today for the private organizations that concern us in this book. Ford is not singularly Mr. Ford's company, Du Pont is not the du Ponts anymore, and neither company is cast in the image of a single powerful leader, whatever his last name. Emerson is not entirely out of date, though. Each modern corporation, for all its diversification and decentralization, despite chains of command and shared authority is still the lengthened shadow of a few people. Those who are board members and senior managers establish the climate within, and casting the shadow is their main work.

Index

About the Authors

IRVING S. SHAPIRO is a lawyer and businessman. Now
a partner in the law firm of Skadden, Arps, Slate,
Meagher & Flom, he previously was chairman of the
board and chief executive officer of the Du Pont
Company. He continues to serve on the Du Pont
board as chairman of its Finance Committee.

A son of Lithuanian immigrants, he was born in
Minneapolis in 1916. He was graduated in 1939 from
the University of Minnesota with a Bachelor's degree,
and in 1941 from the university's law school, beginning what he describes as a lifelong love affair with
the law.

Following graduation in 1941, he worked briefly
for the Office of Price Administration in Washington,
and then joined the Justice Department, where he
specialized in cases being presented to the Supreme
Court and to various circuit courts of appeal.

He joined Du Pont's Legal Department in 1951,
became the company's assistant general counsel in
1965, and five years later was named a vice president,
director, and member of the Executive Committee.
Mr. Shapiro was named vice chairman in 1973, and
the following year, the chairman and CEO. As a corporate executive, he spoke and wrote widely about the
relationships of business and government, and the responsibilities of private-sector organizations in national and community affairs—the topics of this
book. During his seven years as a CEO, he was a
member of the Policy Committee of The Business

Roundtable, and for several years was that organization's chairman.

Currently, Mr. Shapiro is a director of International Business Machines, Citicorp, Continental American Company, Hospital Corporation of America, the Seagram Company Ltd., and the Boeing Company. He is a trustee of the Ford Foundation and is chairman of its Audit and Administration Committee.

He lives and works in Wilmington, Delaware.

CARL B. KAUFMANN is an executive assistant in Du Pont's Public Affairs Department. A former newspaper reporter and magazine writer, he has spent most of his career with Du Pont. He has worked with Mr. Shapiro for more than a decade on speeches, articles, testimony for governmental agencies, and other public presentations.

Born in Memphis in 1926, he studied engineering at MIT and the University of Michigan, then switched to English, in which he was awarded a Bachelor's degree in 1947 at Dartmouth, and to history, in which he earned a Master's at the University of Delaware.

He is author of an earlier book, *Man Incorporate: The Individual and His Work in an Organized Society.*

He too lives and works in Wilmington.